the
American composer speaks

the
American composer speaks
a historical anthology, 1770-1965

edited by
GILBERT CHASE

LOUISIANA
STATE
UNIVERSITY
PRESS

In a healthy culture differing musical
philosophies would be coexistent, not
mutually exclusive. . . .
HARRY PARTCH, *Genesis of a Music.*

foreword

Somewhat over thirty years ago, in 1933, the American composer
Henry Cowell edited a book called *American Composers on American
Music,* which I have always regarded as one of the most valuable
works ever published in this field. But its scope was contemporary,
not historical. It made us acutely aware of the trend of American
music in the 1930's; it did not reach back into our musical beginnings
nor attempt to trace the rather awkward and sometimes painful emergence of "the American composer," both as a type and as an individual,
through the vicissitudes of his social, economic, artistic, and intellectual situation. Cowell's book gave limited shape to an excellent idea
and invited an extension of the same principle, both into the past and
up to the present.

Hence the present collection brings together for the first time,
within the covers of a single book, a representative selection of writings by American composers from Billings to Brown, from the early
New England singing school masters to the avant-garde of the 1960's.
The historical span is just under two hundred years, which is a very
brief time if we take the entire history of music into account. Yet this
is the whole of our national, as distinct from our colonial, history
(actually, Billings' first collection of music appeared six years before
the Declaration of Independence), and one can only marvel at the variety and richness, the originality and force, of the musical culture
developed in the United States during this relatively short period.

As long as we continued to take a limited, one-sided, aesthetically
inhibited, and intellectually snobbish view of this musical culture, the
greater part of its significance remained hidden from sight, like the
bulk of an iceberg under water. But during the past thirty years or
so, thanks largely to the publications of such genuinely "humanistic"
scholars as George Pullen Jackson, John and Alan Lomax, Frederic
Ramsey, Hans Nathan, Rudi Blesh, and Irving Lowens, the rich subsoil of America's musical culture has been more thoroughly worked

over and the fruits thereof revealed for all to taste and enjoy. Some of the most important composers of our time, among them Charles Ives, Virgil Thomson, Roy Harris, and Aaron Copland, have drawn upon this rich subsoil of the American vernacular for many of their compositions. Indeed, the cross-fertilization that has occurred in our music is one of the healthiest signs of cultural maturity. Differing musical expressions do not merely coexist: they exert a reciprocal and salutary influence upon each other. The modern jazz musician is probably a graduate of Juilliard, and "pop" is the password of the avant-garde. All premises have been questioned, all assumptions suspended; anything can happen, and events called "happenings" are arranged for this purpose. Bearing a banner with the strange device SILENCE, John Cage goes about from campus to campus and city to city talking at a great rate. In spite of his emblem, he maintains that there is really no such thing as silence: sound is always going on, even if it be only that of one's own heartbeat—which, after all, is rather important.

It may be said that the American composer has been a victim of silence. Our earliest composers suffered the silence of history, which is the neglect of posterity. The composers of our middle period suffered the silence of criticism, which means indifference. Our composers of today, as a whole—there are individual exceptions—suffer the silence of the concert hall: their works, by and large, have not entered the repertory. Our greatest composer, Charles Ives, suffered the cruelest silence of all: the silence of rejection, which meant the repudiation of originality, the castigation of nonconformity.

At the beginning of the present century, another American composer, Arthur Farwell, declared that "all American music needs is publicity." History and criticism are also forms of publicity; the one publicizes past events, the other current opinion. Both are necessary to a healthy culture, in which, as Harry Partch says, differing musical philosophies would be coexistent, not mutually exclusive. Therefore I have wished to make this anthology historical, to shed the light of a modest publicity (a contradiction in terms—but there are limits to scholarly enterprise) upon our musical past and upon some of its representative figures. After all, there was no false modesty in Francis Hopkinson's claim to be the first native-born composer of the United States. He won immortality by a single well-aimed and well-timed "plug"—the Dedication to George Washington (obviously, he knew the publicity value of a famous name). For the same reason I have wished to make this anthology critical, chiefly in the Introduction, where, with the typical presumption of the critic, I have had my say before letting the composers have theirs. But this, after all, was simply to avoid an anticlimax, as well as to set the scene and point up some issues. The main thing was to break the silence, to speak a kind of prologue before the curtain rises on the *dramatis personae*; after that, I become an offstage voice, continuing my task of quiet publicity with a few biographical facts. What is important here is the voice of the composer who speaks.

CHAPEL HILL, N.C.   GILBERT CHASE
December, 1965

acknowledgments

The following permissions to reprint are gratefully acknowledged: G. Schirmer, Inc., and *The Musical Quarterly* for "The American Composer" by Henry F. B. Gilbert and for "Problems and Issues Facing the Composer Today" by Roger Sessions; W. W. Norton & Co., Inc., for "Epilogue" from *Essays Before a Sonata* by Charles Ives; Alfred A. Knopf, Inc., for material from *New Musical Resources* by Henry Cowell; the estate of Daniel Gregory Mason for "The Dilemma of American Music"; Stanford University Press for "Problems of American Composers" by Roy Harris from *American Composers on American Music*, edited by Henry Cowell (copyright 1933 by the Trustees of the Leland Stanford Junior University; renewed 1961 by Henry Cowell); Coward-McCann, New York, for "The Composer in the Machine Age" by George Gershwin from *Revolt in the Arts*, edited by Oliver M. Sayler; Alan Lomax for the selection from his *Mister Jelly Roll*; McGraw-Hill Book Co., for "Composer from Brooklyn" by Aaron Copland from his *Our New Music*; Random House, Inc., for "How Composers Eat" from *The State of Music* by Virgil Thomson; Harry Partch for "American Musical Tendencies" from *Genesis of a Music*; William Glock for "Stravinsky and the Younger American Composers" by Arthur Berger from *The Score and I.M.A. Magazine*; Wesleyan University Press for "Experimental Music" from *Silence* by John Cage; *High Fidelity Magazine* for "Who Cares if You Listen?" by Milton Babbitt; *The Saturday Review* for "The Future of Form in Jazz" by Gunther Schuller; Earle Brown and the New York Philharmonic Society for "Some Notes on Composing"; Enzo Valenti Ferro, editor of *Buenos Aires Musical*, for "A Further Step" by Elliott Carter and "The Younger Generation" by William Flanagan (both originally published in Spanish translation).

contents

the
American composer speaks

introduction

The image of the American composer is remote and indistinct in our national consciousness. We have no Wagner, no Verdi, no Berlioz—not even a Vaughan Williams—securely immortalized and certified as a national glory, equally suitable for domestic and foreign consumption. Our clearest and most widely accepted images are far removed from the concept of "The Great Composer" that appears in the standard histories of music. Our brightest image is that of the "popular" composer—a Stephen Foster, a John Philip Sousa, a George Gershwin—who made his appeal to the people through the less pretentious forms of musical composition: the plantation melody, the military march, the musical comedy. Such figures have passed from the limbo of history to the realm of legend, where true fame begins and endures.

Gershwin, to be sure, wrote piano concertos, preludes, overtures, and operas, as well as hit tunes and Broadway shows; but it is the popular ingredient in his more ambitious works that gained them universal acceptance. Gershwin, aspiring to be what is called a "serious" composer, remained popular in spite of himself. He was always a creative artist in whatever he wrote, whether it was a musical comedy number or a concerto, and never established a dichotomy between popular and serious music. For him, it was all music, and his desire was to make the best of both worlds.

Stephen Foster, too, would have wished to make the best of both worlds, but time and circumstance were against him. He aspired to make the plantation songs or "Ethiopian melodies" of blackface minstrelsy into something more refined and artistic. Yet in his own day, the guardians of good taste, the promoters of better music, and the "opera-mongers" (as he once called them), observing only that his tunes were catchy and universally popular, turned against him savagely and denounced his beloved songs as "poisonous trash" and "the lowest dregs of music." Nevertheless, in the twentieth century, Stephen Foster became the first musician to be admitted to the American Hall of Fame. He may not have been a great composer in the conventional sense, but of his fame there could be no doubt.

The sentiment persisted, nonetheless, that the American Hall of Fame should enshrine the bust of a genuine Great Composer. It may be questioned whether anyone connected with the project gave much thought to defining the concept of a Great Composer —least of all in terms of American civilization and its cultural characteristics—but it could be taken for granted that a candidate for the title should have written serious works, such as concertos and sonatas, that he should not have been tainted by excessive popularity, and that he should resemble as closely as possible the standard European model of the Classical-Romantic era. Given these hypothetical criteria, the most likely candidate was Edward MacDowell, whose post-Romantic piano concertos, sonatas, and symphonic poems carefully avoided any deviation from accepted notions of serious music. That they also avoided originality could only enhance his candidacy, because this placed his conformity beyond question. Consequently, it is not surprising that in 1964 MacDowell became the second American musician to be admitted to the Hall of Fame.

Such official recognition has little effect on a composer's viable fame. Stephen Foster was already so famous that he did not need it; MacDowell's reputation, always limited to a relatively small circle, has declined so sharply that it can never be effectively revived—not fame, but the semblance of fame, is all that the Establishment can salvage for him. The public image of the American composer remains essentially unaffected by such ceremonial maneuvers. It is the legend that lives. But how is the legend created?

To begin with, it requires good raw material. Some historical figures have the stuff of legend in them; others remain merely historical—neither wholly forgotten nor wholly remembered. A good weaver of legends, too, can achieve small miracles with material that seems rather unpromising: witness Parson Weems and George Washington. And sometimes it happens that the great legendary figure gets the Grand Weaver that he deserves: witness Carl Sandburg and Abraham Lincoln. But who will make a legend of Alexander Hamilton, or of John Quincy Adams, important statesmen though they were? And who, in American music, will make a legend out of Edward MacDowell or Horatio Parker, important though they were in their day?

The ingredients of legendary fame cannot be precisely measured or prescribed, but they can be recognized and manipulated by the trained eye and hand. Often there is an untimely death, usually under tragic or dramatic or particularly distressful circumstances, which cuts the victim down at the height of his fame or at the moment of his greatest glory. George Gershwin is an example of this classical syndrome. Another is Louis Moreau Gottschalk, the celebrated piano virtuoso and composer from New Orleans, whose hour of triumph at the Imperial Court in Rio de Janeiro—following his unprecedented successes in Peru, Chile, Argentina, and Uruguay—was but a brief prelude to his sudden death at the age of forty in the Brazilian capital.

With the exception of Stephen Foster, who represents a special case, Gottschalk is, in my opinion, the American composer of the nineteenth century who offers the best raw material for the building of a legend. The picturesque background of his early years in New Orleans, his youthful years in Paris, his sensational tour of Spain, his brilliant career as the first internationally celebrated American pianist, his numerous love affairs, his years of vagabondage in the West Indies, and the immense popular success of his piano compositions, ranging from the genteel sentimentality of "The Last Hope" to the zestful colloquialism of "The Banjo," are all potential ingredients for legendary fame. The sober historian will quite rightly insist on his importance as the first American composer successfully to exploit elements of the local vernacular in his music; the initiator, in short, of what is generally, though perhaps not very aptly, called "musical nationalism" in the United States.

Critical recognition of the novel and unique qualities in the best of Gottschalk's piano pieces is necessary and just; but this is not sufficient for what I call a "viable fame," which goes beyond historical importance and critical recognition and which is manifested—in the case of a composer—first of all by the widespread and continuous performance of his music. The historian, the critic, and the performer do not themselves create the legend; but they lay the foundation for it. A motion picture on the life of Louis Moreau Gottschalk, taking the spectator from the Place Congo in antebellum New Orleans to the elegant salons of Paris, from adventure and intrigue in Spain to intrigue and disaster in San Francisco, from a liaison with the actress Ada Mencken in New York to the last amorous entanglement in Montevideo—such a picture would out-glamorize the filmed biographies of all the European composers who ever lived and died on the silver screen and would make of Gottschalk as much of a legend as Schubert, Chopin, or Liszt.

William Billings of Boston, who died in the year 1800 and who was our first native-born composer of any consequence, is another potential figure of legend in American music. Having lost his father at the age of fourteen, Billings was apprenticed to a tanner and in the ordinary course of events might have spent the rest of his life in the tanner's trade. But, having received some lessons from a "singing-school" teacher and having studied a *Musical Grammar* that was available to him, Billings, gifted with a pleasing voice, unbounded self-confidence, and tremendous enthusiasm, decided to make music his sole occupation. He was only twenty-four when, in 1770, he published his first collection of compositions, *The New England Psalm Singer, or American Chorister*. Undaunted by his lack of knowledge, unoppressed by the weight of tradition, he boldly declared: "I think it best for every *Composer* to be his own *Carver*."

By the time of his death in 1800, Billings had published five more collections of music, including *The Singing Master's As-*

sistant (1778), popularly known as "Billings' Best," and had become famous as the composer of "Chester," the hymn tune that was adopted as a marching song during the Revolutionary War. Although highly regarded by his contemporaries, he barely managed to make a living and at his death left his family in poverty. He himself was buried in a pauper's grave, and the certificate of his death listed his profession as "tanner." The American composer, in Billings' day, had only *de facto* status: it was a calling to be pursued at one's own peril, and few indeed ventured to commit themselves to it entirely, as he did. Most of his contemporaries and immediate successors exercised a trade while practicing music on the side. Among the trades by which composers of this period made a living were those of carpenter, cooper, fuller (dresser of cloth), hatter, silversmith, storekeeper, tavernkeeper, and breeder of horses (for example, Justin Morgan, whose breed is still famous).

Billings had to overcome other handicaps besides those of poverty and lack of education. A contemporary tells us that "he was a singular man, of moderate size, short of one leg, with one eye, without any address, and with an uncommon negligence of person. Still he spake and sang and thought as a man above the common abilities." He had also more than the common share of conviction and enthusiasm, which he was able to impart to others. "Great art thou O Music!" he once exclaimed, adding, "and with thee there is no competitor." Bill Billings of Boston should be as much of an American legend as Ben Franklin of Philadelphia or Daniel Boone of Kentucky. He was a pioneer, an individualist, a self-made man, an astonishing personality, a composer of and for the people.

The better educated a man is, the more he becomes conscious of history. So it was with Francis Hopkinson, a Philadelphia lawyer who, not content with having been a signer of the Declaration of Independence (after all, there were many others), claimed the unique distinction "of being the first Native of the United States who has produced a Musical Composition." And to make doubly sure that his claim would catch the eye of posterity, he embodied it in a dedication to George Washington prefacing a volume of his songs published in 1788. The evidence of history actually refutes Hopkinson's claim; but since that evidence is buried in scholarly journals, most people who know his name at all continue to think of Francis Hopkinson as the first native-born composer of the United States—so that his spirit may remain satisfied until that moment, always long delayed, when popular belief gives way to historical fact. Hopkinson was the type of musical amateur that was to play a considerable role in the development of musical composition in the United States. Anthony Philip Heinrich, William H. Fry, John Hill Hewitt, and even Charles Ives were amateurs in the sense that they did not make music their profession. But there is a world of difference between a well-trained amateur like Ives and an untrained amateur like Heinrich. The latter, indeed, could more correctly be described as a dilettante.

Heinrich has been permitted to speak here as an American composer—in spite of his musical shortcomings, his eccentricities, and the rather pitiful frustration of his most ambitious schemes, such as the choral-symphonic "Poem on the Emancipation of the Slaves" for which he solicited a libretto from "the venerable Patriarch J. Q. Adams"—because he was apparently the first musician fully to feel and express the excitement of being an *American* (though by adoption) and to identify himself, during his sojourn in Kentucky, with the novel sensations and subject matter (including Indian lore) of the frontier, the newly settled and still strange wilderness of North America.

As a matter of historical fact, in the same year that Heinrich went to Kentucky, a singing-school teacher from Virginia by the name of Ananias Davisson, who was almost his exact contemporary, copyrighted a collection of sacred music called the *Kentucky Harmony* (it had been published the previous year in 1816). Davisson's book was instrumental in bringing to the South and what was then the West the music of Billings and other early New England composers, which continued to be sung in the rural South and throughout the frontier region long after it had fallen into disuse in the urban centers of the Northeast. Davisson and his successors in the South followed the practice of using notes of different shapes (round, square, triangular, diamond-shaped) to facilitate the task of teaching the rural population to sing. Hence the expression "shape-note music" to designate this important grass-roots movement in America's musical culture.

Among the successors of Davisson in the southern shape-note movement, none was more prominent than William Walker, popularly known as "Singin' Billy Walker," who operated out of Spartanburg, South Carolina. His celebrated collection *The Southern Harmony* (1835) went through numerous editions and is said to have sold 600,000 copies. At the present time it is still being used by some shape-note singing groups in the South. The author of a *History of Spartanburg County*, writing about Walker, declared that "his reputation for attainments in his science soon spread all through the South and Southwest." The same author added that Walker "gathered and arranged into meter and melody a wonderful book suitably adapted to the praise and glory of God." This was *The Southern Harmony*, which contained over two hundred "tunes, hymns, psalms, odes, and anthems, selected from the most eminent authors in the United States, together with nearly one hundred new tunes, which have never before been published." Of these new tunes, Walker ascribed some twenty-five to himself. He was one of the many humble but locally influential musicians who, from Atlanta to Cincinnati, were shaping the indigenous tradition of America's music.

But the cities of the eastern seaboard were still the strongest centers of musical attraction, and "Father" Heinrich himself finally settled in New York. The composer and journalist William Henry Fry, after his early years in Philadelphia, where his "grand opera" *Leonora* was produced in 1845, also gravitated to New York, where he was influential as a critic and lecturer. In one of his lectures he called upon American composers to strike out along new paths, to trust their own inspiration, to cast aside their provincialism, and in short to declare their artistic independence. This was good preaching, but Fry could set no example himself, for his own music was glaringly derivative. Yet the theme of creative independence that he announced was to echo and re-echo in the thoughts and words of succeeding generations of American composers.

Although John Hill Hewitt was the son of a professional musician, he himself spoke of music, not as his profession, but as his "frailty." His father had emigrated to America in 1792 and, like many other professionals, had capitalized his European training and prestige into a considerable success—which, among other things, enabled him to make a socially advantageous marriage. With the latter situation went certain prejudices concerning music as a profession: the offspring of such a union should be a "gentleman," not a mere performer or scribbler of music (except, perhaps, as a pastime). The military profession was such as a gentleman might enter; hence young Hewitt was sent to the U. S. Military Academy at West Point. But there he only succeeded in frustrating his parents' plans, first by not graduating; second, by managing to study music with the bandmaster at the post. No wonder that Hewitt *fils* was the victim of a deep dichotomy throughout his life: devoted to music, yet rebelling at the low status—economically and socially—of the American composer; eager to compose in the grand manner, yet with only a rudimentary training in the art of composition; desiring to dedicate himself to music, yet obliged to engage in many miscellaneous activities in order to make a living; ambitious of fame, yet long outliving his reputation, based chiefly on romantic ballads and songs of the Civil War. How many who knew (or know) the song "All Quiet Along the Potomac Tonight" could name Hewitt as the composer?

John Hill Hewitt lived to be eighty-nine. Before he died, other American composers who enjoyed greater advantages of training and opportunity had risen to national and international fame: John Knowles Paine, Horatio Parker, Edward MacDowell, George W. Chadwick. But in the genuine history of American music, which includes the changing fashions of taste, the socioeconomic status of the composer, the struggle to scale heights of artistic composition as well as the temptation to cater to popular taste, the personality and life-work of John Hill Hewitt can no longer be ignored. Here, in an autobiographical excerpt, he speaks for himself and for his generation; before the story of our musical development is fully told, others, with the hindsight of history, must speak for him too.

There is a curious inconsistency between spoken thought and written music in the case of Edward MacDowell, whose compositions ape the European post-Romantic manner, but who in a lecture delivered in New York called for "absolute freedom from the restraint that an almost unlimited deference to European thought and prejudice has imposed on us. . . . What we must arrive at is the youthful optimistic vitality and the undaunted tenacity of spirit that characterizes the American man." In line with this thought, MacDowell scornfully rejected the call for a "national" school of American composition based on Negro and Indian themes, made by the Bohemian composer Antonin Dvořák during his sojourn in the United States (1892-95). Said MacDowell, "Masquerading in the so-called nationalism of Negro clothes cut in Bohemia will not help us." The idea, he affirmed, was "childish."

The fact is that MacDowell had spent twelve of his most formative years in Germany, and he could look at musical composition only through German eyes, hear it only through German ears. A composer from "Bohemia" was not to be taken seriously—especially when he asserted the aesthetic value of Negro music. In *America's Music*, I quote MacDowell's brief statement on national music, in which he maintains that "the vital element in music—personality—stands alone." This belief is reiterated in some of the lectures that he delivered as Professor of Music at Columbia University and which were posthumously published as *Critical and Historical Essays*. From these I have selected the one that seems to have the most general interest and to reflect most completely the essence of MacDowell's ideas on the art of music. Titled "Suggestion in Music," it develops the thesis that the "physical pleasure" of music should be separated from its "ideal significance." Only the latter, he maintains, is important and meaningful. This extreme idealism involves a deprecatory attitude toward all "inferior" types of musical expression: "After dinner, our forefathers were accustomed to sing catches which were entirely destitute of anything approaching music." This sneering contempt for common forms of musical

enjoyment goes far, I believe, to account for the neglect into
which MacDowell's own music has fallen.

In 1903, several years after MacDowell's assertion, the strongest affirmation of American music was made by Arthur Farwell,
a composer from the West who clung to his vision of an American music that would reflect the freedom and grandeur of that
region, divorced from what he considered effete, Europeanized
art of the eastern cities. American music, he declared, must do
justice to "the myriad sights and sounds of our own country."
He was optimistic regarding the emergence of the American
composer as a creative force in the land: "Every year sees them
[the composers] more numerous, fearless, energetic, prolific."
Farwell himself was all of those things—he had to be fearless
to proclaim the death knell of German domination in American
music when that hegemony was at its height. In the same article, he wrote: "All American composition needs is publicity."
Publicity of one kind or another has done wonders for American
music in the second half of the twentieth century, as far as the
contemporary composer is concerned, but it is American composition of the past that needs more publicity—and more performance. No nation can afford to throw away its past.

Farwell's friend and fellow-champion of American music,
Henry F. B. Gilbert, writing in his "The American Composer"
in 1915, was less optimistic about the situation. "One is compelled to admit," he wrote, "that there are as yet no real American composers." He conceded that "we have already developed
a strong and distinctive American *spirit*," but he maintained
that "such composers as we have fail for the most part to grasp
or to express this new spirit." Although he foresaw the development of "an American school of composition," he still felt that
"music by an American is not wanted, especially if it happens to
be *American music*." Here at least it is clearly implied that
there *is* something, however tentative and imperfect, that can
be called "American music"—with the emphasis on *American*.
Much of the writing and talking by American composers during
the next twenty years or so was concerned with discussing the
quality of "Americanism" in musical composition. The essays in

this volume by Farwell, Gilbert, Ives, Mason, Harris, Gershwin, and Copland are all variations on this theme.

Although Edward MacDowell and Charles Ives were antipodal in backround, in temperament, and indeed in their basic world-views as well as in their musical accomplishments, Ives, in the Epilogue of his *Essays Before a Sonata* (1918), agreed essentially with MacDowell's thesis that national music cannot be created simply by "dressing up" folk tunes with instrumental colors. For Ives the issue hinged on his fundamental distinction between "manner" and "substance" — a distinction that he applied to all the arts and which he illustrated in these essays by a comparison between Poe (manner) and Emerson (substance). Ives, who felt a strong spiritual kinship with Emerson, held that music, if it was truly "substantial," was an expression of character. He was thinking of individual character; but he believed— with reference to musical nationalism — that if the composer had assimilated the national component as a vital and necessary part of his own character, then his music (if he was an American), would inevitably have a quality, however indefinable, that deserved to be called American.

Ives, however, warned against "over-insistence upon the national in art." He did not wish to limit or place boundaries on artistic expression and least of all on music. It may be, he said, that music "was not intended to satisfy the curious definiteness of man. Maybe it is better to hope that music may always be a transcendental language in the most extravagant sense." The transcendentalism of Ives not only links him with America's past through his profound affinity with the Concord Transcendentalists (to whom his Second Piano Sonata is dedicated), but also places him above the immediate polemical situation represented by such men as MacDowell, Dvořák, Farwell, and Gilbert. This permits Ives to appear, in the second half of the twentieth century, as the most stimulating historical presence for the new composers who seek to transcend the definiteness of conventional forms and techniques and to make of music a truly "transcendental language in the most extravagant sense." Perhaps Ives's most remarkable achievement was bringing a sense of extrava-

gance into the timid, imitative, conventional enclosure of American art music at the beginning of our century.

Daniel Gregory Mason, a composer of New England anteced-
ents who did a great deal of lecturing and writing about music,
diagnosed the chronic illness of American art music as, "too
much passive reception, too little self-realizing activity. . . ." We
are not only parrots, he said, "but polyglot parrots." Detailing
the plethora of national, racial, regional, and aesthetic ingredients in our musical culture, he characterized American musical
composition from 1914 to 1928 as the "Music of Indigestion."
Much as he favored the Ango-American tradition, he was not
convinced that nationalism was a satisfactory cure for the ills
of musical indigestion. He found that nationalism suffered from
"a fatal defect" — that of excessive narrowness. His ultimate
plea was for "an elastic eclecticism of individual choice."

Roy Harris and Aaron Copland, two of the leading musical
Americanists in the twentieth century, both attempt to be specific in discussing the American quality in music. Harris appears
convinced that "our rhythmic impulses are fundamentally different from the rhythmic impulses of Europeans," and he maintains that "from this unique rhythmic sense are generated different melodic and formal values." He is confident, moreover,
"that a national taste and talent for harmonic balance and
nuance is developing" in the United States. But when he gen-
eralizes he becomes sententious: "Musical literature never has
and never will be valuable to society as a whole until it is created
as an authentic and characteristic culture of and from the people
it expresses." Calling upon the testimony of history to support
his personal convictions (as most of us do), Harris writes: "History reveals that the great music has been produced only by
staunch individuals who sank their roots deeply into the social
soil which they accepted as their own."

Aaron Copland, in his autobiographical sketch titled "Composer From Brooklyn," does not discuss nationalism in general,
but simply tells us that at a certain moment in his career he
"was anxious to write a work that would immediately be recognized as American in character." He does not present this
attitude as something entirely individual, or purely a matter

of personal conviction; on the contrary, he tells us that "this desire to be 'American' was symptomatic of the period." It was the spirit of the time, the *Zeitgeist,* that caused Copland to think of his First Symphony as being "too European in inspiration." It was perhaps also the *Zeitgeist* of the Jazz Age that suggested to Copland the most effective means for writing music that would immediately be recognized as American in character. So he decided "frankly to adapt the jazz idiom" in the composition of symphonic music. The principal fruits of this decision were the suite titled *Music for the Theatre* (1925) and the Concerto for Piano and Orchestra (1926). But Copland did not find it creatively profitable to pursue this vein any further. True, "it was an easy way to be American in musical terms, but all American music could not possibly be confined to two dominant jazz moods: the 'blues' and the snappy number." Eventually Copland found other ways of writing American music, by using folk tunes and cowboy songs; yet he had no desire to be held down by the roots in any particular social soil. Rather he claimed, like Mason, the eclecticism of individual choice.

Neither Harris nor Copland was exclusively concerned with the aesthetics or the social significance of musical Americanism. In discussing problems of the American composer, Harris deplored the lack of performances of American compositions by the country's orchestras ("Why should they sweat over a young American upstart?"); protested against the teaching of obvious formulas in musical composition; attacked the power and the poor preparation of music critics; and indicted the commercialism and materialism of the United States as a hindrance to the freedom of creative expression.

Virgil Thomson, in discussing the situation of the composer in America, became even more specific when he wrote about "how composers eat," thus shifting the problem to the bedrock of economic survival. Apart from having a private fortune or marrying money, he saw the economic status of the American composer—in the 1930's—as highly precarious. He noted that the composer was a member of the professional class while enjoying few of the advantages of that position, especially the opportunity to earn an adequate income. Constricted by economic limitations, the composer does not enjoy complete intellectual freedom but "has that only with regard to the formal, or structural aspects of his art."

At about the same time, a composer of vastly different background and aims, the French-born Edgard Varèse, who had been living in New York since 1915, gave a speech in Los Angeles advocating the most basic of all freedoms for musical composition—the freedom to be heard. Music, he found, "has not gone forward with the other arts today but still turns around and around like a squirrel in a cage." There is no musical institution in America, he pointed out, corresponding to the Museum of Modern Art in New York. "The very basis of creative work is experimentation," he declared; yet where is any support or encouragement to be found for experimental music in the United States? Varèse foresaw not only the possibility but the necessity for electronically produced sounds to give the composer a complete range of freedom and to liberate him, in large measure, from the tyranny of the interpreter.

Among native-born American musicians, the line of innovation runs from Charles Ives and Henry Cowell, through Harry Partch and John Cage, to Earle Brown and the newer "experimental" composers such as Morton Feldman, Robert Ashley, James Tenney, and many others. Ives was an intuitive innovator rather than a systematic theorist, and the conditions under which he worked as a composer—virtually isolated from contemporary musical activity—prevented him from exerting an immediate influence during the most productive period of his life, about 1895 to 1915. He avoided technical considerations in his writings, being more concerned with spiritual and aesthetic values. A sort of homespun musical Emerson, a belated Transcendentalist, he once wrote: "The future of music may not lie with music itself, but rather . . . in the way it makes itself a part with the finer things that humanity does and dreams of."

Henry Cowell, who was Ives's friend, champion, and biographer, felt the need to formulate a theoretical justification for the technical innovations, such as the celebrated tone-clusters, that he had intuitively exploited as a very young man. This led him, in 1919, to write a book called *New Musical Resources*, in which he systematically explored the application of overtone relationships to musical composition—covering not only what had been done but also what might be done. The book was not published until 1930, so that the publication date actually obscures the innovative importance of Cowell's theories. While the work underwent considerable revision in the intervening years, this should not detract from its significance as a pioneering and prophetic treatise — the most important theoretical work by an American composer up to that time.

Harry Partch, writing on American musical tendencies in 1927,[1] found much that was disturbing in the stranglehold that the Establishment had on musical activity in the United States. His key question was pitched on a rather pessimistic note: "Will the American genius for perverting a spark of individual imagination into a commodity for nationwide distribution permit us—ever—to hope for a significant evolution in American music?" Obviously, the riddle consists in knowing what Partch means by "significant evolution." What he means, I believe, might be expressed by the title of Bergson's celebrated work *Creative Evolution*. Partch sees our musical activity as geared primarily to the smooth, mass-reproduction of the standard masterpieces plus the commercial dissemination of a synthetic music that is neither great abstract music nor genuine corporeal music (such as authentic folk song), but a routine sound-product "obviously born of outside pressure and inward weariness." For him, the musical situation is simply one manifestation of what he calls the "general paralysis of individuality" in American life. Partch, like Varèse, makes a plea for freedom in musical expression, and he phrases this specifically as "the opportunity to hear, to create, and to be heard." The desideratum for which he pleads is "a congenial milieu for the music of the creators who do not fit into the Abstractionist framework of 'serious' music . . . ." It is perhaps not too optimistic to say that, since 1947, the milieu—in spots, if not as a whole—has become more congenial to the American musical creator who has other aims

1 Partch's book was published in 1949; but according to the "Foreword," the first draft was finished some twenty years earlier. [Ed.]

than that of joining the Establishment. And Partch himself is a striking illustration of the stubborn survival of individualism in the United States.

There is a vast area of musical composition in the United States whose representatives do not, as a rule, indulge in discursive or ratiocinative statements about their work. What was the aesthetic philosophy of Daniel Decatur Emmett, the composer of "Dixie," or of Scott Joplin, the one-time King of Ragtime, or of William Christopher Handy, composer of the immortal "St. Louis Blues"? No one knows or cares. Yet these men were far from inarticulate, in their own way. Handy wrote an autobiography, *Father of the Blues,* which is an important document of America's musical history. Autobiography, indeed, became the chief historical medium for shedding light on the often obscure processes of the rise and proliferation of the various forms of the American musical vernacular: ragtime, blues, jazz (in its many phases from the archaic to the ultra-modern), the popular song, the musical comedy, the military march (Sousa wrote *his* autobiography too!). To be sure, histories have been written on these aspects of our music; but in the case of popular music they are mostly superficial, and in the case of jazz they are necessarily based largely on hearsay, since no historians were wise enough to document the development of this music while it was actually happening. Now historians are frantically busy, with the assistance of foundation grants, tape-recording the reminiscences of the last survivors of the heroic age of jazz.

It was Alan Lomax who first applied the recorded interview technique to the history of jazz, in his ever-memorable sessions with Ferdinand "Jelly Roll" Morton at the Library of Congress in 1938. The skeptic might say that in these recording sessions, jazz history was not so much made as made up. It is true that "Jelly Roll," whose conceit was colossal, exaggerated his own role in the development of jazz. His reminiscences and declarations are simply primary historical sources which, like any others, need to be critically examined and evaluated by the historian. And, of course, there is the pure gold of the music—for "Jelly

Roll" played as well as talked. Both in his playing and in his talking he was most eager to put across the idea that jazz was *real* music—beautiful music—when properly played. And so he would demonstrate the "wrong" and the "right" way to do it.

All this is fine, even fascinating; but was Jelly Roll Morton a composer in the sense in which that term is generally used? We need, I think, to revive the old concept of the composer-performer, the creator-executant, as an indivisible entity. Charlie Parker, playing the saxophone, was a creative genius of the first magnitude. I am convinced that Morton was also a creative personality—though I prefer not to measure his magnitude— and hence what we call, in music, "a composer." As are also Duke Ellington, Thelonius Monk, Miles Davis, Ornette Coleman, George Russell, Charles Mingus—and other luminaries of modern jazz. I wish that all of them could speak at length in this book as American composers; but as a whole they are not wordy men. The one conspicuous exception is Mingus, who has poured forth his ideas, his memories, his convictions, his resentments, into a mammoth autobiographical work of over 1,500 manuscript pages, which Nat Hentoff describes as "a molten collection of reminiscences, exposés of the music business, and reflections on race relations."[2]

The achievements of such jazz composers as Ellington, Mingus, Jimmy Giuffre, George Russell,[3] Miles Davis, and Charlie Parker are discussed by Gunther Schuller, himself a composer and executant (on the French horn), who is equally at home in the worlds of jazz and of classical music. Indeed, much of his talent and effort have been successfully directed toward bringing about a union of the two in what has been called "Third Stream Music." His article, "The Future of Form in Jazz," written in 1955, is prophetic, for it predicted an increased preoccupation with new musical forms in jazz, a reaching out "for more complex ideas, a wider range of expression." This has certainly come to pass during the decade since Schuller's perceptive article was published; jazz, as he foresaw, has become more and more a *listener's*

2 Mingus is articulate but uncooperative: he refused permission for any statement by him to be included in the present anthology. [Ed.]
3 Russell is the author of an interesting treatise on jazz composition, *The Lydian Chromatic Concept of Tonal Organization* (New York, 1961). [Ed.]

art, with a highly sophisticated aural and aesthetic appeal. Jazz may not be *the* "music of the future" (that eternal historical illusion!), but it is definitely a music with a future.

The German philosopher Wilhelm Dilthey defined historical force as "the influence which any experience has in determining what other experiences shall succeed it." According to this definition, the influence of John Cage would constitute the most powerful historical force in American music since 1950. Although his ideas and his music have upset many people, Cage's own attitude is one of calm and serene confidence. "One need not fear about the future of music," he wrote. "The future of creative art is always safe. It is the *present* that seems difficult and doubtful. And yet it is really all so simple! All we have to do is to accept the proposition that, in musical terms, any sounds may occur in any combination and in any continuity"— also that silences may occur instead of sounds. And what is required for perfect understanding of the new music? "Just an attention to the activity of sounds." In short: "New music: new listening." What could be simpler? Cage offers us the key to that "world of perception beyond knowledge" of which Partch speaks, the "Enchanted Land" of pure perception.

The somewhat flippant title of Milton Babbitt's article, "Who Cares if You Listen?" is actually the gambit to a coolly objective analysis of the situation of the "advanced" composer in the contemporary musical world. Other writers on the subject, such as William Schuman, have tacitly assumed that with sufficient goodwill and "understanding" on either side, the gulf separating the modern composer and the average listener can somehow be bridged. Babbitt, on the contrary, takes the position that the gulf is not only inevitable, but necessary and desirable. Far from trying to build a bridge across it, the advanced (or experimental) composer should simply go about mending his own fences, letting the layman wallow in his ignorance and indifference. Putting the matter bluntly, he inquires, "Why should the layman be other than bored and puzzled by what he is unable to understand, music or anything else?"

Babbitt maintains that it is foolish and unrealistic to expect that this specialized, advanced music can find wide acceptance "in an alien and inapposite world," wherein both popular prejudice and established authority work continually against it. Instead of coming to terms with popular taste, he recommends for the composer a "total, resolute, and voluntary withdrawal from this public world to one of private performance and electronic media, with its very real possibility of complete elimination of the public and social aspects of musical composition." He rests his case for the noncommercial support of experimental music on the premise that music will cease to evolve if there is no experimentation, and hence "in that important sense, will cease to live." More specifically, Babbitt points out that the contemporary composer no longer lives "in a unitary musical universe of 'common practice,' but in a variety of universes of diverse practice." That is why no unilateral approach to the composer–and–public relationship can be valid in today's world. Only by recognizing the "variety of universes" in contemporary musical practice and by granting full autonomy, respect, and support to each can we achieve a mature and civilized attitude toward musical creativity in America.

Writing about the same time as Babbitt and from the standpoint of an "advanced" composer of an earlier generation who is nevertheless much closer to traditional procedures in most of his music, Elliott Carter, thoughtfully and with moderation, analyses the problem of continuity—both in composing and in listening—that arises from the "many different trends" of contemporary music. After the "emancipation of dissonance" achieved by Schoenberg and other composers in the early years of this century—including the Americans, Ives and Cowell— Carter sees the present era as characterized by an "emancipated musical discourse" that enables the composer to use "any system or musical procedure that seems suitable" for a particular work. He believes that "the composer, in spite of all, *does* write for a public," and he is reluctant to follow the road toward "complete hermeticism"—the *selva oscura* where much of the new music remains hidden from public view. On the other hand, he speculates as to whether "this road toward hermeticism" is really a dead end, as generally supposed, since "today we see the poems of Mallarmé and Valéry in our children's high-school French book." In other words, what was once hermetic and accessible only to an élite has become the intellectual pablum of teen-agers. Perhaps the most practically valuable statement in Carter's essay is that which refers to the need for a "restudying of existing music and the elaboration of a more significant kind of music theory that is more widely applicable"—applicable, that is, to all the varied universes of musical discourse instead of to only one variety.

Elliot Carter, pointing to the "vast array of information, of methods and ideas" that are available—as never before in such abundance—to the composer of today, remarks that "even the most erudite composers of the past did not have so much to learn and so much to choose from." Hence many composers feel the need to limit their range, to select a specific area within which they choose to work. "This need for choice," Carter continues, "explains why young composers have relied on one dominating figure after another—following Stravinsky and others in neoclassicism, or Schoenberg in expressionism." This situation is perfectly illustrated in Arthur Berger's article "Stravinsky and the Younger American Composers," written in 1954.

Actually, it was Aaron Copland who, several years earlier, had written: "Among our younger generation it is easy to discover a Stravinsky school: Shapero, Haieff, Berger, Lessard, Foss, Fine." But Berger, who by 1954 was the recognized *chef d'école* of this group, added some half-dozen more names to the list and undertook to defend himself and his colleagues "from the accusation of being servile followers" of Stravinsky. He confirms Carter's thesis when he writes: "The challenge to our newer generation is to consolidate our country's vast new resources and to rehabilitate solid structures after years of sheer effect for its own sake." He also deprecates the cultivation of personality as "old-fashioned" and believes that the main center of attention should rightfully be shifted from the personality of the artist to the work of art itself. While he is concerned with individuality of style, he believes that a discerning critic should be able to perceive and evaluate this individuality in terms of specific detail,

instead of merely dismissing a composer as being just a smaller
Stravinsky.

Ten years after the publication of Berger's article, I communi-
cated with most of the musicians mentioned and found that they
regarded their "Stravinsky period" simply as a passing phase.
In any case, Stravinsky himself continued to evolve, and those of
his neoclassical disciples who turned to twelve-tone writing—
even though they may have done so independently or for different reasons—were still following the example of the Master.

Writing of the "younger generation" in 1958, William Flanagan is somewhat on the defensive because of the widespread notion that "the United States has failed to produce a new generation of composers to rival the vitality, [the] originality . . . that
was so characteristic of men like Roy Harris and Aaron Copland
during the twenties, or David Diamond and William Schuman
during the thirties." While recognizing several factors that enter
into this view, Flanagan holds that "our primary difficulty . . .
rests with our failure to achieve consistent performance with the
major symphony orchestras." This, he believes, is one of the reasons why some young composers have turned to the writing
of operas "with a kind of desperate gusto." At the same time,
he points out that the operatic medium is "not one to attract
young composers working in advanced styles."

In a judicious and revealing retrospective survey, Flanagan
finds that "Copland and Harris are, in all probability, the United
States composers whose work has been most drawn on by the
young." He, too, mentions the Stravinsky movement, which he
characterizes as an example of "reevaluating tradition." Although Flanagan himself, as a composer, is more concerned with
reevaluating tradition than with sheer innovation in the manner
of John Cage, he is objective enough to recognize in the latter's
aesthetic an important creative principle, namely, that of "*depersonalizing* sound, freeing it from its historical commitment
to logical arrangement, formal design and personal expressivity
that the usual composer imposes upon it." Unlike those who ridi-
cule or dismiss Cage's work as nonsense, Flanagan points out
that "Cage is, in the last analysis, questioning the classic definition of music, which he has every right to do."

Admitting that the situation is largely one of chaos, Flanagan nevertheless concludes on a confident and defiant note: "Our generation is venturesome and even defiant in its refusal to cotton to the sociological and critical pressures that would wish it otherwise." Admitting the presence of "a disquieting question mark," he obviously considers this preferable to a self-satisfied full stop.

If Roger Sessions continues to be regarded with great admiration by many of the younger generation, this is in part because he too prefers unceasing search and continual questioning to any kind of self-satisfaction or self-repetition. Neither a "revolutionist" nor a "conservative," he has known how to change with the times—from neoclassicism to dodecaphonism—while always maintaining his creative individuality and intellectual integrity. He readily concedes that "harmony as we have traditionally conceived it has probably reached a dead end"—which definitely takes him out of the conservative camp. He advocates the "responsibility of holding one's mind, ear and heart open to whatever may reveal genuinely new vistas of musical expression and experience"—which indicates that he is receptive to the profound transformations taking place in all the arts of our time. But he also points out that there have been "earlier periods of apparent crisis during which long-established values were brought into deep question," thereby implying that our own age may not be unique in this respect. He scrutinizes such developments as post-Webern serialism and electronic composition with the critical objectivity that is so lacking in most discussions of these trends. Without partisanship, above the melée yet not aloof from its issues, detached and yet involved, Roger Sessions holds fast to the conviction that the creative imagination, which, "at its most vital, has revealed itself through many and often surprising channels," will continue to do so through the surprising and often disconcerting developments of our time.

If it is true, as William Flanagan wrote, that many of the younger American composers are turning toward opera "with a sort of desperate gusto," may not this be because the American composer has so long been frustrated in this area? Up to very recent times, a few performances at the Metropolitan Opera in New York was about all that even the most privileged of

American composers could expect. The few exceptions, such as Marc Blitzstein's *Regina* or Virgil Thomson's *Four Saints in Three Acts*, which enjoyed Broadway runs, only prove the rule; and, besides, these operas were different. Perhaps Charles Hamm is unduly pessimistic in his picture of the operatic situation in the United States; on the other hand, he may simply be more realistic than most writers on the subject. Basically, his attitude is constructive. "We have in this country today," he writes, "all of the necessary ingredients for a thriving operatic life. We have excellent singers, instrumentalists, directors, technicians, and the largest potential audience of well-educated people with time and money to spare that the world has ever known. And we have composers with enough talent to write first-rate operas." Everything now depends, in his view, on the American composer, who must be able to deliver the goods: "We need composers of genius who will have enough respect for opera not to presume to write in this form until they understand it and have mastered some of its techniques . . . [and] who are willing to write half a dozen or more unsuccessful operas in the process of acquiring a technique."

The prescription is not likely to meet with favor in a country where success means quick success and where composers, instead of achieving a reputation by composing one opera after another, rely on their reputation in other fields in order to write an opera that will be assured of production regardless of its merit. In Europe composers became famous by writing operas; in the United States composers become famous in order to write operas.

Charles Hamm's trenchant and challenging article undercuts any complacency that may exist with regard to opera in the United States. His plea, in effect, is for expert professionalism in a highly specialized and exacting field. The American popular musical theater—admired and emulated throughout the world —was developed by skilled professionals who devoted their entire efforts to the task. Can American opera demand less?

Near the end of his lecture on experimental music, John Cage asks, "Where do we go from here?" And his answer is: "Towards theater. . . . We have eyes as well as ears and it is our business while we are alive to use them." What Cage means by theater

is certainly not what Gershwin—or even the successful play-
wrights of his generation—thought of when they used the term.
The term "theater" has to be widened to include not only the
"well-made play"—with or without music—and the "theater
of the absurd," but also those "indeterminate happenings" or
"anarchistic situations," such as Cage's *Theatre Piece* of 1960,
in which the composer took his greatest leap thus far in the
direction that he now considers necessary—"away from art,"
toward nature.

The publicity surrounding some of Cage's most sensational
experiments with "indeterminacy" should not be allowed to obscure the importance of this principle as a motivating force
in the contemporary arts, particularly in music. Indeterminacy
should not be confused with the chance operations upon which
much of Cage's compositional procedure relies. Although the
results of such chance operations are obviously indeterminate—
since they cannot be known in advance—there are other ways
in which a musical work can follow the principle of indeterminacy. For example, indeterminacy can be obtained by what Earle
Brown calls "spontaneous decisions in the performance of a
work and the possibility of the composed elements being 'mobile' " — in the same sense in which the sculptures of Calder are
mobile. That is to say, "there are basic units subject to innumerable different relationships or forms." In Brown's development
of indeterminacy he has aimed at achieving "basic structural
possibilities having more than one conceivable function within
their implied content." As a consequence of the built-in variables,
"no two performances [of a given work] will arrive at the same
formal result, but the work will retain its identity from performance to performance through the unchanging basic character of the events."

Although Earle Brown (born in 1926) was for a time associated with John Cage in New York, his guiding aesthetic ideas
were formulated before his meeting with that composer in 1952.
These ideas, as he explains in the statement included in this volume, were derived from the examples of Jackson Pollock in
painting and Alexander Calder in sculpture, the former providing the principle of spontaneous action, the latter the principle

of mobility. Technically and theoretically, Brown built on the
foundations of Joseph Schillinger's pioneering work, *The Mathematical Basis of the Arts*, even though he reacted against the
excessive rigidity of its concepts.

Composers such as Ives, Cowell, Cage, Earle Brown, and many
others at present active throughout the United States, have succeeded in "breaking the cake of custom"—to use an expression
coined many years ago by the English writer Walter Bagehot in
his book *Physics and Politics* (1876). This occurs, said Bagehot,
"when the sudden impact of new thoughts and new examples
breaks down the compact despotism of the single consecrated
code,"—and history shows that the breakthrough can be accomplished only with great difficulty.

In spite of William Billings' brave admonition to every composer "to be his own Carver," most American composers, in line
with the national trend toward conformity, have been content to
follow the dictates of "the single consecrated code." Yet that
many of them chafed under the yoke of this "compact despotism"
is apparent from their writings. And, on the whole, considering
the unfavorable conditions of the environment and their precarious situation between the Scylla of academicism and the
Charybdis of commercialism, it is surprising—and heartening
—to observe how often, and in how many ways, they have succeeded in breaking the cake of custom.

WILLIAM
BILLINGS (1746–1800), a native and resident of Boston,

Massachusetts, was saluted by a contemporary as "the father of our New England music." Born to poverty, with scant schooling, he was apprenticed to the tanner's trade but found music more alluring. He made music his sole occupation at a time when, among Americans, it was still either an avocation or a sideline. It is no wonder, then, that at his premature death he left his family in poverty and was buried in a pauper's grave.

When Billings, at the age of twenty-four and with only a rudimentary knowledge of music, published his first "tune book," *The New England Psalm Singer, or American Chorister* (1770), he professed little regard for "rules," declaring with youthful brashness, "I think it best for every *Composer* to be his own *Carver.*" Yet, following the customary practice of the early American "singing masters," he himself undertook to explain the rules of music in the introduction to his various books, which made him widely celebrated as one of the most successful choral composers and "singing-school" teachers of his time. And in his last book, *The Continental Harmony* (1794), he publicly confessed—in the form of an imaginary dialogue with a carping critic—his former ignorance and acknowledged with humorous effrontery that "I was fool enough to commence author before I really understood either *time, tune,* or *concord.*"

In addition to these two books, he published several others: *The Singing Master's Assistant* (1778), popularly known as

"Billings' Best"; *Music in Miniature* (1779) ; the *Psalm Singer's Amusement* (1781) ; and *The Suffolk Harmony* (1786). Like most of his contemporaries, Billings wrote unaccompanied choral music, consisting of anthems, hymns, and psalms—the staple musical fare of the American people at that time. Some of these compositions he called "fuges," which meant that they were written in the manner known as "fuging" [*sic*], in which, as he said, "the parts come after each other, with the same notes." The fuging style aroused much opposition among the more conservative musicians, who felt that it was "undignified."

Billings' defence of the fuging tunes—like everything else he wrote—was spirited, humorous, and full of the quirks and conceits that mark him as an unforgettable character. In the words of Dr. Hans Nathan, "He is the fervent and, in his own way, philosophizing preacher, and the chatty and clownish entertainer. At his pleasure he resorts to any literary device at hand: solemn prose, jingling poetry, anecdotes, the homely phrase, and the contemporary catchword. . . ." His partiality for lengthy footnotes is notorious; he called them "a glorious privilege, for which bad memories and dull authors cannot be too thankful." Hence it is not surprising that three of the following selections from his writings consist entirely of footnotes from the introduction to *The Continental Harmony*.

To All Musical Practitioners / (1770)

Perhaps it may be expected by some, that I should say something concerning the Rules for Composition; to these I answer

that *Nature is the best Dictator*, for all the hard dry studied
Rules that ever was [*sic*] prescribed, will not enable any Person
to form an Air any more than the bare Knowledge of the four
and twenty Letters, and strict Grammatical Rules will qualify
a Scholar for composing a Piece of Poetry, or properly adjusting a Tragedy, without a Genius. It must be Nature, Nature
must lay the Foundation, Nature must inspire the Thought. But
perhaps some may think I mean and intend to throw Art intirely
[*sic*] out of the Question, I answer by no Means, for the more
Art is display'd, the more Nature is decorated. And in some sorts
of Composition, there is dry Study requir'd, and Art very requisite. For instance, in a *Fuge*, where the Parts come in after each
other, with the same Notes; but even there, Art is subservient
to Genius, for Fancy goes first, and strikes out the Work roughly, and Art comes after, and polishes it over. But to return to
my Text; I have read several Author's Rules on Composition,
and find the strictest of them make some Exceptions, as thus,
they say that two Eighths [*i.e.*, octaves] or two Fifths may not
be taken together rising or falling, unless one be Major and the
other Minor; but rather than spoil the Air, they will allow that
Breach to be made, and this allowance gives great Latitude to
young Composers, for they may always make that Plea, and say,
if I am not allow'd to transgress the Rules of Composition, I
shall certainly spoil the Air, and Cross the Strain, that fancy
dictated: and indeed this is without dispute, a very just Plea,
for I am sure I have often and sensibly felt the disagreeable and
slavish Effects of such a restraint as is here pointed out, and so
I believe has every Composer of Poetry, as well as Musick, for
I presume there are as strict Rules for Poetry, as for Musick.
But as I have often heard of a Poetical License, I don't see why
with the same Propriety there may not be a Musical License, for
Poetry and Music [*sic*] are in close Connection, and nearly allied,
besides they are often assistants to each other; and like true
friends often hide each others failings: For I have known a
Piece of Poetry that had neither "Rhime nor Reason" in it,[1] pass

---

1 A simple Fellow bro't a Piece of Prose to Sir *Thomas Moore* for his Inspec-
tion; Sir *Thomas* told him to put it into Rhime, accordingly he did; upon
which Sir *Thomas* said to him, now it is *Rhime*; but before it was neither
Rhime nor Reason.

for tolerable good Sense, because it happened to be set to an excellent Piece of Musick, and to get respect rather for its good fortune in falling into such respectable Company than for any Merit in itself; for likewise I have known and heard a very indifferent Tune often sung, and much caress'd, only because it was set to a fine Piece of Poetry, without which recommendation, perhaps it would not be sung twice over by one Person, and would be deem'd to be dearly bo't only at the expense of Breath requisite to perform it—for my own Part, as I don't think myself confined to any Rules for Composition laid down by any that went before me, neither should I think (were I to pretend to lay down Rules) that any who came after me were any ways obligated to adhere to them, any further than they should think proper: So in fact, I think it is best for every *Composer* to be his own *Carver*. Therefore, upon this Consideration, for me to dictate, or pretend to prescribe Rules of this Nature for others, would not only be very unnecessary, but also a great Piece of Vanity.

Dialogue, Between Master and Scholar
Excerpts from *The Continental Harmony* / (1794)

SCHOLAR. Sir, I should be glad to know which key you think is best; the flat, or the sharp key?[2]
MASTER. I believe your question would puzzle the greatest philos-

2 By the "flat key" and the "sharp key," Billings meant, respectively, the minor and the major modes. [Ed.]

opher, or practitioner, upon earth; for there are so many excellent pieces on each key, that we are apt to fall in with a certain man, who heard two very eminent lawyers plead in opposition to each other; after the first had done speaking, the man
was so charmed with his eloquence and oratory, that he thought
it would be an idle (as well as rash) attempt for any one to gainsay, or contradict him; but when he had heard the second, he
said, that his reasons were so nervous and weighty, he was
about to give him the preference; upon which the first made so
forcible a reply, that the man knew not what to say, at last he
concluded they were both best. Similar to this, let us suppose
ourselves to be auditors to a company of musicians: how enrap-
tured should we be to hear the sharp key, express itself in such
lofty and majestic strains as these! *O come let us sing unto the
Lord, let us make a joyful noise, to the rock of our salvation; let
us come before his presence with thanksgiving and make a joyful
noise unto him with psalms. Sing unto the Lord all the earth,
make a loud noise, rejoice and sing praise!* Do I hear the voice of
men, or angels! surely such angelic sounds cannot proceed from
the mouths of sinful mortals: but while we are yet warm with
the thought, and ravished with the sound, the musicians change
their tone, and the flat key utters itself in strains so moving, and
pathetic, that it seems at least to command our attention to such
mournful sounds as these: *Hear my prayer O Lord, give ear to
my supplication, hear me speedily: O Lord my spirit faileth, hide
not thy face from me; O my God, my soul is cast down within me.
Have pity upon me, O ye my friends, for the hand of God hath
touched me.* O how these sounds thrill through my soul! how
agreeably they affect my nerves! how soft, how sweet, how soothing! methinks these sounds are more expressive than the other,
for they affect us both with pleasure and pain, but the *pleasure*
is so great it makes even *pain* be pleasant, so that for the sake of
the pleasure, I could forever bear the pain. But hark! what shout
is that? It seems the sharp key is again upon the wing toward
heaven; jealous, perhaps, that we pay too much deference to his
rival: he not only desires, but *commands* us to join in such exalted strains as these: *Rejoice in the Lord, and again I say, rejoice, O clap your hands all ye people, shout unto God with the*

*voice of triumph; God is gone up with a shout, the Lord with
the sound of a trumpet; sing praises to God, sing praises, sing
praises unto our King, sing praises.* What an ecstasy of joy may
we suppose the Royal Author to be in when he composed this
Psalm of praise! perhaps it might be some such strain as this,
that expelled the evil spirit, and I wish it might expel some of the
evil spirits in these days, who are averse to hearing God's praises
sung, in such a manner as the Psalmist has here pointed out:
but I would refer such persons to King David, for their character, who says, they are like the deaf adder, who floppeth her ear,
and will not hearken to the voice of charmers, charming never
so wisely. But to return, you see the extreme difficulty, and almost impossibility of giving the preference to either of these
keys, both of which are so agreeable to our natures, and are so
excellent that they seem to excel each other; for when we are
about to declare ourselves in favour of one, the other comes and
pleads its own cause so powerfully upon our nerves, that it not
only staggers, but sometimes sets us quite beside our purpose;
for the one is so sublime, so grand, and so majestic, the other
so soft, so soothing, so pathetic; in fact, the key which comes
last seems to be the best, and generally leaves the greatest impression. History gives us an account very similar to this in the
Life of Alexander the Great, viz. that while he was sitting at
table (calmly and quietly) his musician would strike upon a
majestic strain on the sharp key, sounding *to arms, to arms, to
arms*, in such animating and commanding sounds, that the king
being filled with martial rage, would start from table, draw his
sword, and be just about to sally forth, in order to slay his ene-
mies, when none were near him; but even while martial fury had
the ascendancy over reason, the musicians would change the key,
and play such moving and melting airs; viz. *Darius is fall'n,
fall'n, fall'n,* that the king (being melted into pity) would let his
sword drop out of his hand, sit down and weep heartily for him,
whose destruction he had been always seeking, and whose ruin
he had but just accomplished. For my own curiosity I have been
very critical in my observations, and very industrious in my in-
quiries, and I find that most men who are lovers of music, are
affected in the same manner (though not often to such a de-

gree) as Alexander was; but at the same time, if all, who are lovers of music, were to decide the point by vote, I am positive the flat key would have the preference by a great majority.

SCHOLAR. Sir, I do not well understand you, for you have but just given it as your opinion, that the two keys, were to most men equally pleasing; therefore I should be glad to hear you explain yourself further.

MASTER. When I spoke in that manner, I meant to confine the observation to the male sex: but you take it for granted, that the female part of the creation are much the greatest lovers of music; for I scarcely ever met with one but what was more or less entertained with musical sounds, and I am very positive that nine-tenths of them are much more pleased and entertained with a flat, than a sharp air; and I make no doubt, but that the musical world (if upon reading what I have now asserted, they should be induced to make some observations that way) must unavoidably fall into my opinion.

[*The Pleasures of Variety*]³

It is an old maxim, and I think a very just one, viz. *that variety is always pleasing*, and it is well known that there is more variety in one piece of fuging [*sic*] music, than in twenty pieces of plain song, for while the tones do most sweetly coincide and agree, the words are seemingly engaged in a musical warfare; and excuse the paradox if I further add, that each part seems determined by dint of harmony and strength of accent, to drown his competitor in an ocean of harmony, and while each part is thus mutually striving for mastery, and sweetly contending for victory, the audience are most luxuriously entertained, and exceedingly delighted; in the mean time, their minds are surprisingly agitated, and extremely fluctuated; sometimes declaring in favour of one part and sometimes another.—Now the solemn bass demands their attention, now the manly tenor, now the lofty counter, now the volatile treble, now here, now there, now

---

3 This selection occurs as a footnote (!) on page xxviii of *A Commentary on the preceding Rules; by way of Dialogue, between Master and Scholar*. It was prompted by mention of "fuging music," which always put Billings on the defensive. [Ed.]

here again—O inchanting! [*sic*] O ecstatic! Push on, push on ye sons of harmony, and

> Discharge your deep mouth'd canon, full fraught with
>   Diapasons;
> May you with Maestoso, rush on to Choro-Grando,
> And then with Vigoroso, let fly your Diapentes
> About our nervous system.

[*The Composer and the Critic*][4]

Ah! well, what says the critic? "I think, Mr. Author, your *precept* is excellent, and your *practice* but indifferent, for in your New England Psalm Singer, you seem to take but little notice of either *emphasis* or *accent*, and whether the reason is founded either upon ignorance or inattention, I am not able to determine, but I am rather inclined to think the former." Hark you, Mr. Critic, a word in your ear, hear and be astonished, and let me assure you, upon the word and honour of an author, that what I am about to confess is neither ambiguous nor ironical, but you may depend upon my sincerity, when I acknowledge, I was fool enough to commence author before I really understood either *tune, time,* or *concord.* "Indeed, this from your heart." This from my very soul. "Amazing, what condescension is this, in an author of your popularity? But sure, Mr. Author, you do not intend to publish this acknowledgment in the world." O, by no means, as I told you before, this is only a word in your ear. "But if my opticks inform me right, I saw this same confession, inserted, verbatim, in a dialogue between you and your pupil, how then do you suppose it possible to conceal it from the world, when it is typically conveyed to every reader." Softly Sir, not quite so loud, if my pupil (who is hard by) should chance to hear your interrogation or my confession, his great opinion of my infallibility, would be entirely destroyed, and instead of respect for my

4 This selection also appears as a "footnote," in the above-mentioned Dialogue, occupying almost the whole of page xxix and part of the next page. It was prompted by a remark made by the Master, concerning the need for "a better agreement about using Forte for Piano, so that one voice would not be so apt to swallow up the other, as is sometimes the case, when they are at a loss about accenting." [Ed.]

knowledge, he would, no doubt, show his contempt of my ignorance, and he might also (with great propriety) express his in-
dignation at my impudence in attempting to instruct him in a
science of which I have confessed myself entirely ignorant; although such teachers are no *novelty*, yet no doubt the consequences to me would be this; the loss of my character, which
would be attended with the loss of my business, and consequently
the loss of my bread; therefore Sir, in the name of charity, I
must entreat you not to be so clamorous. "But indeed, Mr. Author, your manner of answering my last question is very foreign
from the purpose, and entirely evasive; but I am resolved your
equivocation shall not excuse you from answering this concise
question. How do you expect to keep private, what you have already made public?" I do not intend to have it inserted in the
body of the work, but by way of whisper in a marginal note, and
I intend to order the printer to print it on a very small type, in
an obscure part of the book, and as near the bottom of the page
as possible. I suppose, Mr. Critic, I need not inform you that all
readers may be divided into these two classes, viz. the *curious*
and *incurious*; the curious reader, by perusing this work, will
(without this information of mine) be fully satisfied that the
composition is both inaccurate and indifferent; therefore, as I
tell him no more than he knew before, my popularity will not be
diminished by this frank confession; but if he has a spark of
generosity, he will bestow large encomiums both on my honesty
and modesty; and if he does not (I still further confess) I shall
be prodigiously chagrined, and confoundedly disappointed. As to
the incurious readers (by way of gratitude) I confess they are
a set of people I have great respect for; because they constitute
the greater part of my admirers; and as they seldom trouble
themselves with marginal notes (unless some Type-Master-Gen-
eral should be so illnatured as to inform against me) they would
be none the wiser, and (by this artful evasion) I presume I shall
be none the worse for this honest declaration. And now Sir, in
my turn, I shall take it upon me (however you may receive it)
to interrogate you. Pray Sir, how came you so impertinently
officious in your criticisms upon me? You syllable catcher, if you
are but half so honest as I am condescending, you will acknowl-

edge I have made game out of your own hand, and beat you at
your own weapons! You comma hunter, did I not inform you
that I intended to discharge you from my service, and do my own
drudgery; and now Mr. Semi-critic, once more I command you
to quit my Consonance, with the velocity of a Demisemi; and

> If you ever be so hardy as to traverse my Quartas,
> Or score off your Eptachords with my Diapasons,
>   I solemnly protest,
> By the graveness of Adagio, and vivacity of Allegro,
> The forte of my Canon well charg'd with Septi Nonas,
> Shall greet your Auditory with terrible Sensations,
>   And fill you with tremor.
> I'll beat your empty bars in the twinkle of a pendulum,
> By way of a syncopation I'll score your composition,
> And with a single solo I'll close up your Chorus
>   In tacitness eternal.

FRANCIS
HOPKINSON (1737-1797), born in Philadelphia, belonged
to a prominent family and received an excellent education, graduating from the College of Philadelphia, where he became known as an amateur composer and performer on the harpsichord and the organ. A lawyer by profession, he cultivated music as one of the "polite arts" to which he was strongly attracted by taste and temperament. He supported the revolutionary cause with fervor, was a delegate to the Continental Congress and a signer of the Declaration of Independence, and took an active part in the Constitutional Convention of 1787. From 1779 until his death he served as Judge of the Admiralty from Pennsylvania.

John Adams, who met Hopkinson in 1776 at the studio of the artist Charles Willson Peale, wrote to his wife giving his candid impression of the meeting: "He is one of your pretty, little, curious, ingenious men. His head is not bigger than a large apple. . . . I have not met with anything in natural history more amusing and entertaining than his personal appearance; yet he is genteel and well-bred, and is very social." Adams added that Hopkinson took delight in "those elegant and ingenious arts of painting, sculpture, statuary, architecture, and music."

Hopkinson spent many of his leisure hours copying out the music of vocal compositions by celebrated European musicians of his day, which he collected into a volume of over two hundred pages. Scattered among the hundred or more pieces in this collection are six songs signed with the initials "F. H.," presum-

38

ably composed by him. It is on the basis of these songs that
Francis Hopkinson earned a place in the musical history of the
United States as the first native-born composer—the first, that is,
whose music has been definitely dated. The first of his six songs
in the manuscript collection mentioned above, "My Days Have
Been So Wondrous Free," bears the date 1759.

In 1788, Hopkinson published a collection titled *Seven Songs
for the Harpsichord or Forte-Piano*, advertised as "intended for
young practitioners" and as "the first work of this kind attempted in the United States." The volume, which actually contains eight songs, was dedicated to General George Washington.

**Dedication to His Excellency George Washington,
Esquire / (1788)**

SIR,

I embrace, with heart-felt satisfaction, every opportunity that
offers of recognizing the personal Friendship that hath so long
subsisted between us. The present Occasion allows me to do this
in a manner most flattering to my Vanity; and I have accordingly taken advantage of it, by presenting this Work to your
Patronage, and honouring it with your Name.

It cannot be thought an unwarrantable anticipation to look
up to you as seated in the most dignified situation that a grateful
People can offer. The universally avowed Wish of America, and
the Nearness of the Period in which that Wish will be accomplished, sufficiently justify such an Anticipation; from which

arises a confident Hope, that the same Wisdom and Virtue which has so successfully conducted the Arms of the United States in Times of Invasion, War, and Tumult, will prove also the successful Patron of Arts and Sciences in Times of national Peace and Prosperity; and that the Glory of America will rise conspicuous under a Government designated by the *Will*, and an Administration founded in the *Hearts* of THE PEOPLE.

With respect to the little Work, which I have now the honour to present to your notice, I can only say that it is such as a Lover, not a Master, of the Arts can furnish. I am neither a profess'd Poet, nor a profess'd Musician; and yet venture to appear in those characters united; for which, I confess, the censure of Temerity may justly be brought against me.

If these Songs should not be so fortunate as to please the *young* Performers, for whom they are intended, they will at least not occasion much Trouble in learning to perform them; and this will, I hope, be some Alleviation of their Disappointment.

However small the Reputation may be that I shall derive from this Work, I cannot, I believe, be refused the Credit of being the first Native of the United States who has produced a Musical Composition. If this attempt should not be too severely treated, others may be encouraged to venture in a path, yet untrodden in America, and the Arts in succession will take root and flourish amongst us.

I hope for your favorable Acceptance of this Mark of my Affection and Respect, and have the Honour to be

> Your Excellency's most obedient, and
>
> Most humble Servant,

PHILADELPHIA   F. HOPKINSON
Nov. 20th, 1788.

ANTHONY PHILIP

HEINRICH (1781–1861) was born in Bohemia of German descent and became through inheritance a wealthy wholesale merchant and banker. Indulging his taste for travel throughout Europe, he also dabbled in music and learned to play the piano and violin. In 1810 he came to the United States in the hope of expanding his export business; but a year later the financial crash in Austria ruined him completely, and he decided to remain in America. After a stay in Philadelphia, he made his way on foot to Pittsburgh, where he had been offered a position as musical director of a theater. With the collapse of that enterprise, he set out for Kentucky via the Ohio River, and in 1817 he arrived at Lexington, where he proceeded to organize and conduct some concerts that included a performance of Beethoven's First Symphony. A severe illness caused him to withdraw from public activity and, in the beautiful setting of Bardstown, Kentucky, he began to compose assiduously, undaunted by his lack of formal training. Many of his compositions reflected the enthusiasm he felt for his adopted land—an enthusiasm that, in spite of many disappointments, he maintained to the end of his long life. All these pieces written in Kentucky he gathered into a volume titled *The Dawning of Music in Kentucky, or the Pleasures of Harmony in the Solitudes of Nature*, which he published in 1820. This was followed by another collection called *The Western Minstrel*.

The self-styled "Loghouse Composer of Kentucky" then moved

41

on to Boston and New York, where his music was performed and on the whole well received, notwithstanding some critical misgivings about "those strange and elaborate works of his." Heinrich was ambitious beyond his powers: he wanted to compose the great American Epic in such works as *The Columbiad: A Grand National Chivalrous Symphony* and *The Jubilee,* "a grand national song of triumph" (from the landing of the Pilgrim fathers to the consummation of American liberty). He was proud, as he says, of being *an American musician* and claimed with justice that "the majority of his compositions . . . are those of purely American sentiment." Although his music is only of antiquarian interest, Heinrich was a pioneer of "musical nationalism" in the United States. He was poverty stricken at the time of his death in New York City.

Preface to *The Dawning of Music in Kentucky* / (1819)

In presenting this work to the world, the Author observes, that he has been actuated much less by any pecuniary interest, than zeal, in furnishing a Volume of various *Musical Compositions,* which, it is hoped, will prove both useful and entertaining.

The many and severe animadversions, so long and repeatedly cast on the talent for Music in the Country, has been one of the chief motives of the Author, in the exercise of his abilities; and should he be able, by this effort, to create but one single *Star* in the *West,* no one would ever be more proud than himself, to be

called an *American Musician*—He however is fully aware of the
dangers which, at the present day, attend talent on the crowded
and difficult road of eminence; but fears of just criticism, by
Competent Masters, should never retard the enthusiasm of genius, when ambitious of producing works more lasting than too
many *Butterfly-effusions* of the present age—He, therefore, rely-
ing on the candour of the Public, will rest confident, that justice
will be done, by due comparison with the works of other Authors
(celebrated for their merit, especially as regards Instrumental
execution) but who have never, like him, been thrown, as it were,
by *discordant events*, far from the emporiums of musical science,
into the isolated wilds of nature, where he invoked his Muse, tu-
tored *only* by ALMA MATER.

A. P. HEINRICH,
KENTUCKY.

Letter to Mr. Seaton, Mayor of Washington, D.C. / (1843)

TO THE HONORABLE MAYOR OF WASHINGTON CITY

GEORGETOWN, 2 March 1843

I hear that your accomplished daughter, Miss Seaton, is a very
distinguished Amateur Pianist. I regret that no suitable occasion
would offer, to hear her perform and join in the Chorus of admiration. Will you have the kindness to present her in my name
the following few stragglers of my compositions for the Piano-

forte with my best apologies, as for the moment I am not provided with copies from my printed effusions of more execution and effect. During 2 weeks, I have at least been trotting about 40 miles, by day and night, to and fro, from the *Tiber* to the *Capitol*, inclusive of many Zig Zags, taken with heavy letters of introduction, Pitts, Patts, Puffs and Packages of music to the Colossuses of learning and patriotism of the Commonwealth, abounding so much in these parts, in quest of Patronage for my Grand National Musically historical work. One night, as an utter stranger, I was actually lost in the swamps of Washington City and the Quagmires of Georgetown, thus sustaining many rough Counterpoints but not one cheering subscription corresponding to my harmonious enterprise. . . . I shall forthwith return very independent, nay stoically to my loft garret in New York, reflect on my haps in Washington City and most likely upset the Musical Consumation [*sic*] of American Liberty (Vide my Prospectus)[1] which is by no means a profitable current or tolerated subject in Europe and other parts of the world, where the divine art however is a particular attribute of the pious and the great in Civilization. If the venerable Patriarch J. Q. Adams, so exalted as a Statesman and Poet, would furnish me a Poem on the Emancipation of the Slaves, as huge as that immense Roulade of Signatures from the Abolitionists which was apparently his Symbol before his seat in the Congress hall,[2] I will compose and arrange a Score or an Oratorio, whose gigantic effects may possibly reverberate more stentorian through the welkin and impressive through the World, than all the ponderous dissonant speeches of his opponents, or the Thunders of Niagara. If necessary, my strains shall also flow as gently as the invitations of the "Lovely Ohio." If you please, mention this little "Fantasia or Cappricio" of mine with "Gran Gusto e Amore" to the enthusiastic and philanthropic John Quincy Adams as coming from the ardent Loghouse Composer of Kentucky, who always strives to fulfill his

1 This refers to the oratorio, *The Consummation of American Liberty*, composed by Heinrich. [Ed.]
2 John Quincy Adams, the former President of the United States, was at this time a member of Congress from Massachusetts and at the age of seventy-five was still active in support of abolitionism. [Ed.]

promises to the best of his powers. Pardon my frank and un-
cerimonious [*sic*] rhapsodizing—remaining with perfect esteem,
honored sir!

Your very obliged humble svt.

A. P. HEINRICH

WILLIAM
HENRY
FRY (1813-1864) was born into a prominent Phila-
delphia family; his father was the founder and publisher of the
National Gazette, and the son began his journalistic career on
the editorial staff of that paper, covering music, theater, and
art. Fry graduated from the University of Pennsylvania in 1830,
received his M.A. there in 1833, and was eventually admitted to
the bar. But music—and opera in particular—was his absorbing
interest. He received music lessons from local teachers and by
the age of fourteen had already begun to write orchestral overtures. Four years later one of his overtures was publicly performed by the Philharmonic Society. He was deeply impressed
by the season of French opera given at Philadelphia by the
French Opera Company from New Orleans in 1827. A season
of Italian opera, by the Montressor Company, followed in 1833.
By this time, Fry was determined to be a composer of operas
himself. After an early uncompleted opera, *Christians and Pa-
gans* (1838), he finished his first complete opera *Aurelia the
Vestal* (1841). He then embarked immediately upon the writing
of his second opera, *Leonora*, with a libretto adapted from Bul-
wer-Lytton's *The Lady of Lyons*; he finished this opera in 1845.
First produced at the Chestnut Street Theatre, Philadelphia, on
June 4, 1845, *Leonora* received about a dozen performances in
that month. The principal singers were Arthur Seguin and his
wife, Anna, both from England. Fry himself paid the costs
of the production. In 1858, with the libretto translated into

46

Italian, *Leonora* was performed at the Academy of Music in New York.

Leonora was the first grand opera written by a native-born American. Fry wrote other operas: *Giulio e Leonora, Notre Dame of Paris, Esmeralda*; choral works (including a *Stabat Mater* and a Mass); at least four descriptive symphonies (including the *Santa Claus: Christmas Symphony* in 1853); several overtures, chamber music, and songs. The first native American to try his hand at most of the larger forms of composition, Fry was also influential as a critic and lecturer and was one of the first to champion the "cause" of the American composer.

Prefatory Remarks to *Leonora* / (1845)

This lyrical drama was produced on the stage with a view of presenting to the American public, *a grand opera*, originally adapted to English words. The class of opera technically so designated, is, on the continent of Europe, employed for works of a serious or tragic character. Its peculiarity lies in the absence of all spoken monologue or dialogue; every word being sung throughout, and accompanied by the orchestra. This is essentially the high, complete, and classic form to give to the opera; it imparts proper uniformity of style to the entire declamation; does not confound the strictly musical with the acting drama; and with an artistic performance confirms the interest of the representation.

It would seem, however, that in England, to which America should naturally look for such a union of art and literature, the theory and practice have been to preclude the grand opera from the language, in original works. A late English writer on the subject of dramatic music, speaking of the opera of *Artaxerxes*, by Dr. Arne (composed during the last century, for the purpose of introducing recitative in place of spoken language) has the following remarks:

The attempt to apply Italian recitative to English dialogue was unsuccessful.—Italian speech can be made to take a musical form by merely enforcing and heightening the natural accents and inflections of the language; and thus the dialogue of the Italian opera may be sung, or rather spoken, in recitative: but in no other language is this practicable; and in English, German, and French, it is only where the natural inflections of the voice are supposed to be strengthened by the influence of emotion or passion, that recitative can be used with effect, or even without absurdity.—Hence in the German opera, *simple recitative* is very rarely used. The ordinary dialogue is merely spoken, and it is only when the actor is supposed to give vent to his feelings in broken phrases and passionate exclamations, that *accompanied recitative* is employed. Though the recitative of *Artaxerxes*, accordingly, has passed current in consequence of the popularity of the airs, no other English composer has ever made the experiment, unless in the way of burlesque.

This *simple recitative*, or semi-vocal style of singing in Italian operas, is only supported by the stringed basses of the orchestra; and with such a bald accompaniment it is without musical interest, but is considered necessary to the narrative or conversation, in the same manner that spoken dialogue is in the operas of other nations. There is, however, no reason why in English serious opera, both *simple recitative* and dialogue may not be equally avoided; and all language which has sufficient dignity to merit a place in such an opera, may be sung in *recitative accompanied by the orchestra*. So far from it being "an absurdity," as the authority, above quoted, thinks, to carry on an English dialogue in recitative, an intelligent and critical audience may be as much interested in a prolonged English dialogue in recitative, as in any melody exhibiting the vocal skill of the performer. The postulate being granted that music may be rendered the mean of human expression, there need be no exception to the rule that the whole operatic language of the stage may be carried on in singing. And it is hardly a forced comparison to say, that there is no better reason why a tragic or serious singer should be required to speak on the stage, than a tragic actor to sing. Each may properly confine himself to his respective art. It is a fixed apprehension of this principle of musical propriety that induces the masters of vocal music, the Italians, to substitute even in their comic operas, the simple recitative in place of spoken dialogue. I have, indeed, too much admiration for the resources of the English language, to admit of the supposition that it is excluded, by its nature, from the highest form of opera; and I believe that the original grand opera (using the word, original, in contradistinction to the translated adaptations) would, if produced by English composers, take permanently as a class the preference over mixed speaking opera.

It is a matter of regret that English genius, so fertile in letters and arts, should have neglected this complete form of opera, or attempted only in "burlesque" what should have been accomplished with sobriety and truth. The want of such a standard of dramatic music in our language, has necessarily resulted in a cognate deficiency of literature for the same purpose. According to English authorities, strong complaints are prevalent in this regard. If the musico-dramatic capabilities of the language be considered to their fullest extent, there can be lyrical works, which, as far as the nature of such compositions admits, may hold a high rank in English literature. Upon this point it may be remarked, that it is a fatal mistake to suppose, that feebleness, obscurity, or nonsense, in the drama, will be overlooked because it is connected with music. Plot, incident, and character, are as necessary for the lyrical as for the spoken drama; and the neglect of these requisites has prevented the success of operas whose music deserved a better fate. The literature of the opera so far from being of easy achievement, is indeed more perplexing to the writer, than that of the spoken drama. Apart from the consideration that the author must so detail his scenes, and dispose of his characters, as to produce specially musical effects, which is of itself a difficult task, he must also treat the English language with reference to the peculiarities necessary to effective stage declamation, and to the genius of melody as a universal dialect, which claims, indeed, supremacy over words; and as the ordinary structure of English verse ill coincides with such requisites, an amount of eccentric lyrical labors is necessary, that must deter dramatic writers from the undertaking, unless a proper estimate be set upon this required mastery of the language, rendering it flexible to the musical touch, and malleable for all the forms into which composition requires it to be beaten.

The plot of *Leonora*, it will be seen, is identical with that of Bulwer's *Lady of Lyons*; which, as an acting drama, holds a first rank in public estimation. Certain modifications have been made in the scenes and characters for musical purposes: in the omission of some persons; in the increased prominence given to others; in the change of place, and of the time to a more distant and hence romantic era. This change of time and place was readily effected, as there was no imperative delineation of national characteristics or localities in a purely domestic plot, to prevent it. For this reason, too, there has been no attempt made to infuse any popular or patriotic temper into the melodies. The tone of polite society—of "cavaliers and ladies," is much the same the world over. The action and expression of pointedly national characters, however, might suggest local music. But composers are not, and cannot always be, particular on this head. A scene laid in ancient Greece or Rome would preclude a national style of music, now lost, if it ever existed. The action of an opera laid in this country, also, could not be illustrated with national music, since the original type is wanting.

The success which attended the production of *Leonora* has been as great as I could desire. The public attention so given to the first American work of the kind, induces the trust that in this country, which has the accumulating wealth, taste, and knowledge conferred by freedom and peace, and a coincident prosperity, there may be a rapid, and at the same time, a vigorous growth of this branch of Art. But it will be requisite to have a lyrical drama free from whatever is gross, so that it become essentially moral in its character, and thus disarm all opposition to its progress. A sense of public justice should, at the same time, establish an international copyright law—a republic of letters—by which American authorship shall be rendered secure, and the rights of Intellect be regarded, even though it be of foreign birth and politics. The hope may be indulged, that the period is not far distant, when, as a people, we shall not reap where we have not sown; and we shall be too honorable to enjoy the fruits of European genius without rewarding it.

It is a clear proposition, that no Art can flourish in a country until it assume a genial character. It may be exotic experimentally, for a time, but unless it becomes indigenous, taking root and growth in the hearts and understandings of the people generally, its existence will be forced and sickly, and its decay quick and certain. And it may be remarked, emphatically, that, as vocal music must ever take precedence in general estimation of other music, for the reason that no musical instrument equals the human voice in quality and expression, it will be necessary to render national the lyrical drama, as being the only means by which great singers can be formed, and a school of music reared. Upon the stage alone can the expression of the master passions be adequately given; and the identification of music with action and character, being an artistical exhibition of man's nature, while it gives lyrical representation the strongest hold upon the common heart, renders it necessary for the singer to attain to the perfection of his art, and be pathetic, eloquent, great. The church has ever been obliged to call upon the theatre for its chief devotional singers; and it must ever be thus, while the drama covers a spiritual as well as a tangible ground. All times and places are subservient to the illustrations of the stage. The mists of antiquity and the divination of the future; the abodes of the gods, of fairies, and of demons, as well as of men; earth, air, sea, and sky are searched for the facts and imaginings of the dramatist. To fight against such a material and immaterial array, is like a war upon the seven prismatic colors, upon the seven essential sounds, upon the very spirit of ideality which clothes all visible things with romance and beauty. To destroy dramatic music is to endanger all music; to bring back monkish formality and abused mathematics in the science. The chief interest of all instrumental music, of the passion displayed in the modern Oratorio and the Mass, lies in the dramatic expression derived originally from the universal lyrical delineations of the stage. Composers of religious works have learned to avoid frigid calculation and to attain the expression of devotional fervor, by the study directly or indirectly of Humanity in the lyrical drama.

My particular acknowledgments are due to the principal vocalists and other performers engaged in producing the work, for the manner in which they executed their parts. I am likewise under signal obligations to the many kind friends who manifested interest in the success of the opera.

I cannot omit to mention the enterprise of Messrs. FERRET & Co. for the manner in which they issue this volume.

PHILADELPHIA, 1845

STEPHEN COLLINS FOSTER

(1826–1864), America's best-loved songwriter, lived at a time when it was extremely difficult, if not impossible, for an American composer—even of popular songs—to make a living at his trade. His contemporary Daniel Decatur Emmett, the composer of "Dixie" and of many other successful minstrel songs, made a living primarily as a blackface minstrel performer. Another contemporary, William Russell, made money by singing his own songs in public. But Stephen Foster had no special talent as a singer or performer; he was a *composer*, and he tried desperately to make a living from his music for himself and his wife and child.

Foster's songs were unquestionably popular. There were many poor ones among the more than two hundred that he wrote (in later years his inspiration was dulled by drink, hardship, and disappointment), but the goods ones, such as "Susanna," "Camptown Races," "Old Folks at Home," "Old Black Joe," "My Old Kentucky Home"—and many others—were the hit tunes of their day. Foster was industrious and tried to arrange his time as though he were a business man, renting an office in Pittsburgh where he could work steadily and undisturbed at his songwriting; but he lacked good business sense. He sold many of his songs outright to publishers and was very pleased when he received one hundred dollars for "Susanna"—the publisher made thousands from it!

Blackface minstrelsy was then the chief form of popular entertainment in the United States. When the minstrel performers took up a song it was bound to become nationally known and to enjoy wide popularity with consequent high sales. Stephen had been attracted to minstrelsy ever since his boyhood when he and his friends blackened their faces with burnt cork and imitated the celebrated entertainers who were as popular then as movie stars are today. Many of his songs were written specifically for minstrel troupes, including the famed "Christy Minstrels" led by E. P. Christy. But here again, his business judgment proved faulty, for he allowed Christy, for the sum of fifteen dollars[1] to place his own name on the title page as the composer of "Old Folks at Home"! When Stephen understood his mistake, it was too late; Christy refused to release him from the contract.

1 Stephen's brother, Morrison, stated that the sum was $500, but other evidence contradicts this.

Letters to E. P. Christy / (1850–52)

PITTSBURGH, Feb. 23, 1850

DEAR SIR:

Herewith I send you copies of two of my late songs "Gwine to run all night," and "Dolly Day." I regret that the title page had been ordered, and probably cut before I was informed of your desire that your name should not be used in connection with other bands. I have accordingly ordered my publisher in Baltimore to have a new title page cut bearing the name of your band alone like that used by Messrs. Firth, Pond & Co., N.Y. as I wish to be united with you in every effort to encourage a taste for this style of music so cried down by opera mongers. I hope to be in New York in the Spring when I will probably have an opportunity to gratify the desire which I have to hear your band. Please inform me how you are pleased with the accompanying songs.

Very respectfully yours,

STEPHEN C. FOSTER

ALLEGHENY CITY, June 12, 1851

DEAR SIR:

I have just received a letter from Messrs. Firth, Pond & Co. stating that they have copy-righted a new song of mine ("Oh! boys, carry me 'long") but will not be able to issue it for some little time yet, owing to other engagements. This will give me time to send you the m.s. and allow you the privilege of singing it for at least two weeks, and probably a month before it is issued, or before any other band gets it (unless they catch it up from you). If you will send me $10 immediately for this privilege I pledge myself, as a gentleman of the old school, to give you the m.s. I have written to F. P. & Co. not to publish till they hear from me again. This song is certain to become popular, as I have taken great pains with it. If you accept my proposition I will make it a point to notify you hereafter when I have a new song and send you the m.s. on the same terms, reserving to myself in all cases the exclusive privilege of publishing. Thus it will become notorious that your band brings out all the new songs. You can state in the papers that the song was composed expressly for you. I make this proposition because I am sure of the song's popularity.

Very respectfully yours,

S. C. FOSTER

June 30, 1851

DEAR SIR:

Your favor of the 12th inst., inclosing ten dollars for the first privilege of singing "Oh! boys, carry me 'long" is received. Accept my thanks. Herewith, I send you the m.s. according to agreement. I am not certain that you use a piano in your band; but I have arranged an accompaniment for that instrument at a venture. If you have a tenor voice in the company that can sing up to "g" with ease (which is very probable) it will be better to sing the song in the key of "g." Thus you will not carry the bass voice quite so low. I hope you will preserve the harmony in the chorus just as I have written it, and practice the song well before you bring it out. It is especially necessary that the person who sings the verses should know all the words perfectly, as the least hesitation in the singing will damn any song—but this of course you know as well as myself. Remember it should be sung in a pathetic, not a comic style. You will find the last three verses on another page of this letter. I regret that it is too late to have the name of your band on the title page, but I will endeavor to place it (alone) on future songs, and will cheerfully do anything else in my humble way to advance your interest.

Very respectfully yours,

S. C. FOSTER

I have not yet done anything at the "night funeral &c" but will probably make something out of it one of these days.

May 25, 1852

DEAR SIR:

As I once intimated to you, I had the intention of omitting my name on my Ethiopian songs, owing to a prejudice against them by some, which might injure my reputation as writer of another style of music, but I find that by my efforts I have done a great deal to build up a taste for the Ethiopian songs among refined people by making the words suitable to their taste, instead of the trashy and really offensive words which belong to some songs of that order. Therefore I have concluded to reinstate my name on my songs and to pursue the Ethiopian business without fear or shame and lend all my energies to making the business *live,* at the same time that I will wish to establish my name as the best Ethiopian song-writer. But I am not encouraged in undertaking this so long as "The Old Folks at Home" stares me in the face with another's name on it. As it was at my own solicitation that you allowed your name to be placed on the song, I hope that the above reasons will be sufficient explanation for my desire to place my own name on it as author and composer, while at the same time I wish to leave the name of your band on the title page. This is a little matter of pride in myself which it will certainly be to your interest to encourage. On the receipt of your free consent to this proposition, I will if you wish, willingly refund you the money which you paid me on that song, though it may have been sent me for other considerations than the one in question, and I promise in addition to write you an opening chorus in my best style, free of charge, and in any other way in my power to advance your interests hereafter. I find I cannot write at all unless I write for public approbation and get credit for what I write. As we may probably have a good deal of business with each other in our lives, it is best to proceed on a sure basis of confidence and good understanding, therefore I hope you will appreciate an author's feelings in the case and deal with me with your usual fairness. Please answer immediately.

Very respectfully yours,

S. C. FOSTER

LOUIS
MOREAU
GOTTSCHALK (1829–1869) was born in New Orleans
and received most of his musical training in Paris, where he
was sent as a boy to study piano and theory. Immensely talented,
handsome, and ingratiating, he was praised and befriended by
such eminent musicians as Berlioz and Chopin and was lionized
in the salons of Paris. In 1845 he composed "La Bamboula, Negro
Dance" for piano, which delighted sophisticated Parisian audiences by its rhythmic bravura and exotic flavor.

After a triumphant tour of Spain—where he composed several
works in Spanish style—he returned to the United States. His
career as a piano virtuoso took him not only across the United
States to California but also to the Caribbean, and particularly
to Cuba, where he gave some sensational concerts in Havana
and conducted his symphony *A Night in the Tropics*. In 1856
he returned to Cuba and then went on from one island to another
in the West Indies, for a period of vagabondage that lasted some
six years—"yielding myself up indolently to the caprice of Fortune," as he later wrote.

During the Civil War, his sympathies being with the North,
he composed a piece for piano called "The Union." He was
always proud of being an American, and when he was touring
abroad he would play fantasias on American themes, such as
Recuerdos de mi Patria ("Memories of my Fatherland"), in
which he used "Old Folks at Home" as the principal theme.
He also wrote some elaborate variations on "America" ("My

58

Country, 'Tis of Thee I Sing"). But his most popular piano pieces—and they were very popular indeed—were such sentimental compositions as "The Dying Poet" and "The Last Hope" ("gems of the genteel tradition," we might call them) and, more original and significant, the compositions based on Louisiana themes, such as "Le Bananier" and "La Savanne," or "The Banjo" with its effective evocation of the syncopated banjo tunes of American minstrelsy.

Gottschalk died in Rio de Janeiro during a tour of South America, where he had been greatly admired and applauded.

From *Notes of a Pianist* / (1862–64)

Killed by the gross attacks of which I had been the object, discouraged by the injustice of *soi-disant* musical judges, who denied me every species of merit, undeceived, disgusted at a career which, even among my own countrymen, did not promise the means of providing for the wants of my family and myself, I returned to New York.

My compositions continued to have a large sale in Paris. Then it was that I received a letter from one of my old friends and patrons, the respectable and old Countess de Flavigny, who afterwards was appointed lady of honour to the Empress Eugénie. She exhorted me to return to Paris, and held out to me the probability of my being soon appointed pianist to the Court. But I was withheld through bashfulness. It was painful for me to return to Paris, first theatre of my great success, and confess that I had not succeeded in my own country, America, which at this epoch was the Eldorado, the dream of artists, and which from the exaggerated accounts of the money which Jenny Lind had made there, rendered my ill success more striking.

I had composed a few pieces, one of them of a melancholy character, and with which was connected a touching episode of my journey to Santiago de Cuba, that seemed to me to unite the conditions requisite for popularity. A publisher purchased it from me for fifty dollars, advising me to endeavour to copy the style of the pianist Gockel, of whom a certain piece—how I do not know—had just obtained a great run.

At last one day I played some of my compositions to Mr. Hall, the publisher. "Why do you not give a concert to make them known?" he said to me. "Ma foi," I answered him, "it is a luxury that my means no longer permit me!" "Bah! I will pay you one hundred dollars for a piano concert only at Dodsworth's Rooms."

Eight days after I played in this small hall (whose proportions are such that I should never wish to see them exceeded, as they are those that make the piano heard advantageously before a select audience) my new pieces, "Le Banjo," the "Marche de Nuit," the "Jota Aragonesa," and "Le Chant du Soldat." Its success surpassed my most brilliant expectations. During *five months* I continued, without interruption, a series of weekly concerts for the piano only, in the same place, without being forsaken by the public. "Le Banjo" and "La Marche," and many other pieces purchased by Hall, were published and sold with a rapidity which left no doubt as to the final result of Hall's speculation, and which time has only corroborated. Everybody knows of the enormous edition which was published of "Banjo," and "Marche de Nuit." I then concluded a contract which assured to Hall the exclusive property in all my compositions for the United States. As Hall wished to possess my works anterior to those which he had just published, and having faith in my talent as a composer, he addressed the publisher of the melancholy piece of which I have already spoken, for the purpose of purchasing it. "Willingly," was the reply; "it does not sell at all; pay me the fifty dollars which it has cost me, and it is yours."

This little piece was "Last Hope," of which more than thirty-five thousand copies have been published in America, and which still produces yearly to its publisher, after a run of more than twelve years, twenty times the amount which it cost him. I have always kept at the bottom of my heart a sentiment of gratitude for the house of Hall, who first discovered that I was worth something; and from that moment dates this friendship which unites me to that family, and which time has only ripened.

But my ill-will toward those publishers who, when I stood in most need of them, continued only to discourage me, increased with my success. Returned to-day to New York, after an absence of six years, and in a position which I have conquered inch by inch, I revenged myself by refusing all those who approached me to offer, one five hundred, another one thousand dollars for one piece only. One publisher, the one who had first purchased the "Last Hope" (a gentleman, I must say, toward whom I have no grudge), offered me one thousand dollars for my "Murmures Eoliens." This sum made me smile on comparing it with the thirty dollars, at which price I had offered in vain my pieces some years before. It then was gratifying to me to give a proof of my gratitude to General Hall, with whom my contract had expired. I sent to him "Murmures Eoliens," "Pastorella e Cavaliere," "Ojos Criollos," and many other pieces, asking him to fix the conditions of a new contract, which I was ready to sign.

. . . . . .

There is a class of individuals for whom the arts are only a fashionable luxury, and music, in particular, an agreeable noise and elegant superfluity that agreeably revives at a soirée the conversation when it languishes, and commodiously serves to fill up the interval that separates the time for lemonade from the time for supper. For them all philosophical discussions on the aesthetics of art, are no more than puerilities, analogous to that of the fairy who occupied herself in weighing grains of dust in a scale of spider's web. The artists (to whom, through a prejudice which goes back to the barbarism of the Middle Ages, they persist in refusing a place in the higher sphere of social order) are for them only merchants of the lowest rank who trade in questionable products, the most of the time awkwardly, since they rarely make a fortune.

Performers are for them mountebanks or jugglers, who ply the agility of their hands, like dancers or acrobats that of their legs. The painter, whose *chefs-d'oeuvre* decorate the wall of their saloons, figures in the budget of their expenses under the same title with the upholsterer who has covered their floor with an *Aubusson*; and if they were left to themselves, they would value according to the price of the canvas and the oil, the "Heart of the Andes" of Church, or the "Le Marché aux Chevaux" of Rosa Bonheur. It is not for these, who are disinherited by thought, that I write, but there are others, and it is to those that I address myself, who recognize in the artist the privileged instrument of a moral and civilizing influence, and who appreciate art because they draw from it pure and unspeakable enjoyment; who respect it, because it is the highest expression of human thought aspiring toward the Eternal Ideal, and love it as the friend into whose bosom they pour their joys and their griefs to find there a faithful echo of the emotions of their soul.

Lamartine has rightly said, "La musique est la littérature du coeur, elle commence là où finit la parole." Indeed, music is a psycho-physical phenomenon. It is in its essence a sensation, and in its development an ideal. It suffices not to be deaf, if not to understand, at least to perceive music. Idiots and furious maniacs have submitted to its influence; not being confined to the precise and restricted meaning of a word, and expressing only the status of the soul, music has the advantage over literature that every one can assimilate it to his own passions, and adapt it to the sentiments which dominate him. Its power, limited, in the intellectual order of things, to the imitative passions, is illimitable in that of the imagination. It answers to that innate, undefinable feeling which everyone possesses, the *Ideal*. Literature is always objective; it speaks to our understanding, and determines in us impressions in harmony with the limited sense which it expresses. Music, on the contrary, is perhaps by turns objective and subjective, depending on our state of mind at the time we hear it. It is objective when, under the wholly physical sensation of sound, we listen passively, and it suggests to us impressions. A warlike march, a waltz, the flute's imitation of a nightingale, the chromatic scales imitating the murmuring of the wind in the "Pastoral Symphony," are examples of it. It is subjective when, under the influence of a secret impression, we discover in its general character an agreement with our physical state and assimilate it. It is then like a mirror in which we see reflected the emotions which agitate us with a fidelity so much the more exact as we ourselves without being aware of it are the painters of the picture which is unfolded before the eyes of our imagination. I will explain myself: Play a melancholy passage to an exile thinking on his distant country, to an abandoned lover, to a mother mourning for her child, to a conquered warrior, and be assured that each one of these various griefs will appropriate to itself these plaintive harmonies, and will recognize in them the voice of its own suffering.

· · · · · ·

We have no traditions in America. Archaeology, the worship of the past, could not exist in a society born but yesterday, which has not yet had time to think of resting in order to dream, occupied as it still is with providing for its material requirements. We are all, more or less, like that American who found Rome very *shattered*. To look back at the past is the business of a satiated and idle man; it is a luxury which only old societies satiated with civilization, and discounting the future, can indulge in. Our Churches, our landscapes, strike our senses, but do not appeal to our imagination. I have never been profoundly moved by a very large landscape. My emotion is dissipated by the multiplicity of things. I desire to bind together the details, but the string breaks. I remain cold. A very small brook softly murmuring at the bottom of an obscure and shady glade sets me to dreaming. All my emotions are awakened by it.

· · · · · ·

I am daily astonished at the rapidity with which the taste for music is developed and is developing in the United States. At the time of my first return from Europe I was constantly deploring the want of public interest for pieces purely sentimental; the public listened with indifference; to interest it, it became necessary to strike it with astonishment; grand movements, *tours de force*, and noise had alone the privilege in piano music, not of pleasing, but of making it patient with it. I was the *first* American pianist, not by my artistic worth, but in chronological order. Before me, there were no piano concerts except in peculiar cases, that is to say, when a very great name arriving from Europe, placed itself by its celebrity before the public, which, willing or unwilling, through curiosity and fashion rather than from taste, made it a duty to go and see the lion. Now, piano concerts are chronic, they have even become epidemic; like all good things they are abused. From whatever cause, the American taste is becoming purer, and with that remarkable rapidity which we cite through our whole progress. For ten years a whole generation of young girls have played my pieces. "Last Hope," "Marche de Nuit," "Murmures Eoliens," "Pastorella e Cavaliere," "Cradle Song" have become so popular that it is difficult for me to find an audience indisposed to listen to me with interest since the majority has played or studied the pieces which compose the programme.

We should all, however narrow may be our sphere of action, bear our part in the progressive movement of civilization and I cannot help feeling a pride in having contributed within the modest limits of my powers in extending through our country the knowledge of music.

· · · · · ·

There is a class of persons who wish to learn what was the artist's intention. The artist is an instrument through which God inspires good things to men. He is passive. You might as well ask of the sun his intention in producing the marvellous effects of light and shade in a landscape. The inspired artist is like a key-board which sounds correctly under the tremor which agitates it. We, all of us, have in us a finger-board, but some have broken the cords of their soul in such a way that the finger-board no longer produces a sound. Others sound false, although feeling everything deeply. These are generally those artists who, to express it, are not endowed with the faculty of formulating what they feel. Sometimes by dint of slow and patient researches,

assisted by their insatiable desire to express what they experience, they attain to creating something which approaches to
genius, but the effort and the labour are apparent, two shackles
which genius does not know.

WILLIAM
WALKER (1809–1875), a native of Union County in upper South Carolina, was a leading figure in the Southern singing-school and rural hymnody movement. A member of the Baptist church, he received some rudimentary training in music and composed his first hymn-tune at the age of eighteen. By the time he was twenty-six he had published his first and most popular tune-book *The Southern Harmony and Musical Companion* (New Haven, 1835), which went through at least seven editions by 1854 and was reported to have sold 600,000 copies by 1866. As a contemporary of Walker wrote: "*The Southern Harmony* and his name, the name of the distinguished author, are as familiar as household duties in the habitations of the South."

In 1846 Walker published the *Southern and Western Pocket Harmonist,* which was printed in Philadelphia. Meanwhile, he had married and settled in Spartanburg, South Carolina, where he operated a bookstore. As an itinerant singing-school teacher who, in his own words, "travelled thousands of miles in the Middle, Southern, and Western States," he earned the nickname of "Singing Billy" Walker. He, in turn, trained many other singing-school teachers in that area.

Another collection of music composed or compiled by William Walker, titled *The Christian Harmony,* was published in 1866 (revised edition, 1873). His last work, *Fruits and Flowers,* intended for children, appeared in 1869.

Like his New England predecessor William Billings, Walker

was a musician of the people, who composed or arranged music
for the people, emphasizing the popular type of folklike hymn
or religious song that was the staple musical diet of rural Amer-
ca in his day.

Preface to *The Christian Harmony* / (1866)

Since publishing the Revised Edition of the SOUTHERN HAR-
MONY, we have travelled thousands of miles in the Middle, Southern, and Western States, and taught a number of singing schools,
—all the time consulting the musical taste of the clergy, music
teachers, and thousands of others who love the songs of Zion,—
and all the time trying to ascertain the need and wants of the
Church, in a musical point of view, and selecting all the good
tunes we could find, with a design to publish them at some future
period. During our travels, we were often asked and urged to
publish a tune-book in the seven-syllable and seven-character
note system, containing more music suitable for church use, and
a greater variety of metres, than could be found in any of our
books. After many years' labor and effort to comply with these
urgent requests, we have been enabled, through the blessing of
God, to bring out THE CHRISTIAN HARMONY as the result of our
labor. In treating on the rudiments of music, we have taken them
as they naturally present themselves,—viz.: *Melodics, Rhythm,*
and *Dynamics,*—leading the learner on gradually from the easier
to the more abstruse parts of this delightful science.

The tunes have been selected from about fifteen thousand (15,000) pages of printed music, and a great number of manuscript tunes kindly given to us and sent by mail by brother teachers, ministers of the gospel, and many other musical friends, embracing a great many standard church tunes (some of them composed in the days of the Reformation), which are as necessary in a music book for church use as ballast for a ship; together with a large number of splendid pieces of more modern dates,—*some perfect gems*;—also some right fresh from the author's pen. We have also inserted a few Odes and Anthems.

We have been careful in trying to get a large variety of metres suitable to the different Hymn and Psalm-Books used by the different denominations of Christians. Our *aim* has been to make our work A COMPLETE BOOK OF HARMONY FOR ALL CHRISTIANS.

Where the names of the authors of the tunes were positively known, they have been given; but where several persons claimed the same tune, we have dropped all names, fearing we might not do justice to some of the parties. Many of the tunes appear without any name as author; but we hope no author will think hard of us on this account, for we would have given names with pleasure had they been known. Our own name is placed over several pieces in this work, some of them original; others are melodies too good to be lost, which we set to music and composed the parts.

We have tried, in selecting music for our work, to gratify the taste of all. We have tunes that are used mostly in the country (that is generally called rural music), but the most of them are those used everywhere, in the *cities, towns, villages,* and *country,* from the *seaboard to the mountains*—over the whole land, East, West, North, and South. The *aged* and youth will find tunes in THE CHRISTIAN HARMONY that they will love to sing in the praise of our God and Redeemer.

Several authors have kindly given us the free use of their works, from which we have selected many valuable tunes for our book: but it is possible we may have inadvertently inserted some without leave that are copyrighted; if so, and if we are informed of the fact, we will try and arrange the matter satisfactorily, for we do not want to do anything that is not high-toned and gentlemanly.

We would here express our sincere thanks and heart-felt gratitude to a generous public and music-loving people for the very hearty and unparalleled patronage given to the various editions of the SOUTHERN HARMONY, there having been sold (as we understand from one of the publishers) about six hundred thousand copies. May we not reasonably hope that THE CHRISTIAN HARMONY—a work of mature years and tenfold more experience—will merit and receive a still more extensive patronage from the millions who love to praise God in his sanctuary? We earnestly ask the kind assistance, which has heretofore been given, of ministers of the gospel, brother teachers, pupils, and other friends, in the circulation and sale of this work (maybe the main work of our life),—in employing teachers of good moral character, forming large singing schools, and improving music generally.

The compiler now commends this work to the public, humbly praying God's blessing upon it, that it may be the means of advancing this important, sacred, and delightful science, and of cheering the weary pilgrims of Zion on their way to the Celestial City.

SPARTANBURG, S. C., October, 1866

JOHN
HILL
HEWITT (1801–1890) was the son of an English musician,
James Hewitt (1770–1827), who had migrated to America in
1792 and who was active in New York as violinist, composer,
concert manager, and music publisher. The elder Hewitt's most
celebrated composition was a sonata for piano titled *The Battle
of Trenton*, dedicated to General Washington. He married twice
and had six children, several of whom became musicians, as did
some of their descendants. Although John Hewitt was born in
New York, the family moved to Boston when he was eleven,
and he attended public school there. Hewitt *père*, who had married above his station and had pretensions to gentility, did not
favor a musical career for his son. Rebelling against his father's
authority, young Hewitt ran away from home and for the next
few years led an adventurous existence. In 1818, however,
through his father's influence, he received and accepted an appointment to the military academy at West Point. He remained
there the full four years, but was not permitted to graduate because of academic deficiencies. Having in the meantime studied
music with the bandmaster at West Point, he decided to be a
musician.

It was not easy, in those days, to be a musician—especially
a composer—in the United States. Hewitt had several precarious
years as actor, law student, publisher, music teacher, composer,
and poet. His first song, "The Minstrel's Return from the War,"
was successful but brought him no money because he failed to

have it copyrighted. His next song, "The Knight of the Raven Black Plume," was one of more than three hundred that he was to write and which were to earn him the title, "Father of the American Ballad." He also wrote one of the favorite songs of the Civil War, "All Quiet Along the Potomac Tonight." His large works include several oratorios, among them *Jephtha*, performed in the principal cities of the East.

From 1828 until his death Hewitt lived chiefly in Baltimore, where for a time he edited the *Saturday Visitor*. In spite of his industry and *succès d'estime*, he was unable to make a living from music. "The publisher pockets all," he wrote, "and gets rich on the brains of the poor fool who is chasing that *ignis fatuus*, reputation."

From *Shadows on the Wall, or Glimpses of the Past* / (1877)

Music and Musicians

Music has always been, and still is, my frailty. Since my earliest youth I have sought its gentle influence; and though in early days I prepared myself for another and quite a different pursuit, yet the fondness of it clung to me, and it finally became my profession, though my parents were solicitous that I should adopt any other honorable calling but that. I studied it as an art and as a science; but only for the sake of the accomplishment, never thinking that I should use it as the means of support. I was educated at the Military Academy at West Point, and prepared for the army, but never went into active service, for I resigned at the end of my fourth year, and commenced the study of law in South Carolina, thinking the law a less dangerous way of achieving honors than the sword. Whenever I failed in any enterprise I fell back on music; it was my sheet-anchor.

But I would avoid the charge of egotism. My ballads are (or rather *were*) well known throughout the country; for I have not published for many years. Why? the reader may ask. For the simple reason that it does not pay the author. The publisher pockets all, and gets rich on the brains of the poor fool who is chasing that *ignis fatuus*, reputation.

While editing or writing for various journals, I did not neglect my profession [*i.e.*, music], during the practice of which I became acquainted with nearly all of my compeers. . . .

Henry Russell. The descriptive songs and ballads of this composer and vocalist are still much in vogue. He spent much of his time in Baltimore, though New York was his headquarters. In person he was rather stout, but not tall. His face was quite prepossessing, of the Hebrew cast, dark and heavy whiskers and curly hair. He was an expert at wheedling audiences out of applause, and adding to the effect of his songs by a brilliant pianoforte accompaniment. With much self-laudation he used often to describe the wonderful influence of his descriptive songs over audiences. On one occasion he related an incident connected with "Woodman, Spare that Tree." He had finished the last verse of the beautiful words, written by his highly esteemed friend, Gen. George P. Morris. The audience were spellbound for a moment, and then poured out a volume of applause that shook the building to its foundation. In the midst of this tremendous evidence of their boundless gratification, a snowy-headed gentleman, with great anxiety depicted in his venerable features, arose and demanded silence. He asked, with a tremulous voice: "Mr. Russell, in the name of Heaven, tell me was the tree spared?" "It was, sir," replied the vocalist. "Thank God! thank God! I breathe again!" and then he sat down, perfectly overcome by his emotions. This miserable bombast did not always prove a claptrap; in many instances it drew forth hisses. . . .

Father Heinrich. The eccentric Anthony Philip Heinrich, generally known as "Father Heinrich," visited Washington while

I resided in that city, with a grand musical work of his, illustrative of the greatness and glory of this republic, the splendor of its institutions and the indomitable bravery of its army and navy. This work Heinrich wished to publish by subscription. He had many names on his list; but, as he wished to dedicate it to the President of the United States, and also to obtain the signatures of the Cabinet and other high officials, he thought it best to call personally and solicit their patronage.

He brought with him a number of letters of introduction, among them one to myself from my brother, a music-publisher in New York. I received the old gentleman with all the courtesy due to his brilliant musical talents; and, as I was the first he had called upon, I tendered him the hospitalities of my house— "pot-luck" and a comfortable bed; promising to go the rounds with him on the following morning and introduce him to President Tyler (whose daughter, Alice, was a pupil of mine), and such other influential men as I was acquainted with.

Poor Heinrich! I shall never forget him. He imagined that he was going to set the world on fire with his "Dawning of Music in America"; but alas! it met with the same fate as his "Castle in the Moon" and "Yankee Doodliad."

Two or three hours of patient hearing did I give to the most complicated harmony I have ever heard, even in musical dreams. Wild and unearthly passages, the pianoforte absolutely groaning under them, and "the old man eloquent," with much self-satisfaction, arose from the tired instrument, and with a look of triumph, asked me if I had ever heard music like that before? I certainly had not.

At a proper hour we visited the President's mansion, and after some ceremony and much grumbling on the part of the *polite* usher, were shown into the presence of Mr. Tyler, who received us with his usual urbanity. I introduced Mr. Heinrich as a professor of exalted talent and a man of extraordinary genius. The President, after learning the object of our visit, which he was glad to learn was not to solicit an office, readily consented to the dedication, and commended the undertaking. Heinrich was elated to the skies, and immediately proposed to play the grand conception, in order that the Chief Magistrate of this great nation might have an idea of its merits.

"Certainly sir," said Mr. Tyler; "I will be greatly pleased to hear it. We will go into the parlor, where there is a piano, and I will have Alice and the ladies present, so that we may have the benefit of their opinion; for, to confess the truth, gentlemen, I am but a poor judge of music."

He then rang the bell for the waiter, and we were shown into the parlor, and invited to take some refreshments at the sideboard. The ladies soon joined us, and in a short space of time we were all seated, ready to hear Father Heinrich's composition; I, for the second time, to be *gratified*. The composer labored hard to give full effect to his weird production; his bald pate bobbed from side to side, and shone like a bubble on the surface of a calm lake. At times his shoulders would be raised to the line of his ears, and his knees went up to the keyboard, while the perspiration rolled in large drops down his wrinkled cheeks.

The ladies stared at the maniac musician, as they, doubtless, thought him, and the President scratched his head, as if wondering whether wicked spirits were not rioting in the cavern of mysterious sounds and rebelling against the laws of acoustics. The composer labored on, occasionally explaining some incomprehensible passage, representing, as he said, the *thaw* of the ice, and the dash of the mass over the mighty falls. *Peace* and *plenty* were represented by soft strains of pastoral music, while the thunder of our naval war-dogs and the rattle of our army musketry told of our prowess on sea and land.

The inspired composer had got about half-way through his wonderful production, when Mr. Tyler restlessly arose from his chair, and placing his hand gently on Heinrich's shoulder, said: "That may all be very fine, sir, but can't you play us a good old Virginia reel?"

Had a thunderbolt fallen at the feet of the musician, he could not have been more astounded. He arose from the piano, rolled up his manuscript, and, taking his hat and cane, bolted toward the door, exclaiming:

"No, sir; I never plays [*sic*] dance music!"

I joined him in the vestibule, having left Mr. Tyler and family enjoying a hearty laugh at the "maniac musician's" expense.

As we proceeded along Pennsylvania Avenue, Heinrich grasped my arm convulsively, and exclaimed:

"Mein Got in himmel! [*sic*] de peeples vot made Yohn Tyler Bresident ought to be hung! He knows no more apout music than an oyshter!"

He returned to New York by the next train, and I never heard any more of the "Dawning of Music in America."

Musical Snobs

Though music is considered all the world over as the hand-maid of pleasure and the soother of our cares and sorrows, yet the professional musician—I mean the teacher—knows that it has its miseries. One of them is the mortification a master is subjected to in consideration of his being *number two* in the scale of society. There are legions of *parvenus*—aristocratic mushrooms—who hold the education of the teacher as naught, believing him to be a "one-idea" man, educated exclusively in the school of demi-semi-quavers. Now, with me music was made a mere stand-by; I learnt it as an accomplishment, and it has proved a means of buoying me up on the ocean of life. I have always imagined that I could hold my own in science and litera-ture; but with the purse-proud men of letters and science, I have imagined I was thrown out of the scale as mere chaff—a man who, beyond the concord of sweet sounds, knew nothing. This reads like egotism, but I feel that I am reasoning for others of my profession whom I have met with—men and general scholars who follow the calling of music-teacher from inclination, or more probably because it is profitable.

For instance, while sojourning in South Carolina many years ago, I was invited to a dinner-party given by a wealthy planter. Cards of invitation had been extended to some of the leading spirits of the South, and "a feast of reason and flow of soul" was anticipated. I prepared myself for an intellectual treat, and rejoiced in the thought that music, which was almost a drug to me, was, at least for a brief period, to be placed on the shelf.

I found the company everything that I could have wished for. The ladies were bright and beautiful, and the gentlemen, among whom were John C. Calhoun, George McDuffie, Warren R. Davis, and other politicians of the South, full of that genial hilarity and warmth of heart so peculiar to Southerners. The dinner was sumptuous, the wit brilliant, and the conversation edifying. All I had to do was to listen, for no one ever dreamed that I had an opinion to express, and therefore did not ask it.

. . . . . .

The viands of the table discussed, the dishes were removed and a variety of wines placed in their stead. The best part of the feast was of course in anticipation, and the ladies, having no predilections for wine and cigars, adjourned to the parlor. Now, thought I, for an intellectual *olla prodrida,* a highly seasoned *pot-pourri,* a well-savored *medley.* Vain hope!

I had barely lighted my cigar and drawn myself up, *vis-à-vis* with a bottle of sparkling sherry, when a servant informed me that the ladies desired my company in the parlor; they wanted some music. Politeness dictated that I should not say nay to an order from that quarter, but the mortifying thought came over me that the hospitality of the host was not genuine. I had been invited merely for my musical abilities.

I arose from my seat with a very bad grace, and rather sulkily responded to the message of the lady of the house, who led me to the piano with many smiles, at the same time whispering in my ear that I must "do my best," as there were two heiresses in the room, both passionately fond of music, and both marriageable, though she forgot to introduce me to them.

I played and sang for an hour, while they conversed on trifling topics—the fashions of the day, the wedding of a mutual friend, the style of the dresses there exhibited, with an effort to solve the problem as to whether the bride and groom were destined to be happy together. No one thought of listening to me. I was compelled to labor on, for I had been *honored* with an invitation to the fete only to amuse the company. My mortification did not end with a solo or two or a ballad, for one of the heiresses proposed a quadrille, which was heartily agreed to by all but myself. I played, of course, for I was determined to do my best to prove myself a gentleman, if *they* lacked the requisites of the lady.

EDWARD A. MACDOWELL (1861–1908) was at one time looked

upon as *the* "Great American Composer." Born in New York City, he was taken to Europe at an early age to continue his musical training, first in Paris (which he did not like), then in Germany (which he loved). He became an excellent pianist, but with encouragement from Raff and Liszt he decided to concentrate his major effort on composition. Finding the musical and cultural climate of Germany extremely congenial, he remained there some twelve years, returning to the United States permanently in 1888. His fame had preceded him, and in Boston, where he lived for the next eight years, he was acclaimed as pianist, praised as composer, and sought after as teacher. His two concertos for piano and orchestra, in the Romantic manner, were especially successful. One critic hailed his piano sonatas as "far the best since Beethoven."

In 1896, when the trustees of Columbia University in New York established the first professorship of music there, they invited MacDowell to occupy that chair, citing him as "the greatest musical genius America had produced." MacDowell accepted the appointment, full of idealistic aspirations about developing musical education on a high technical and aesthetic plane; but differences with President Nicholas Murray Butler led to disappointment and frustration, and in January, 1904, he resigned. In a statement to the press, he said: "There is certainly individual idealism in all universities, but the general tendency of modern education is toward materialism."

The essay that follows is taken from *Critical and Historical Essays*, a selection from the lectures delivered at Columbia University by MacDowell during the years from 1896 to 1903. These lectures, mostly historical, were edited by W. J. Batzell and published posthumously in 1912. The essay on "Suggestion in Music" contains the key to MacDowell's own attitude toward musical composition, for he believed that "it is in the power of suggestion that the vital spark of music lies."

Toward the end of the essay, MacDowell reveals an often unsuspected phase of his character, when he confesses, after discussing the "stunning" effect of Richard Strauss's tone poem *Thus Spake Zarathustra*, that he recalls having once heard in London, "sung in the street at night, a song that seemed to me to contain a truer germ of music."

Suggestion in Music / (*ca.* 1896)

In speaking of the power of suggestion in music I wish at the outset to make certain reservations. In the first place I speak for myself, and what I have to present is merely an expression of my personal opinion; if in any way these should incite to further investigation or discussion, my object will in part have been attained.

In the second place, in speaking of this art, one is seriously hampered by a certain difficulty in making oneself understood. To hear and to enjoy music seems sufficient to many persons, and an investigation as to the causes of this enjoyment seems to them superfluous. And yet, unless the public comes into closer touch with the tone poet than that objective state which accepts with the ears what is intended for the spirit, which hears the sounds and is deaf to their import, unless the public can separate the physical pleasure of music from its ideal significance, our art, in my opinion, cannot stand on a sound basis.

The first step toward an appreciation of music should be taken in our preparatory schools. Were young people taught to distinguish between tones as between colors, to recognize rhythmic values, and were they taught so to use their voices as to temper the nasal tones of speech, in after life they would be better able to appreciate and cherish an art of which mere pleasure-giving sounds are but a very small part.

Music contains certain elements which affect the nerves of the from want of familiarity with its material. Thus, after dinner, our forefathers were accustomed to sing catches which were entirely destitute of anything approaching music.

Music contains certain elements which affect the nerves of the mind and body, and thus possesses the power of direct appeal to the public,—a power to a great extent denied to the other arts. This sensuous influence over the hearer is often mistaken for the aim and end of all music. With this in mind, one may forgive the rather puzzling remarks so often met with; for instance, those of a certain English bishop that "music did not affect him either intellectually or emotionally, only pleasurably," adding "every art should keep within its own realm; and that of music was concerned with pleasing combinations of sound." In declaring that the sensation of hearing music was pleasant to him, and that to produce that sensation was the entire mission of music, the Bishop placed our art on a level with good things to eat and drink. Many colleges and universities of this land consider music as a kind of *boutonnière*.

This estimate of music is, I believe, unfortunately a very general one, and yet, low as it is, there is a possibility of building on such a foundation. Could such persons be made to recognize the existence of decidedly unpleasant music, it would be the first step toward a proper appreciation of the art and its various phases.

Mere beauty of sound is, in itself, purely sensuous. It is the Chinese conception of music that the texture of a sound is to be valued; the long, trembling tone-tint of a bronze gong, or the high, thin streams of sound from the pipes are enjoyed for their ear-filling qualities. In the *Analects* of Confucius and the writings of Mencius there is much mention of music, and "harmony of sound that shall fill the ears" is insisted upon. The Master said, "When the music maker Che first entered on his office, the finish with the Kwan Ts'eu was magnificent. How it filled the ears!" Père Amiot says, "Music must fill the ears to penetrate the soul." Referring to the playing of some pieces of Couperin on a spinet, he says that Chinese hearers thought these pieces barbarous; the movement was too rapid, and did not allow sufficient time for them to enjoy each tone by itself. Now this is color without form, or sound without music. For it to become music, it must possess some quality which will remove it from the purely sensuous. To my mind, it is in the power of suggestion that the vital spark of music lies.

Before speaking of this, however, I wish to touch upon two things: first, on what is called the science of music; and secondly, on one of the sensuous elements of music which enters into and encroaches upon all suggestion.

If one were called upon to define what is called the intellectual side of music, he would probably speak of "form," contrapuntal design, and the like. Let us take up the matter of form. If by the word "form" our theorists meant the most poignant expression of poetic thought in music, if they meant by this word the art of arranging musical sounds into the most telling presentation of a musical idea, I should have nothing to say: for if this were admitted instead of the recognized forms of modern theorists for the proper utterance, we should possess a study of the power of musical sounds which might truly justify the title of musical intellectuality. As it is, the word "form" stands for what have been called "stoutly built periods," "subsidiary themes," and the like, a happy combination of which in certain prescribed

keys was supposed to constitute good form. Such a device, originally based upon the necessities and fashions of the dance, and
changing from time to time, is surely not worthy of the strange
worship it has received. A form of so doubtful an identity that
the first movement of a certain Beethoven sonata can be dubbed
by one authority "sonata-form," and by another "free fantasia,"
certainly cannot lay claim to serious intellectual value.

Form should be a synonym for *coherence*. No idea, whether
great or small, can find utterance without form, but that form
will be inherent to the idea, and there will be as many forms as
there are adequately expressed ideas. In the musical idea, *per se*,
analysis will reveal form.

The term "contrapuntal development" is to most tone poets
of the present day a synonym for the device of giving expression
to a musically poetic idea. *Per se*, counterpoint is a puerile jug-
gling with themes, which may be likened to high-school mathematics. Certainly the entire web and woof of this "science," as
it is called, never sprang from the necessities of poetic musical
utterance. The entire pre-Palestrina literature of music is a conclusive testimony as to the non-poetic and even uneuphonious
character of the invention.

In my opinion, Johann Sebastian Bach, one of the world's
mightiest tone poets, accomplished his mission, not by means of
the contrapuntal fashion of his age, but in spite of it. The laws
of canon and fugue are based upon as prosaic a foundation as
those of the rondo and sonata form; I find it impossible to imagine their ever having been a spur or an incentive to poetic musical speech. Neither pure tonal beauty, so-called "form," nor what
is termed the intellectual side of music (the art of counterpoint,
canon, and fugue), constitutes a really vital factor in music.
This narrows our analysis down to two things, namely, the physical effect of musical sound, and suggestion.

The simplest manifestations of the purely sensuous effect of
sound are to be found in the savage's delight in noise. In the
more civilized state, this becomes the sensation of mere pleasure
in hearing pleasing sounds. It enters into folk song in the form
of the "Scotch snap," which is first cousin to the Swiss *jodel*,
and is undoubtedly the origin of the skips of the augmented and

(to a lesser degree) diminished intervals to be found in the music of many nations. It consists of the trick of alternating chest tones with falsetto. It is a kind of quirk in the voice which pleases children and primitive folk alike, a simple thing which has puzzled folklorists the world over.

The other sensuous influence of sound is one of the most powerful elements of music, and all musical utterance is involved with and inseparable from it. It consists of repetition, recurrence, periodicity.

Now this repetition may be one of rhythm, tone tint, texture, or color, a repetition of figure or of pitch. We know that savages, in their incantation ceremonies, keep up a continuous drum beating or chant which, gradually increasing in violence, drives the hearers into such a state of frenzy that physical pain seems no longer to exist for them.

The value of the recurring rhythms and phrases of the march is well recognized in the army. A body of men will instinctively move in cadence with such music. The ever recurring lilt of a waltz rhythm will set the feet moving unconsciously, and as the energy of the repetition increases and decreases, so will the involuntary accompanying physical sympathy increase or decrease.

Berlioz jokingly tells a story of a ballet dancer who objected to the high pitch in which the orchestra played, and insisted that the music be transposed to a lower key. Cradle songs are fashioned on the same principle.

This sensuous sympathy with recurring sounds, rhythms, and pitch has something in common with hypnotism, and leads up to what I have called suggestion in music.

This same element in a modified form is made use of in poetry, for instance, in Poe's "Raven,"

> Quoth the Raven, "Nevermore,"

and the repetition of color in the same author's "Scarlet Death." It is the mainspring (I will not call it the vital spark) of many so-called "popular" songs, the recipe for which is exceedingly simple. A strongly marked rhythmic figure is selected, and incessantly repeated until the hearer's body beats time to it. The well-known tunes "There'll Be a Hot Time," etc., and "Ta-ra-ra, Boom-de-ay" are good examples of this kind of music.

There are two kinds of suggestion in music: one has been called tone-painting, the other almost evades analysis.

The term tone-painting is somewhat unsatisfactory, and reminds one of the French critic who spoke of a poem as "beautifully painted music." I believe that music can suggest forcibly certain things and ideas as well as vague emotions encased in the so-called "form" and "science" of music.

If we wish to begin with the most primitive form of suggestion in music, we shall find it in the direct imitation of sounds in nature. We remember that Helmholtz, Hanslick, and their followers denied to music the power to suggest things in nature; but it was somewhat grudgingly admitted that music might express the emotions caused by them. In the face of this, to quote a well-known instance, we have the "Pastoral Symphony" of Beethoven, with the thrush, cuckoo, and thunderstorm. The birds and the storm are very plainly indicated; but it is not possible for the music to be an expression of the emotions caused by them, for the very simple reason that no emotions are caused by the cuckoo and thrush, and those caused by thunderstorms range all the way from depression and fear to exhilaration, according to the personality of individuals.

That music may imitate any rhythmic sounds or melodic figure occurring in nature, hardly needs affirmation. Such devices may be accepted almost as quotations, and not be further considered here. The songs of birds, the sound made by galloping horses' feet, the moaning of the wind, etc., are all things which are part and parcel of the musical vocabulary, intelligible alike to people of every nationality. I need hardly say that increasing intensity of sound will suggest vehemence, approach, and its visual synonym, growth, as well as that decreasing intensity will suggest withdrawal, dwindling, and placidity.

The suggestion brought about by pattern is very familiar. It was one of the first signs of the breaking away from the conventional trammels of the contrapuntal style of the sixteenth and seventeenth centuries. The first madrigal of Thomas Weelkes (1590) begins with the words, "Sit down," and the musical pattern falls a fifth. The suggestion was crude, but it was caused by the same impulse as that which supplied the material for Wagner's "Waldweben," Mendelssohn's "Lovely Melusina," and a host of other works.

The fact that the pattern of a musical phrase can suggest kinds of motion may seem strange; but could we, for example, imagine a spinning song with broken arpeggios? Should we see a spear thrown or an arrow shot on the stage and hear the orchestra playing a phrase of an undulating pattern, we should at once realize the contradiction. Mendelssohn, Schumann, Wagner, Liszt, and practically everyone who has written a spinning song, has used the same pattern to suggest the turning of a wheel. That such widely different men as Wagner and Mendelssohn should both have adopted the same pattern to suggest undulating waves is not a mere chance, but clearly shows the potency of the suggestion.

The suggestion conveyed by means of pitch is one of the strongest in music. Vibrations increasing beyond two hundred and fifty trillions a second become luminous. It is a curious coincidence that our highest vibrating musical sounds bring with them a well-defined suggestion of light, and that as the pitch is lowered we get the impression of ever-increasing obscurity. To illustrate this, I have but to refer you to the Prelude to *Lohengrin*. Had we no inkling as to its meaning, we should still receive the suggestion of glittering shapes in the blue ether.

Let us take the opening of the "Im Walde" Symphony by Raff as an example; deep shadow is unmistakably suggested. Herbert Spencer's theory of the influence of emotion on pitch is well known and needs no confirmation. This properly comes under the subject of musical speech, a matter not to be considered here. Suffice it to say that the upward tendency of a musical phrase can suggest exaltation, and that a downward trend may suggest depression, the intensity of which will depend upon the intervals used. As an instance we may quote the "Faust" overture of Wagner, in which the pitch is used emotionally as well as descriptively. If the meaning I have found in this phrase seems to you far-fetched, we have but to give a higher pitch to the motive to render the idea absolutely impossible.

The suggestion offered by movement is very obvious, for music admittedly may be stately, deliberate, hasty, or furious, it may march or dance, it may be grave or flippant.

Last of all I wish to speak of the suggestion conveyed by means of tone-tint, the blending of timbre and pitch. It is essentially a modern element in music, and in our delight in this marvellous and potent aid to expression we have carried it to a point of development at which it threatens to dethrone what has hitherto been our musical speech, melody, in favor of what corresponds to the shadow languages of speech, namely, gesture and facial expression. Just as these shadow languages of speech may distort or even absolutely reverse the meaning of the spoken word, so can tone color and harmony change the meaning of a musical phrase. This is at once the glory and the danger of our modern music. Overwhelmed by the new-found powers of suggestion in tonal tint and the riot of hitherto undreamed of orchestral combinations, we are forgetting that permanence in music depends upon melodic speech.

In my opinion, it is the line, not the color, that will last. That harmony is a potent factor in suggestion may be seen from the fact that Cornelius was able to write an entire song pitched upon one tone, the accompaniment being so varied in its harmonies that the listener is deceived into attributing to that one tone many shades of emotion.

In all modern music this element is one of the most important. If we refer again to the "Faust" overture of Wagner, we will perceive that although the melodic trend and the pitch of the phrase carry their suggestion, the roll of the drum which accompanies it throws a sinister veil over the phrase, making it impressive in the extreme.

The seed from which our modern wealth of harmony and tone color sprang was the perfect major triad. The *raison d'être* and development of this combination of tones belong to the history of music. Suffice it to say, that for some psychological reason this chord (with also its minor form) has still the same significance that it had for the monks of the Middle Ages. It is perfect. Every complete phrase must end with it. The attempts made to emancipate music from the tyranny of this combination of sounds have been in vain, showing that the suggestion of finality and repose contained in it is irrefutable.

Now if we depart from this chord a sensation of unrest is occasioned which can only subside by a progression to another triad or a return to the first. With the development of our modern system of tonality we have come to think tonally; and a chord lying outside of the key in which a musical thought is conceived will carry with it a sense of confusion or mystery that our modern art of harmony and tone color has made its own. Thus, while any simple low chords accompanying the first notes of Raff's "Im Walde" Symphony, given by the horns and violins, would suggest gloom pierced by the gleams of light, the remoteness of the chords to the tonality of C major gives a suggestion of mystery; but as the harmony approaches the triad the mystery dissolves, letting in the gleam of sunlight suggested by the horn.

Goldmark's overture to *Sakuntala* owes its subtle suggestion to much the same cause. Weber made use of it in his *Freischütz*, Wagner in his "Tarnhelm" motive, Mendelssohn in his *Midsummer Night's Dream*, Tchaikovsky in the opening of one of his symphonies.

In becoming common property, so to speak, this important element of musical utterance has been dragged through the mud; and modern composers, in their efforts to raise it above the commonplace, have gone to the very edge of what is physically bearable in the use of tone color and combination. While this is but natural, owing to the appropriation of some of the most poetic and suggestive tone colors for ignoble dance tunes and doggerel, it is to my mind a pity, for it is elevating what should be a means of adding power and intensity to musical speech to the importance of musical speech itself. Possibly Strauss's *Thus Spake Zarathustra* may be considered the apotheosis of this power of suggestion in tonal color, and in it I believe we can see the tendency I allude to. This work stuns by its glorious magnificence of tonal texture; the suggestion, in the opening measures, of the rising sun is a mighty example of the overwhelming power of tone color. The upward sweep of the music to the highest regions of light has much splendor about it; and yet I remember once hearing in London, sung in the street at night, a song that seemed to me to contain a truer germ of music.

For want of a better word I will call it ideal suggestion. It has to do with actual musical speech, and is difficult to define. The possession of it makes a man a poet. If we look for analogy, I may quote from Browning and Shakespeare.

> Dearest, three months ago
> When the mesmerizer, Snow,
> With his hand's first sweep
> Put the earth to sleep.
>
> Browning, "A Lover's Quarrel"

> Daffodils,
> That come before the swallow dares, and take
> The winds of March with Beauty; Violets dim,
> But sweeter than the lids of Juno's eyes.
>
> Shakespeare, *Winter's Tale*

For me this defies analysis, and so it is with some things in music, the charm of which cannot be ascribed to physical or mental suggestion, and certainly not to any device of counterpoint or form, in the musical acceptance of the word.

ARTHUR
FARWELL (1872–1951) was born in St. Paul, Minnesota.

He was trained as an engineer at the Massachusetts Institute of Technology, and it was after hearing the Boston Symphony Orchestra that he decided to make music his career. He studied with Homer Norris in Boston, with Humperdinck and Pfitzner in Germany, and with Guilmant in Paris. He was also influenced by the ideas of Antonin Dvořák, who was in the United States from 1892 to 1895, and whose "New World Symphony" was first performed in the same year that Farwell graduated from M.I.T., 1893. Dvořák declared that in Negro and Indian folk music, American composers could find the material "for a great and noble school of music." Dvořák, in brief, was preaching "musical nationalism," as that term was then understood by European composers.

Farwell himself became greatly interested in American Indian music around 1900 and spent some time in the Southwest studying and assimilating the tribal melodies and rhythms. But his interests were never narrow. He believed that American composers should familiarize themselves with *all* aspects of their native heritage: "Notably, ragtime, Negro songs, Indian songs, Cowboy songs. . . ." At the same time, he made a plea for liberation from the dominant German influence, claiming that (in 1903) American composers had more to learn from French and Russian music. He foresaw the day when the United States

would witness (if not welcome), "new and daring expressions
of our composers, sound-speech previously unheard."

In 1901, Farwell founded the Wa-Wan Press for the publication of new American music. In his initial declaration he said:
"We shall ask of the composer, not that he submit to us work
which is likely to be in demand, but that he express himself.
We shall do our utmost to foster individuality." Thus he struck
at the two blights of American music: commercialism and conformity.

Farwell's own music has fallen into unjust neglect; it should
be revived, performed, and recorded. Among his orchestral
works are *Mountain Vision* (with piano, 1931), *Mountain Song*
(with mixed chorus, 1931) and *Rudolph Gott Symphony* (1934).

An Affirmation of American Music / (1903)

Art evolution moves by waves. Progress is made not so much
through the random appearance of the works of individuals here
and there as in the successive impacts of successive groups of
workers. The Elizabethan poets, the Lake School, the German
Romanticists, the Barbizon painters—such groups show us how
powerful a bond is community of interest, of purpose, and ideal.
Sometimes, however, individuals appear who are large enough
to stir up quite a wave single-handed, but it is rare that even
one of these Titans has not some connection with a clearly defined group. As random instances we may name Millet, Tschai-

kovsky, and Flaubert, and respectively their allied groups, the Barbizon painters, the modern Russian composers, and the French school of literary naturalists. When the creative ideas of a certain group have spread and fulfilled their purpose, when their work has carried the day and proceeds constructively along accepted lines rather than striking out new ones, at this juncture arises a new group whose work is necessarily an evolution, a reaction, or, at the least, a demand for greater freedom, a search for a more direct and forcible expression of the spirit of the times. In a country geographically small, as Greece or England, or in a larger country whose intellectual force is concentrated in a small area, such a group will be in close contact and will stand for a clearly perceived and clearly defined cause. But in a land as large as the United States, with irrepressible intellects and wills springing up inconsiderately in regions more or less remote from each other and divergent in interests, the common impulse, the newly born cause, is less easy to perceive and define. But this divergence is only superficial. Despite many dialects, we still speak the American language, and despite local variations in government, we still stand for broad and universal principles. And what with variations in education and culture, we have the spirit of a new land to express in art; we have allied impulses to obey. Defined, or undefined, the fact remains that the new cause is with us. Nature, the self-contained, cares not, nor, in the language of a new Western bard, "does she give a whoop," whether we perceive it or not; her whole concern is in producing it.

And through a new group, with new needs and powers, an irresistible force is born into a country. Rawness, inexperience, obstacles, neglect,—no force, internal or external,—can finally prevail against the new accretion of will. With a sublime disregard for artistic precepts of however ancient a lineage, yet not without reverence for truth and power of expression, it will insist on producing works in accordance with its own need and environment.

In the United States the period of gestation is over, and at the present moment conditions prevail which are particularly favorable to the birth of such a new force. For the land is con-

quered from east to west, and for the first time it is possible
for a generation whose energies were not absorbed in planting
cities and establishing trade, to grow up, having peacefully gathered, in the enormously receptive period of childhood, impressions of the rivers and plains, the mountains and valleys, the
native atmosphere and genius of their own land. These impressions are as certain to dictate and compel characteristic expressions in art, later, as a tree is to put forth leaves. Natural environment exerts as definite an influence upon the respective and
sensitive creative mind as biological or hereditary conditions.
Only he is impervious to it who, unobservant of nature about
him, and its teeming wealth of creative suggestion, pedantically
copies the art forms of other races and periods instead of dis-
solving them, that they may recrystallize in forms having an obvious and vital meaning to people who are alive and present.

Until Wagner pointed out the absurdity of trying to mould
German Romantic drama into Greek iambic hexameter, a quantity born of conditions of life diametrically opposite to the German, no one realized its folly, and yet all Germany had been seeking out the causes of the ineffectualness of that drama. Germany
was never wholly satisfied with music and drama until Beethoven and Wagner bombarded the severe classic forms and riddled
them with Gothic cannon balls; nor was Russia, until Tschai-
kovsky broke the new German classicism on the wheel of Slavic
feeling. And this is no narrowing of results, but a universalizing
of them, for the world at large was never satisfied nor finally
impressed by German and Russian music until each had broken
free from the bondage of imported tradition.

Normal art evolution, however, does not come by skipping
steps, but by periodic action and reaction. It was natural that
as the conditions for peaceful life were being wrung, step by
step, from the land, there should follow the standards and the
enjoyment of European culture. During this period it was the
destiny of American musical activity to perpetuate the fundamental principles of the musical aspects of that culture in
the New World. This accomplished simultaneously several important things. It gave crude America a general view of the
spirit and the form of European music. Through its own un-

avoidable crudeness it cleared that music of the ultra-refinement appropriate to an alien and venerable art evolution, but without meaning for pioneers about to face the task of expressing the broader feelings of a new and vast land, innocent of culture ideals. Moreover, it secured the distribution of trained musicians throughout the land, and thus provided a tolerably complete outfit of musical machinery, ready to be set into more purposeful operation when the right time and the right controlling minds should appear. But the life breath of this activity was drawn from European sources, and expended upon the performance of European works. Even native composition was dominated by this influence. With German sentiment or stability, with Slavic intensity and recklessness of expression, with the suavity of Italy or the vigor of the north, we had, in music, nothing of our own to compare. Here was a vacuum, ripe for Nature's abhorrence.

But to-day this is past history. A new day of American music is not about to dawn,—it had already dawned with the appearance of an appreciable number of persons who no longer demanded solely the product of European art, and the appearance of an appreciable number of composers to supply that demand. And now the number has vastly increased. It makes not the slightest difference that these pioneers are not yet in command of the symphony orchestras and the newspaper columns. Their existence is sufficient. They do not herald *the* day of American music, but merely *a* day, between which and yesterday a shadowy night has intervened. They know well enough, too, that yesterday evening's fête has been carried over into the new day, with curtains drawn and candles lit. And they know that those revellers will never raise the curtains of their own free will and look out.

But the swiftly increasing group of American composers of the present generation has tasted of the regenerative sunlight flooding the wide stretches of our land, has caught glimpses of the wealth of poetic lore in the traditions of Negroes and Indians, and seen that justice must be done at last to the myriad sights and sounds of our own country. Europe will never respect America artistically, until she sees the results of this rebirth.

And American composers are pressing to the mark. Every year sees them more numerous, fearless, energetic, prolific. Their compositions are sounding less German, less European, and more untrammelled and redolent of a new composite spirit, insistent, yet still undefined. And this we must bear in mind: that their shelves are already laden with an incredible number of completed manuscripts of all degrees of size and value; the very existence of which will not be generally known until their champions have a little longer "nourished active rebellion."

Any student of history and ethnology knows that an invading race must always finally be repulsed, or absorb into itself the life and characteristics of the conquered nation. As for the Indians, it is not to be supposed that an American art is to be gained by a trivial and pedantic copying of their rhythms and songs; but because we have conquered them, mingled with them (to an extent not dreamed of by the dwellers in our Eastern cities), been thrilled in turn by the land which thrilled them, we will inevitably have inhaled great draughts of their splendid optimism and faith, their freedom of spirit and largeness of feeling, and their power to appropriate nature's teeming stores of energy. This is not only a poetic but also a scientific fact.

Meanwhile it is certainly suicidal, and would be fratricidal—were not our brothers so strong—to deny that we have a worthy and distinctive musical life of our own, when already many persons are joyously living that life to the end of their finger tips. All American composition needs is publicity. We can trust our sincere music lovers and sincere critics to discriminate between sheep and goats.

Let those of us who have caught a glimpse of the dawn feel no shame in letting others know that we have been up so early. And let us not lack the moral courage to waken others, believing that, at heart, they would rather be thrilled by to-day's realities than by the dreams of yesterday. And let us remember that it is impossible for us to be a power in any cause until, from our turbid and cloying doubts, we have distilled our living convictions, and converted these, in the retort of the will, into visible acts.

HENRY
F.B.

GILBERT (1868–1928) was born in Somerville, Massachusetts, and died not far from there, in Cambridge. But in his musical interests he went far afield, for eclecticism was his creed. As he wrote of himself: "More than the music of any individual composer; more than the music of any particular school, the folk tunes of the world, of all nationalities, races, and peoples, have been to me a never-failing source of delight, wonder and inspiration."

Although he studied with MacDowell in Boston, he shared a much deeper spiritual kinship with Farwell, who was his close friend. Like Farwell, he was keenly interested in all aspects of American folk music, but in his own compositions he gave priority to American Negro music, upon which he drew for his *Comedy Overture on Negro Themes* (1905), his *Negro Rhapsody* (1912), and the symphonic poem, *The Dance in Place Congo* (1906), an evocation of slavedays in New Orleans (also performed as a ballet-pantomime at the Metropolitan Opera House in New York). Regarding this last-mentioned work, he said: "It has been for a long time an ideal of mine to write some music which should be in its inspiration native to America." He continued his explorations of the American musical vernacular in *American Dances in Rag-time Rhythm* (1915) and *Jazz Study* (1924). A writer in 1917 called him "the 'Mark Twain' of American music." Farwell wrote of him: "Often rough in technique, though greatly resourceful, and rich in orchestral imagination, it is to the spirit of the time and nation that Gilbert makes his contribution and his appeal."

Gilbert's eclecticism is evident in such compositions as the "Indian Scenes" for piano, the "Celtic Studies" for voice and piano, "Two South American Gypsy Songs," the symphonic prologue to Synge's *Riders to the Sea* (1904), and *Salâmmbo's Invocation to Tanith* for orchestra (1901-1902).

The American Composer / (1915)

In a truthful and honest consideration of the art of Musical Composition in America, one is compelled to admit that there are as yet no real American composers. That is, speaking in the sense in which we consider Beethoven, Wagner or Strauss as German composers; Delibes, Massenet or Saint-Saëns as French composers, and Verdi, Rossini and Donizetti as Italian composers. There is a family resemblance between the music of the various German composers which in its ultimate essence constitutes a racial distinction to the music of any other nation. The same is true of the French composers *in toto*; also of the Italians and of other nations whose native culture has been allowed to develop for a period of time during which it has been protected from the disturbing effects of outside influences. This especial characteristic attaching to the music or other culture of a nation, or race, is a well-nigh impossible thing to define, although comparatively easy to recognize. If we contemplate sequentially, say fifty or more compositions by German composers, without allowing any serious diversions of attention to interfere with the process, we shall get a fair mental equivalent of the composite photograph. Certain common characteristics will be felt rather than perceived. If we now repeat the process with say fifty compositions by French composers, we shall get an impression which we shall have no difficulty in feeling to be of a mental color quite distinct from that of the German group.

Papa Haydn declared that *his* language was understood all over the world. This remark has given rise to the curious corollary that music is a universal language. Many persons hold that music is music, no matter whether composed by a German or a Frenchman, Italian or whoever it may be, that the laws of beauty are the same for all and far above any racial influence. This appears to be so, as long as we confine our attention to the externals of music such as melody, harmony, counterpoint, etc. But when we consider the inner meaning, the spiritual color of the music of a particular race, we immediately perceive something which differentiates it from the music of any other race. We feel the presence of a characteristic which we cannot define, but it would be foolish and unscientific to ignore this simply because we cannot analyze it. While music is quite universal in its appeal, it is not universal in its expressive power but in some esoteric manner reflects that particular racial spirit of which its individual composer is a fragment and as it were a mouthpiece.

In the sense of the foregoing we certainly do not have *American* composers. Possibly one reason for this, and perhaps the greatest reason, is that we have hardly as yet developed an American race. The population of America is, as every one recognizes, a general hodge-podge of almost all conceivable racial elements. These racial elements are not as yet amalgamated. Each still retains to a very large degree its original physical and mental characteristics, and that particular brand of conservatism peculiar to the race to which it originally belonged. However, environment, the enforced contact with other individuals of different races, and intermarriage are rapidly doing their work and an American race is only a question of time. Meanwhile we have already developed a strong and distinctive

American *spirit*. As compared with that of Europe it is the spirit of youth in contrast to the spirit of age. We are filled with a glorious will for accomplishment, an impatience of restraining bonds of tradition, and a buoyant and incontrovertible optimism. The dominant tone of America is ever onward. We *have* hitched our wagon to a star, the star of youth which shall indeed eventually drag us out of the slough of vulgarity. Inasmuch as we, as a nation, are infused with the spirit of youth we have the faults of youth as well as the virtues. These faults are ever present and indeed are the only things that certain critics and satirists perceive. But the main point is that with all our shortcomings we do possess the pristine and indomitable will of youth and it is this spirit which is the very mother and father of invention, culture, science, the arts and all which in the end tends to make life of value and beauty. In our literature this free and self-reliant characteristic has found from time to time an unmistakable expression. The writings of Emerson and Thoreau are filled with it. Walt Whitman continually suggests to us that in America humanity having touched the bedrock of primitive conditions is arising Antaeus-like, endowed with new and pristine vigor. And in quite another manner that most glorious of recent Americans, Mark Twain, strongly reflects the same spirit. But when we turn our attention in an earnest and unprejudiced manner to our native musical culture we must confess that not only are we lacking in composers of equal distinction, vigor, and originality, but we must admit that such composers as we have fail for the most part to grasp or to express this new spirit. With the exultant life of America throbbing vigorously about them they still turn to Europe, asking, that she not only teach them technique (which is right) but unconsciously absorbing and expressing her ideals of beauty (which is wrong). Here and there appears a gleam of the right sort but as it does not receive much encouragement it usually fails to develop. One always feels that music by an American is not wanted, especially if it happens to be *American music*. It is merely tolerated with a sort of good-natured contempt. It is true that American music as such is still very much in its infancy. But an unwelcome child always has a very hard time and sometimes fails to grow up.

The position of the native composer of music in America is, to say the least, peculiar. The art of music plays a large and important part among the present-day diversions of the American public, but it is in the nature of an imported toy and is not a significant part of the life of the people. We have much music, it is true; the greatest in the world; and probably a more catholic and broader view of the world's musical achievements than can be obtained in any other country. But the reverse side of the fact is, that the poor, struggling, and as yet not very individual native musical product has perhaps a harder time than it has had in other countries.

In America, Symphony Orchestras and Opera Companies spring up as it were overnight. Beside which there is always an abundance of piano and vocal recitals. The members and directors of these opera companies, the conductors of the symphony orchestras, besides the vast majority of the players, and by far most of the recitalists, are Europeans. Even when they have not been born in Europe, all their training has been European, and all their mental bias is in accordance with European musical tradition. Naturally almost all the music performed is European and thus the public is educated to an ideal of musical beauty which though great and wonderful in itself is perforce exclusive of anything which differs from it.

The American composer, even one of the best and most earnest sort, in submitting a composition of his to one of our European-American symphony-orchestra conductors, must abide by his decision respecting its worthiness of performance. The decision of the orchestral conductor respecting the value of the work submitted is naturally influenced by the degree in which the new work approaches those great European models with which his life-training has made him familiar. It therefore happens that many works which are not in the least significant, nor important to the development of an *American* school of composition, are given the high honor of a finished performance and a widespread publicity.

To this it should be added that the great body of our professional critics is likewise educated exclusively to European standards of musical beauty. There are of course a few brilliant exceptions who are doughty champions of the new note wherever it appears. But the vast majority proceed to judge the work performed in accordance with their European-derived standards of taste; to praise it wherever it coincides, however weakly, with these standards; and to condemn it whenever it departs, with no matter how much intrinsic justification, from these standards.

There have also been instituted numerous prize competitions such as the Paderewski prize, founded by the munificence of Mr. Paderewski; the annual prize competition held by the Federation of Music Clubs, and numerous others of smaller caliber. At first sight these competitions would appear to be most excellent encouragers of the art of musical composition in America. They undoubtedly do this to a certain extent, but inasmuch as the judges who award the prizes in these competitions are usually veteran composers, whose training and sympathy is entirely in accordance with European ideals, it almost invariably happens that the composition which, though technically well made, is least offensive by reason of any new or significant features which it might present, gets the prize. In other words, the most un-American composition stands about the best chance of a prize. I am well aware that in prize competitions generally, in no matter what country, the most academic and frequently the least significant composition gets the prize. In America, however, the operations of these prize competitions would seem to be one degree worse than anywhere else. Not only does the most academic composition usually get the prize, but the one which is the least American also, owing to the European training of the judges.

Prize competitions in general certainly encourage activity but their immediate effects tend to retard progress. For they emphasize and raise to a high point of honor those still-born works in which the form is quite in accordance with existent traditions of musical beauty but which are lacking in vitality, in new and convincing spirit. The world *does* move. There is progress in Art as in other things. The gentlemen who act as judges in prize competitions continually forget to remember that new wine refuses to be confined in old bottles!

Then again there is the attitude of the government; Music, and indeed the fine arts in general, have no official recognition or government support and encouragement in this country. The attitude of the government of the United States toward the fine arts is indeed one of apathy if not complete indifference. Almost without exception civilized countries have a minister of fine arts, and by means of endowment of art schools, subsidies to theatres and opera-houses, and pensions given to creative artists such as poets and composers, do much to encourage and make possible the growth of a native culture. But the government of the United States of America offers the most flagrant exception to this custom. Our legislators, if they do not express open scorn at the idea of governmental patronage of the fine arts, consider the issue of no importance whatsoever. In fact, if we consider the indifference and inaction of the government in this matter we cannot take a very high rank as a civilized country. We are certainly true barbarians in this matter. Even Russia, a country which it is much the fashion to look down upon, is inestimably in advance of us in this particular. She has developed a vigorous and distinctive native culture, and this largely through the aid, encouragement and financial support of the government. It is perhaps a trite saying that "Art is not a business," but the truth of it cannot be emphasized too often, especially in this country. It needs to be fostered and substantially encouraged if it is to take root and grow among a people and in turn react upon them as a civilizer. The encouragement of Art and particularly of Music is therefore left to the care of a few wealthy individuals; and were it not for the generosity and public spirit of certain of our citizens in supporting our Symphony Orchestras, Opera Companies, and in certain very rare instances giving financial aid to our serious composers, our country would indeed be a barren desert as far as the art of music is concerned.

The endowment or financial aid given to a composer is too often looked at as charity, or as temporary aid until the time when he shall eventually be able to stand upon his own feet. But this is wrong. True Art seldom pays for itself; at least not for a long time. And the finer it is the less likelihood there is of its paying for itself. Money, advanced to a composer to free him from the necessity of earning it, should be regarded in the light of an investment; not as a material investment which shall eventually bring returns in kind, but as a spiritual investment which shall eventually bring rich returns of an artistic or cultural nature.

With the many prevailing ideas of music which however excellent in themselves nevertheless militate against the success of the American composer, he has much difficulty in getting proper public performances of his works. Numerous societies have been formed from time to time for the purpose of bringing to public performance worthy American Musical work. Such are the Manuscript Society of New York; the American Music Society; and the Women's Musical Clubs in various parts of the country. There is a slight tendency on the part of the European-trained conductors of our symphony orchestras to give the American composer a little fairer show than formerly.

About 1904 the investigation of Professor Will H. Monroe, covering the six principal symphony orchestras of the country, showed that of all the music given by these orchestras less than one per cent was by American composers. This is really a shameful condition of things and should cause both composer and public to take thought. This condition, however, has slightly improved since then.

Let us now examine a few of the prejudices against the American composer and his work. In the first place there is the feeling, which is widely spread, that he can only produce works of an inferior order of merit. This feeling I am bound to say is somewhat justified by the facts. Many American composers (and would-be composers) hardly as yet realize the intense and utterly self-sacrificing amount of concentration necessary to produce a real masterpiece. Our country is so rich; life is so royally easy here. It seems that in this as in other things the prize may be had for the plucking. That symphonies may be built by main strength even as are fifty-story buildings. But this rough and ready optimism, this objective and materialistic heroism with which America is filled, is not the kind which creates great music. For that a finer, a more spiritual strain of heroism is necessary. Our Brooklyn bridges and fifty-story buildings are fine, heroic and masterful and fill one with an exultant joy in the compelling power of the mind of man over material things. But it takes a yet sterner and deeper mastery for the mind to compel and to control itself. And this must be done before great art can arise. Is it not written that he who controls his own spirit is greater than he that taketh a city? And Emerson writing in 1840 says:

> The hero is not fed on sweets,
> Daily his own heart he eats.

This kind of heroism is all too rare in America, even among such as aspire to fill the sacred rôle of creative artist.

But there is yet another reason why the work of the American composer, taken as a whole, can hardly win our highest respect. That is, that it is so largely imitative of the art of Europe. Most of us realize, even though unconsciously, that imitative art can never be great art. And even though its very lack of individual distinctive quality may procure it a temporary recognition and quasi-success, at the same time it fails to win for it a permanent respect. American music in its development as such, has this problem to face: that it can only become ultimately distinctive by leaving the paths of imitation, and that by leaving the paths of imitation it must temporarily sacrifice both immediate success and the respect, such as it is, of both public and academician. However, this principle is not at all confined to the development of American music but applies to all things of any distinction or ultimate value which have ever been developed in any age or country.

In addition to this there is the somewhat provincial but nearly always present objection to the home product as opposed to the imported article. This is also a very old and widely operative principle. It is mentioned in the New Testament, Matt. 13:57. Without resorting to any cheap jingoism, which I hate as does I believe every true American, I will merely observe that as long as we run after foreign gods with too great an assiduity we shall never have a god of our own really worthy of our respect and worship.

Considering the lack of aesthetic consciousness in the American people, the apathy of the government toward the fine arts, and the prejudices of various kinds against the serious-minded American composer, we are fain to give him considerable credit for his struggle against such overwhelming odds. During the last quarter of a century or so there may be observed a slight tendency on the part of our composers to kick over the traces of European tradition, and to treat American subjects, to use fragments of melody having an American origin as a basis for musical structure. Indian and Negro tunes and rhythms, Spanish-American tunes, and even the familiar Foster songs have been made use of in this way. Many of these compositions are probably not of lasting art value. The high-water mark that has thus far been reached by this method of procedure is undoubtedly MacDowell's *Indian Suite*. But these compositions taken as a whole indicate a fine, healthy tendency on the part of the American composer, one which we should certainly congratulate ourselves upon. This is but a tendency as yet and the compositions arising therefrom can certainly not express the large and complete spirit of America. It seems to indicate that our composers are gradually beginning to realize that we cannot arrive at a distinctive adulthood in our music until we have left the home nest of European tradition and struck out for ourselves. Now these first steps are naturally somewhat blundering and unsure and can hardly give any true indication of what may be arrived at ultimately. But the main point, on which we should all congratulate ourselves, is, that the first step toward an American music has actually been taken. Its subsequent arrival is merely a question of time.

The foundations of culture in a new and only partially civilized country are always laid in imitation of the culture of a completely developed and civilized country. Thus, early Italy imitated Greece; France and Germany imitated Italy; Russia imiated Germany, and in the nineteenth century we have seen America imitating England in literature and Germany in music. All the European countries mentioned have eventually developed a fine, sturdy, and distinctive culture of their own. Something native to themselves and expressive of their own race consciousness. But what of America?

To the minds of all thinkers and the hearts of all who sincerely love our country and have a living faith in its future, this question must be big with interest. We have already, as has been said, struck a distinctive note in our literature. But the spirit of our music is still largely imitative. In the order of the development of the arts music usually comes last, and it is perhaps too early to look for a distinctive note in American music. Still I see here and there a gleam of something big and vital.

But it is the potentialities, the latent possibilities of American music which arouse my most earnest enthusiasm. Here we are in America with a population composed of all European racial stocks. Each having its own distinctive race consciousness, yet all bound together by a free, liberated and onrushing national spirit. When the amalgam is complete—shall there not arise eventually a strong and beautiful music in whose texture is woven all those various strands of race consciousness? For all these threads shall be here gathered together and harmoniously blended, and I, for one, look with great interest to the ultimate development of an art of music, which, while containing these many elements, shall yet be superior in expressive power to any of the single elements from which it has been built.

CHARLES
IVES (1874–1954) was a musical genius of such orig-
inality and daring that only now, more than ten years after his
death, are we beginning to understand the nature and importance of his unique contribution to American music. Born and
raised in Danbury, Connecticut, he received his early training
in music from his father, leader of the local band and a man
with a keen interest in acoustical problems; his influence on his
son was decisive. Before he was twenty, Charles Ives had written at least two compositions using polytonality. He then matriculated at Yale University, where during the next four years
he studied composition with Horatio Parker, who frowned on
his musical experimentation. Upon graduating, Ives was faced
with a difficult choice as a musician: whether to conform to
the prevailing standards and tastes of the time, or to go his
own independent way as a composer, regardless of the consequences. He decided on the latter course. This meant, obviously,
earning his livelihood by some means other than music. He chose
to enter the insurance business, in which he was extremely successful.

All his composing was done in his spare time, chiefly late at
night and on holidays. In 1918 he suffered a serious illness, from
which he never fully recovered, and after that he was able to
do very little composing. In 1919 he began to have some of his
compositions privately printed. His *Essays Before a Sonata*, apparently written between 1916 and 1918, was published with

the Second Piano Sonata ("Concord Sonata") in 1920. But it was many years before his music obtained significant public recognition. An important breakthrough occurred in 1939, when John Kirkpatrick gave the first complete public performance of the "Concord Sonata" in New York. The audience reaction and the critical acclaim were encouraging; yet the Third Symphony, completed in 1904, was not performed until 1947; and the Second Symphony, composed in 1897–1902, received its first performance in 1951.

Receptive to all expressions of the American musical vernacular, from old-time fiddle tunes to ragtime, from camp-meeting hymns to circus marches, Ives also explored new realms of sound, particularly in the use of simultaneous sound-masses of strongly contrasted character moving with complete independence of each other. Spiritually, he felt a deep kinship with Emerson, Thoreau, Hawthorne, and others of the Concord group, to whom he dedicated his Second Piano Sonata.

The *Essays Before a Sonata* begins with a "Prologue" and concludes with an "Epilogue." What follows here is a longish excerpt from the Epilogue, which in its entirety consists of nine sections.

Epilogue from *Essays Before a Sonata* **/ (1920)**

The futility of attempting to trace the source or primal impulse of an art inspiration may be admitted without granting that human qualities or attributes which go with personality cannot be suggested, and that artistic intuitions which parallel them cannot be reflected in music. Actually accomplishing the latter is a problem, more or less arbitrary to an open mind, more or less impossible to a prejudiced mind.

That which the composer intends to represent as "high vitality" sounds like something quite different to different listeners. That which I like to think suggests Thoreau's submission to nature may, to another, seem something like Hawthorne's conception of the relentlessness of an evil conscience—and to the rest of our friends, but a series of unpleasant sounds. How far can the composer be held accountable? Beyond a certain point the responsibility is more or less undeterminable. The outside characteristics—that is, the points furthest away from the mergings—are obvious to mostly anyone. A child knows a strain of joy from one of sorrow. Those a little older know the dignified from the frivolous—the Spring Song from the season in which the "melancholy days have come" (though is there not a glorious hope in autumn!). But where is the definite expression of late spring against early summer, of happiness against optimism? A painter paints a sunset—can he paint the setting sun?

In some century to come, when the school children will whistle popular tunes in quarter-tones—when the diatonic scale will be as obsolete as the pentatonic is now—perhaps then these borderland experiences may be both easily expressed and readily recognized. But maybe music was not intended to satisfy the curious definiteness of man. Maybe it is better to hope that music may always be a transcendental language in the most extravagant sense. Possibly the power of literally distinguishing these "shades of abstraction"—these attributes paralleled by "artistic intuitions" (call them what you will)—is ever to be denied man for the same reason that the beginning and end of a circle are to be denied.

II

There may be an analogy—and on first sight it seems that there must be—between both the state and power of artistic perceptions and the law of perpetual change, that ever-flowing stream, partly biological, partly cosmic, ever going on in our-

selves, in nature, in all life. This may account for the difficulty
of identifying desired qualities with the perceptions of them in
expression. Many things are constantly coming into being while
others are constantly going out—one part of the same thing
is coming in while another part is going out of existence. Perhaps this is why the above conformity in art (a conformity
which we seem naturally to look for) appears at times so un-
realizable, if not impossible. It will be assumed, to make this
theory clearer, that the "flow" or "change" does not go on in
the art-product itself. As a matter of fact it probably does, to
a certain extent—a picture or a song may gain or lose in value,
beyond what the painter or composer knew, by the progress and
higher development in all art. Keats may be only partially true
when he says that a work of beauty is a joy forever—a thing
that is beautiful *to me* is a joy *to me*, as long as it remains beautiful *to me*—and if it remains so as long as I live, it is so forever; that is, forever *to me*. If he had put it this way, he would
have been tiresome, inartistic, but perhaps truer. So we will assume here that this change only goes on in man and nature, and
that this eternal process in mankind is paralleled in some way
during each temporary, personal life.

A young man, two generations ago, found an identity with
his ideals in Rossini; when an older man, in Wagner. A young
man, one generation ago, found his in Wagner, but when older,
in César Franck or Brahms. Some may say that this change
may not be general, universal, or natural, and that it may be
due to a certain kind of education, or to a certain inherited or
contracted prejudice. We cannot deny or affirm this, absolutely,
nor will we try to even qualitatively—except to say that it will
be generally admitted that Rossini, today, does not appeal to this
generation as he did to that of our fathers. As far as prejudice
or undue influence is concerned, and as an illustration in point,
the following may be cited—to show that training may have but
little effect in this connection (at least not as much as usually
supposed), for we believe this experience to be to a certain extent normal, or at least not uncommon. A man remembers, when
he was a boy of about fifteen years, hearing his music teacher
(and father), who had just returned from a performance of

Siegfried, say with a look of anxious surprise that somehow or
other he felt ashamed of enjoying the music as he did, for beneath it all he was conscious of an undercurrent of make-believe
—the bravery was make-believe, the love was make-believe, as
was the dragon—P. T. Barnum would have been brave enough
to have gone out and captured a live one! But, that same boy
at twenty-five was listening to Wagner with enthusiasm; his
reality was real enough to inspire a devotion. The "Pries-
Lied" [Preislied], for instance, stirred him deeply. But when
he became middle-aged—and long before the Hohenzollern hog
marched into Belgium—this music had become cloying, the melodies threadbare—a sense of something commonplace—yes—of
make-believe came. These feelings were fought against for association's sake, and because of gratitude for bygone pleasures—
but the former beauty and nobility were not there, and in their
place stood irritating intervals of descending fourths and fifths.
Those once transcendent progressions, luxuriant suggestions
of Debussy chords of the 9th, 11th, etc., were becoming slimy.
An unearned exultation—a sentimentality deadening something
within—hides around in the music. Wagner seems less and less
to measure up to the substance and reality of César Franck,
Brahms, d'Indy, or even Elgar (with all his tiresomeness); the
wholesomeness, manliness, humility, and deep spiritual, possibly religious feeling of these men seem missing, and not made
up for by his (Wagner's) manner and eloquence, even if greater
than theirs (which is very doubtful).

    From the above we would try to prove that as this stream
of change flows toward the eventual ocean of mankind's perfection, the art-works in which we identify our higher ideals
come by this process to be identified with the lower ideals of
those who embark after us when the stream has grown in depth.
If we stop with the above experience, our theory of the effect
of man's changing nature, as thus explaining artistic progress,
is perhaps sustained. Thus would we show that the perpetual
flow of the life stream is affected by and affects each individual
river-bed of the universal watersheds. Thus would we prove that
the Wagner period was normal, because we intuitively recognized
whatever identity we were looking for at a certain period in our

life, and the fact that it was so made the Franck period possible
and then normal at a later period in our life. Thus would we
assume that this is as it should be, and that it is not Wagner's
content or substance or his lack of virtue—that something in us
has made us flow past him and not he past us. But something
blocks our theory! Something makes our hypotheses seem purely
speculative if not useless. It is men like Bach and Beethoven.

Is it not a matter nowadays of common impression or general
opinion (for the law of average plays strongly in any theory
relating to human attributes) that the world's attitude toward
the substance and quality and spirit of these two men, or other
men of like character, if there be such, has not been affected by
the flowing stream that has changed us? But if by the measure
of this public opinion, as well as it can be measured, Bach and
Beethoven are being flowed past—not as fast perhaps as Wagner,
but if they are being passed at all from this deeper viewpoint—
then this "change" theory holds.

Here we shall have to assume, for we haven't proved it,
that artistic intuition can sense in music a weakening of moral
strength and vitality, and that it is sensed in relation to Wagner, and not sensed in relation to Bach and Beethoven. If, in
this common opinion, there is a particle of change toward the
latter's art, our theory stands—mind you, this admits a change
in the manner, form, external expression, etc., but not in substance. If there is no change here toward the substance of these
two men, our theory not only falls but its failure superimposes
or allows us to presume a fundamental duality in music, and in
all art for that matter.

Does the progress of intrinsic beauty or truth (we assume
there is such a thing) have its exposures as well as its discoveries? Does the nonacceptance of the foregoing theory mean that
Wagner's substance and reality are lower and his manner higher
—that his beauty was not intrinsic—that he was more interested
in the repose of pride than in the truth of humility? It appears
that he chose the representative instead of the spirit itself; that
he chose—consciously or unconsciously, it matters not—the lower
set of values in this dualism. These are severe accusations to
bring—especially when a man is a little down, as Wagner is to-

day. But these convictions were present some time before he was
banished from the Metropolitan.

Wagner seems to take Hugo's place in Faguet's criticism of
de Vigny—that the staging to him (Hugo) was the important
thing, not the conception—that in de Vigny, the artist was inferior to the poet; finally that Hugo and so Wagner have a certain
pauvreté de fond. Thus would we ungenerously make Wagner
prove our sum! But it is a sum that won't prove! The theory
at its best does little more than suggest something which, if
it is true at all, is a platitude; viz., that progressive growth in
all life makes it more and more possible for men to separate, in
an art-work, moral weakness from artistic strength.

III

Human attributes are definite enough when it comes to their
description, but the expression of them, or the paralleling of
them in an art-process, has to be, as said above, more or less
arbitrary; but we believe that their expression can be less vague
if the basic distinction of this art-dualism is kept in mind. It is
morally certain that the higher part is founded, as Sturt suggests, on something that has to do with those kinds of unselfish human interests which we call knowledge and morality—
knowledge not in the sense of erudition, but as a kind of creation or creative truth. This allows us to assume that the higher
and more important value of this dualism is composed of what
may be called reality, quality, spirit, or substance against the
lower value of form, quantity, or manner. Of these terms, "substance" seems to us the most appropriate, cogent, and comprehensive for the higher, and "manner" for the undervalue. Substance in a human art-quality suggests the body of a conviction
which has its birth in the spiritual consciousness, whose youth
is nourished in the moral consciousness, and whose maturity as
a result of all this growth is then represented in a mental image.
This is appreciated by the intuition, and somehow translated
into expression by manner—a process always less important than
it seems, or as suggested by the foregoing (in fact we apologize
for this attempted definition). So it seems that substance is too
definite to analyze in more specific terms. It is practically inde-

scribable. Intuitions (artistic or not?) will sense it—process, un-known. Perhaps it is an unexplained consciousness of being nearer God, or being nearer the devil—of approaching truth or approaching unreality—a silent something felt in the truth of nature in Turner against the truth of art in Botticelli, or in the fine thinking of Ruskin against the fine surroundings of Kipling, or in the wide expanse of Titian against the narrow expanse of Carpaccio, or in some such distinction that Pope sees between what he calls Homer's "invention" and Virgil's "judg-ment"—apparently an inspired imagination against an artistic care, a sense of the difference, perhaps, between Dr. Bushnell's *Knowing God* and knowing *about* God. A more vivid explanation or illustration may be found in the difference between Emerson and Poe. The former seems to be almost wholly substance, and the latter, manner. The measure in artistic satisfaction of Poe's manner is equal to the measure of spiritual satisfaction in Emer-son's substance. The total value of each man is high, but Emer-son's is higher than Poe's because substance is higher than man-ner—because substance leans toward optimism, and manner [to-ward] pessimism. We do not know that all this is so, but we feel, or rather know by intuition that it is so, in the same way we know intuitively that right is higher than wrong—though we can't always tell why a thing is right or wrong, or what is always the difference or the margin between right and wrong.

Beauty, in its common conception, has nothing to do with it (substance), unless it be granted that its outward aspect, or the expression between [*read: of*] sensuous beauty and spiritual beauty can be always and distinctly known, which it cannot, as the art of music is still in its infancy. On reading this over, it seems only decent that some kind of an apology be made for the beginning of the preceding sentence. It cannot justly be said that anything that has to do with art has nothing to do with beauty in any degree—that is, whether beauty is there or not, it [substance] has something to do with it. A casual idea of it, a kind of a first necessary physical impression, was what we had in mind. Probably nobody knows what actual beauty is—except those serious writers of humorous essays in art maga-zines, who accurately, but kindly, with club in hand, demonstrate for all time and men that beauty is a quadratic monomial—that it *is* absolute—that it *is* relative—that it is *not* relative—that it is *not* . . . . The word "beauty" is as easy to use as the word "degenerate." Both come in handy when one does or does not agree with you. For our part, something that Roussel-Despierres says comes nearer to what we like to think beauty is: "an infinite source of good . . . the love of the beautiful . . . a constant anxiety for moral beauty." Even here we go around in a circle—a thing apparently inevitable, if one tries to reduce art to philosophy. But personally, we prefer to go around in a circle than around in a parallelepipedon, for it seems clearer and perhaps freer from mathematics; or for the same reason we prefer Whittier to Baudelaire, a poet to a genius, or a healthy to a rotten apple—probably not so much because it is more nutritious, but because we like its taste better; we like the beautiful and don't like the ugly —therefore, what we like is beautiful, and what we don't like is ugly—and hence we are glad the beautiful is not ugly, for if it were we would like something we don't like. So having unsettled what beauty is, let us go on.

At any rate, we are going to be arbitrary enough to claim, with no definite qualification, that substance can be expressed in music, and that it is the only valuable thing in it; and, moreover, that in two separate pieces of music in which the notes are almost identical, one can be of substance with little manner, and the other can be of manner with little substance. Substance has something to do with character; manner has nothing to do with it. The substance of a tune comes from somewhere near the soul, and the manner comes from—God knows where.

IV

The lack of interest to preserve, or ability to perceive, the fundamental divisions of this duality accounts to a large extent, we believe, for some or many various phenomena (pleasant or unpleasant according to the personal attitude) of modern art, and all art. It is evidenced in many ways—the sculptor's overinsistence on the "mold," the outer rather than the inner subject or content of his statue—over-enthusiasm for local color—over-interest in the multiplicity of techniques, in the idiomatic, in the effect as shown by the appreciation of an audience rather than in the effect on the ideals of the inner conscience of the artist or the composer. This lack of perceiving is too often shown by an over-interest in the material value of the effect. The pose of self-absorption which some men in the advertising business (and incidentally in the recital and composing business) put into their photographs or the portraits of themselves, while all dolled up in their purple dressing gowns, in their two-fold wealth of golden hair, in their sissy-like postures over the piano keys— this pose of "manner" sometimes sounds out so loud that the more their music is played, the less it is heard. For does not Emerson tell them this when he says, "What you are talks so loud that I cannot hear what you say?" The unescapable impression that one sometimes gets by a glance at these public-inflicted trademarks, and without having heard or seen any of their music, is that the one great underlying desire of these appearing-artists is to impress, perhaps startle and shock their audiences, and at any cost. This may have some such effect upon some of the lady-part (male or female) of their listeners, but possibly the members of the men-part, who as boys liked hockey better than birthday-parties, may feel like shocking a few of these picture-sitters with something stronger than their own "forzandos."

The insistence upon manner in its relation to local color is wider than a self-strain for effect. If local color is a natural part (that is, a part of substance), the art-effort cannot help but show its color—and it will be a true color, no matter how colored; if it is a part (even a natural part) of manner, either the color part is bound eventually to drive out the local part, or the local drive out all color. Here a process of cancellation or destruction is going on—a kind of "compromise" which destroys by deadlock; a compromise purchasing a selfish pleasure—a decadence in which art becomes first dull, then dark, then dead, though throughout this process it is outwardly very much alive —especially after it is dead. The same tendency may even be noticed if there is over-insistence upon the national in art. Substance tends to create affection; manner, prejudice. The latter tends to efface the distinction between the love of both a country's virtue and vices, and the love of only the virtue. A true

love of country is likely to be so big that it will embrace the
virtue one sees in other countries, and in the same breath, so
to speak. A composer born in America, but who has not been
interested in the "cause of Freedmen," may be so interested in
"Negro melodies" that he writes a symphony over them. He is
conscious (perhaps only subconscious) that he wishes it to be
"American music." He tries to forget that the paternal Negro
came from Africa. Is his music American or African? That is
the great question which keeps him awake! But the sadness
of it is that if he had been born in Africa, his music might have
been just as American, for there is good authority that an African soul under an X-ray looks identically like an American soul.
There is a futility in selecting a certain type to represent a
"whole," unless the interest in the spirit of the type coincides
with that of the whole. In other words, if this composer isn't
as deeply interested in the "cause" as Wendell Phillips was when
he fought his way through that anti-abolitionist crowd at Faneuil
Hall, his music is liable to be less American than he wishes. If
a middle-aged man, upon picking up the *Scottish Chiefs,* finds
that his boyhood enthusiasm for the prowess and noble deeds
and character of Sir William Wallace and of Bruce is still present, let him put, or try to put that glory into an overture; let
him fill it chock-full of Scotch tunes, if he will. But after all is
said and sung, he will find that his music is American to the
core (assuming that he is an American and wishes his music to
be). It will be as national in character as the heart of that Grand
Army Grandfather, who read those *Cragmore Tales* of a summer
evening, when that boy had brought the cows home without
witching. Perhaps the memories of the old soldier, to which this
man still holds tenderly, may be turned into a "strain" or a
"sonata"; and though the music does not contain, or even suggest any of the old war-songs, it will be as sincerely American as
the subject, provided his (the composer's) interest, spirit, and
character sympathize with, or intuitively coincide with that of
the subject.

Again, if a man finds that the cadences of an Apache war-
dance come nearest to his soul—provided he has taken pains to
know enough other cadences, for eclecticism is part of his duty;

sorting potatoes means a better crop next year—let him assimilate whatever he finds highest of the Indian ideal so that he can
use it with the cadences, fervently, transcendentally, inevitably,
furiously, in his symphonies, in his operas, in his whistlings on
the way to work, so that he can paint his house with them, make
them a part of his prayer-book—this is all possible and necessary, if he is confident that they have a part in his spiritual consciousness. With this assurance, his music will have everything
it should of sincerity, nobility, strength, and beauty—no matter
how it sounds; and if, with this, he is true to none but the highest of American ideals (that is, the ideals only that coincide with
his spiritual consciousness), his music will be true to itself and
incidentally American, and it will be so even after it is proved
that all our Indians came from Asia.

The man "born down to Babbitt's Corners" may find a deep
appeal in the simple but acute gospel hymns of the New England "camp meetin'" of a generation or so ago. He finds in
them—some of them—a vigor, a depth of feeling, a natural-soil
rhythm, a sincerity, emphatic but inartistic, which, in spite of
a vociferous sentimentality, carries him nearer the "Christ of
the people" than does the *Te Deum* of the greatest cathe-
dral. These tunes have, for him, a truer ring than many of
those groove-made, even-measured, monotonous, non-rhythmed,
indoor-smelling, priest-taught, academic, English or neo-English
hymns (and anthems)—well-written, well-harmonized things,
well-voice-led, well-counterpointed, well-decorated, and well O.K.'d,
by well-corrected Mus. Bac. R.F.O.G.'s—personified sounds, correct and inevitable to sight and hearing—in a word, those proper
forms of stained-glass beauty which our over-drilled mechanisms
—boy choirs—are limited to. But, if the Yankee can reflect the
fervency of "Aunt Sarah," who scrubbed her life away for her
brother's ten orphans, the fervency with which this woman, after
a fourteen-hour work-day on the farm, would hitch up and drive
five miles through the mud and rain to "prayer meetin'"—her
one articulate outlet for the fullness of her unselfish soul—if he
can reflect the fervency of such a spirit, he may find there a local
color that will do all the world good. If his music can but catch

that "spirit" by being a part with itself, it will come somewhere near his ideal, and it will be American too—perhaps nearer so than that of the devotee of Indian or Negro melody. In other words, if local color, national color, any color, is a true pigment of the universal color, it is a divine quality, it is a part of substance in art—not of manner.

DANIEL
GREGORY
MASON (1873–1953), born in Brookline, Massachusetts,

son and grandson of prominent musicians, studied composition
with John Knowles Paine and George W. Chadwick in Boston,
and with Vincent d'Indy at the Schola Cantorum in Paris. On
Thanksgiving Day in the year 1895 he wrote in his journal:
"Thank God Wagner is dead and Brahms is alive. And here's
to the great classical revival of the 20th century in America."
Later, in his autobiography *Music in My Time*, he said: "One
of my deepest convictions has always been a sense of the supreme
value in art of balance, restraint, proportion—in a word, of classic beauty."

During his long lifetime he was a leading spokesman for the
conservative view in American musical thought. He was the
author of numerous books dealing with the music of the great
composers and also surveyed and criticized the American musical scene in two books that made a stir in their time: *The Dilemma of American Music* (1928) and *Tune In, America* (1931).
From 1910 until his death he was a member of the music faculty
at Columbia University and in 1929 was appointed MacDowell
Professor of Music there.

Mason considered himself "a musical humanist," a firm be-
liever in "the unbroken stream of tradition." He held that the
Anglo-American heritage was the mainstream of the American
tradition; hence he was disturbed by the intrusion of what he
regarded as extraneous elements, such as the Jewish influence in

American music, which he saw as a "menace to our artistic integrity."

Although he wrote a *String Quartet on Negro Themes* (1919), Mason was especially attracted by English folk music, as evidenced in his orchestral *Suite After English Folk Songs* (1924) and *Folk Song Fantasy ("Fanny Blair")* for string quartet (1929). He tried to express "the American spirit" in two of his major works: the *Chanticleer Overture* (1928), inspired by certain optimistic statements in Thoreau's *Walden* ("All climates agree with brave Chanticleer. He is more indigenous than the natives. His health is ever good.") ; and in his *Lincoln Symphony* (1936), a musical portrait of the "Great Emancipator."

The Dilemma of American Music / (1928)

Although it is impossible nowadays to mention American music without hearing someone murmur, as if in echo, "jazz," there is, as a matter of fact, a great deal more in the best American music of our day than "pep," "punch," and "kick," and we have a number of composers, of competent technical skill and distinctive personality, who have no commerce with the ragtime jerk.[1] American music, indeed, is already a sturdy offshoot of the great tree of European music, and sufficiently flourishing to deserve respectful attention. No doubt the work of even our best composers still leaves something to be desired, for they labor under great

1 This essay appears here in abridged form. [Ed.]

impediments, chiefly psychological; but they have given us nevertheless a music, and a music that is not jazz.

Perhaps it would be better to say that they have given us ten or a dozen musics. It is highly characteristic of their situation that instead of working in one clear tradition, as their German, French, or Italian brothers more or less do, they are bewildered by the multiplicity of the traditions which with us subsist side by side, mutually diluting, confusing, or even cancelling one another. This confusion of tradition is a peculiarity of American artistic life. If anyone thinks it a small or an academic matter, let him consider for a moment how large a proportion of all that is finest in the musical art of the world owes its existence to tradition: how much of Bach's style, for instance, is reflected directly from his predecessors; how impossible Beethoven would have been without Haydn and Mozart, or Wagner without Meyerbeer and Weber; how fully are already present in Beethoven the germs of Schubert and Schumann, and in them those of Brahms and César Franck.

To consider these things is to get a sense of how small is even the greatest individual, how all-determining is the tradition he works in. Weismann asks what would have happened to Mozart had he been born in the Samoan Islands: what would he have been able to do? At most, he thinks, he might have extended the native gamut of three or four tones to seven, and created melodies a little more complicated; but "he would have been as incapable of composing symphonies as Archimedes would have been incapable of inventing an electric dynamo." Art is a coral reef, and the greatest artist is only one more insect, owing his virtue more to his attachments than to himself. Hence it is no small matter that there is in American music no main reef, but only a confusion of tendencies. With us even the most gifted individuals find it difficult to attach themselves anywhere; instead, they swim distractedly about, make head-on collisions, and generally get in one another's way.

II

The first of all our traditions—indeed, for a long time the only one that powerfully affected us—was that of German Romanticism. Roughly speaking, it dominated our music from its first timid beginnings about 1850 until, let us say, 1890. Those of us who studied with the first serious American composer in larger forms, Professor John Knowles Paine of Harvard, remember how submissively his music reflected the romanticism of Schumann and Mendelssohn, just as most of American literature of that period reflected English models. His "Island Fantasy" was supposed to be inspired by the Isles of Shoals, off Portsmouth, but artistically speaking it was within easy sailing distance of Mendelssohn's "Hebrides."

His younger colleagues and followers, Arthur Foote and George W. Chadwick, did valuable work, but belong on the whole, like him, to the epoch when our music was dominated by German models. MacDowell was of the same heredity, his line coming out of Schumann through Joachim Raff. His greater distinction came largely from his narrower assimilativeness, and was purchased at a price. Three Rheinberger pupils contributed much to our music: Henry Holden Huss, a composer of unusual romantic charm but inadequate constructive and self-critical power; Arthur Whiting, one of our most genuinely native talents despite the meagerness of his output; and Horatio Parker, so facile and so voluminous, and on the whole so characterless. Then there is Edgar Stillman Kelley, whose *New England Symphony*, technically one of the most competent works our country has produced, is German to the backbone. Despite its title, there is in it scarcely more of New England than there is of Old England in the works of Bennett, Macfarren, and other composers of the period when England was dominated by Handel and Mendelssohn. Like most of the works of its generation it is, as Mr. Arthur Whiting once called the songs of a young American composer, "as German as kraut." In most of these works the dominance of a foreign model seems to paralyze personal feeling. MacDowell is almost the only exception, and he purchased individuality at the price of a terrible limitation of style and emotional reach.

The first powerful rival influence to that of Germany, beginning to make itself felt about 1890, came from France, quickened to national self-consciousness by the Franco-Prussian war.

It assumed two strongly contrasted forms: first, the modification of romantic sentiment toward the classic reserve, balance, and plastic beauty naturally produced by French love of clearness and order, as manifested in the work of César Franck and his greatest disciple, Vincent d'Indy; second, the distrust of all sentiment and the devotion of sensuous charm typically represented by the impressionism of Debussy and the irony of Ravel. Some of us who were in college in the nineties found the mysticism and spirituality of Franck and d'Indy quite as potently persuasive as the less subtle romanticism of Schumann and Brahms, and were irresistibly led to try to incorporate in our style both streams of influence. Others were more attracted by the novelty of the sensuous appeal of the impressionists, who enjoyed moreover an infinitely greater vogue.

Debussy and Ravel are reflected in such contemporary American composers as Edward Burlingame Hill and John Alden Carpenter, both of whom studied under Paine at Harvard in the nineties, as unmistakably as Schumann and Raff are reflected in MacDowell. Hill, as he has shown in his orchestral suite, *Stevensoniana,* can score with a richness and clarity of color evidently learned at the feet of the French impressionists, though combined with a naiveté and tenderness of feeling quite personal. In other works, such as "The Fall of the House of Usher," he is less personal, more conventional, more purely reflective. Many of Carpenter's clever and refined—almost too refined—songs and piano pieces might have been written by Debussy, while his suite for orchestra, *Adventures in a Perambulator,* is essentially Gallic in its economy of means, its distinctiveness of color, and its ironic wit.

Of all the cases of French influence no doubt the most striking is that of Charles Martin Loeffler. Alsatian by birth, something of an exotic in America, Loeffler is surely one of our most distinguished composers, distinguished especially through the singleness and complete unity of his style, entirely French in its fastidious reticence, its refinement of sentiment, and its delicacy of color. And what is more, he is not only exclusively French, but inclusively French: there is in his string quartet in memory

of Victor Chapman, for instance, the noble seriousness and
earnest though reticent feeling of d'Indy, and there is, in works
like the *Pagan Poem* for orchestra, the sensuous fascination of
Debussy. Such works are as fine as anything that modern France
itself has produced.

III

At the end of the nineteenth century, then, two traditions
dominated our American music, both imported, one from Germany, the other from France. Those composers who through
singleness of temperament and concentration of mind succeeded
in thoroughly assimilating one tradition and one only, as Mac-
Dowell did German Romanticism and Loeffler did French impressionism, succeeded in producing works that still have a life
of their own, however narrow, and a permanent artistic validity.

During the first quarter of the twentieth century, however,
when traditions began to multiply among us with alarming rapidity, such concentration became more and more difficult to
achieve. We must remember that one does not master a tradition merely by defining it academically or understanding it intellectually; one has to live with it, to make it by long habit a part
of one's point of view; and the more traditions one is sensitive
to, and the more various and perhaps even opposed they are,
the more arduous is this assimilation. We have had from the
beginning, unfortunately, too many parrot composers, clever
enough in imitating any prevalent idiom of musical speech, but
too superficial to ponder its meaning. Our path is littered with
still-born "masterpieces," once acclaimed and now forgotten. The
more traditions there are to follow the more featureless does
such an eclecticism become; and in our day the traditions have
become so tangled that only the most powerful intelligences can
find their way through them, only the simplest spirits can proceed
undismayed by them to the goals appointed by their temperaments.

There were, for instance, several minor national traditions
which, though far less powerful than the German and the French,

began to make definite claims upon our attention. There was what we may call Russian barbarism, which came to us from Moussorgsky and Rimsky-Korsakoff, via Prokofieff and Stravinsky. Leo Ornstein was the chief American composer, if such he may be called, to listen to that formidable Amazonian siren. Then the torrid sunlight of subtropical Spain was flashed into our cooler atmosphere by Albéniz, Granados, and others, and reflected for our dazzlement by Ernest Schelling. Musical speech began to fall upon our ears in many strange and outlandish dialects. Grieg beguiled us with a Norwegian accent, Dvořák with a Bohemian, Sibelius with a Northern wail, Elgar with a bit of British drawl, and Stanford with a brogue. Quick to take a hint, we began to exploit our own "local color," and blossomed forth in Indian suites and Negro rhapsodies.

Once started, the process of differentiation did not stop with nationalism, but began to produce many conflicting schools, groups, and cliques. In Europe itself music, already decadent in the preciousness and exaggerated sensuousness of Debussy and in the distrust of its own feelings betrayed by the irony of Ravel, lost unity and balance altogether, and broke into fragments. Differentiation became disintegration. Musicians ranged themselves in rival camps, all more or less partial and futile. In one were pedants like Reger and Schönberg, trying to ratiocinate their way to a beauty that comes only through feeling. In another were hysterics like Scriabine, striving to refine the soul of art out of its body. In still another were the impatient and the disillusioned who like irritable children smashed the toys they could not mend (the Italian *bruiteurs*, for instance), or who, like the Dadaists or the French Group of Six, finding reality too slow, exacting and laborious for them, reverted to infantility and took to riding rocking horses.

At the very moment of this disintegration in Europe, we in America, through the economic effects of the war, were put more than ever into the position of a receiver nation. Already before the war we looked to Europe for guidance with all the conscious inferiority of youth and inexperience; now, without increasing our wisdom, the war vastly increased our power, by placing

Europe in the relation to us of bankrupt parents forced to defer to immature children in order to live. Since 1914 musicians of every country on earth have flowed in upon us in an unending stream. The music of the whole world has battered our ears. For us, the only ones with wherewithal to pay the piper, the habitable globe has danced and sung.

How could we hope to stand against such a flood? What was there for us to do but open our mouths and shut our eyes, and try to swallow as much of it all as we could without drowning? Too much passive reception, too little self-realizing activity— that had always been the characteristic danger of our situation. Under the vast mass and variety of influences that now swept in upon us our modest powers of assimilation were hopelessly deluged and gutted. We became vast stomachs to swallow at one gulp the music of the universe, while our legs and arms, just timidly sprouting, gave up the unequal struggle and withered away. In short, American music from 1914 to 1928 is the Music of Indigestion.

Go to a concert of any of the "advanced" organizations of the day, such as the International Composers' Guild, and listen to the rumblings and belchings of this indigestion. Listen to the confusion worse confounded of our house of a hundred traditions, our modern Babel. Hear Emerson Whithorne's Chinese tunes, as insulated in their European harmonies as the inhabitants of Pell Street in modern New York. Watch Samuel Gardner's Russian folk-song bacteria bombinating in a matrix vapidly German-sentimentalist. Study Henry F. Gilbert's Negroes in his "Comedy Overture on Negro Themes": not full-blooded, you will observe, but half-breeds—quadroons—octoroons—descended by some repellent miscegenation from Beethoven and Mendelssohn. Notice Charles Wakefield Cadman's Indians, whose only arrows are collars from Troy, and who wear derby hats. Even John Powell, the most gifted of all our "folk" composers apparently does not recoil when, in his "Rhapsodie Nègre" (French titles have appealed to American composers ever since the days of Gottschalk) the swarthy faces of his protagonists suddenly assume the Jesuitical smile of Liszt.

Alas, the confusion of traditions among us is disastrously bewildering, even to the greatest talents. We are not only parrots,
but polyglot parrots. Where shall we recapture our native tongue,
or at least learn to speak the Esperanto of cosmopolitanism with
voices recognizably our own and an authority not borrowed?
This has become the insistent aesthetic question of the day, upon
our finding a right answer to which seems to depend our artistic
salvation.

IV

One answer which has attracted much attention, both by the
plausibility of its theory and by the interest of practical results
already obtained, is that of the nationalists. It is based on the
analogy of the various national awakenings that have taken place
in European music: such as that of Germany, throwing off the
yoke of Italian opera in the work of Mozart, Weber, and Wagner;
of France, finding itself in the activities of the *Société Nationale*
and other organizations and individuals after 1870; of Russia,
reaching national self-consciousness in Borodin, Moussorgsky,
and Rimsky-Korsakoff; and finally of England, asserting itself
only in our own day through the work of Vaughan Williams,
Gustav Holst and other living composers.

This last nationalism, that of England, is quite naturally, and
for several reasons, the one that has most deeply impressed us
here in America. It is not only the most recent but the nearest,
since we are conscious of a closer kinship with the English,
aesthetically, temperamentally, and socially, than with any European people. Moreover, exactly the same kind of featureless
eclecticism that has blighted so much of our own music was imposed on England for generations by the prestige of Handel and
Mendelssohn; and to hear at last Elgar, Holst, and Vaughan Williams, after so many Sterndale Bennetts, Cowens, Macfarrens,
and Prouts, fills us with a great hope. In this we have been
encouraged by observant visitors. Vaughn Williams himself did
not hesitate to prophesy, after his first visit to us, that we should
go through the same evolution as England. We were about a
generation behind the mother country, he told us; our present

men were doing the educational and preparatory work accomplished there by Perry, Stanford, and their fellows; and in
twenty-five years we might hope to see such a school of native
composers as flourishes there now.

English nationalism is undeniably a vital movement. No doubt
its claims may be sometimes exaggerated, as the claims of all
nationalisms seem to have a way of being; we may see reasons,
as we go on, for questioning the universal applicability of its
theory, and the exclusive validity of its practice, especially under
other conditions. But that it has breathed new life into English
music in the last twenty years seems certain. The extraordinary
beauty and variety of the native songs and dances of Britain
were first revealed through the work of enthusiasts like Cecil
Sharp, who devoted a laborious life to discovering, recording,
arranging, and publishing them. Through the British Folk-Song
Society, founded by Sharp, they were given wide vogue. Attractive settings of them were made by many composers, slightly
elaborated but preserving their essential naiveté.

Interest quickly spread from them to the less popular, more
artistic music of early England, and such labors as Fellowes'
monumental collection of sixteenth-century madrigals revealed
an undreamed of richness in the native musical background.
Scholars began to discuss the melodic, modal, and rhythmic peculiarities of this music, and composers more or less consciously
to mold their style upon it. The result was what may fairly be
called a new voice in the chorus of the world's music. Such works
as Vaughan Williams' *Variations on a Theme of Thomas Tallis*
and his "London" and "Pastoral" Symphonies are as unmistakably English as d'Indy's *Symphony on a Mountain Song* is
French, or Balakireff's "Islamey" Russian. Vaughan Williams
has carried the same methods into opera in his *Hugh the Drover*,
in which, appropriately enough, the hero fights the villain not
with sword or poniard but with good British fists; and Holst has
woven an entire one-act opera, *At the Boar's Head*, out of thirty-
odd traditional tunes.

Meanwhile Sharp himself was carrying his investigations into
America, discovering in the Appalachian Mountains and other
rural districts little affected by civilization many survivals of

songs brought from England generations ago. His publications contain curious examples of songs less corrupted by time in America than in England, or differently corrupted here, just as our speech is said to preserve Elizabethan words obsolete in their native land. Howard Brockway in his two collections, *Songs of the Kentucky Mountains* and *Lonesome Tunes* (as these melodies are quaintly called by the mountaineers), has made available much material of great historic interest and, what is better, refreshing artistic simplicity and charm. Both Brockway and Leo Sowerby have made folk-music settings as attractive as those of Percy Grainger, and David Guion has given us in "Turkey in the Straw" as fetching and as Anglo-Saxon a dance as "Shepherd's Hey" itself. So far as the large forms are concerned our composers have been slower to venture on the new ground. John Powell is almost the only one who has as yet worked there successfully, in such pieces as his "Sonata Virginianesque," his Violin Concerto, and above all his orchestral overture, "In Old Virginia." This work is American-English in the sense in which Vaughan Williams' "Pastoral" Symphony is English-English; and in its own way it is as beautiful.

Is it necessary, however, we are likely to find ourselves asking at this point, that all of our music in America should be of this American-English variety? Is it indeed even desirable? Why should not some of our American music be American-German (from Pennsylvania), or American-French (from New Orleans), or American-Jewish (from New York), or even American-Negro or Red Indian? May it not be, in fact, that a nationalistic theory which works out well enough for a tight little island like England, or even for the four tight little islands of Britain, must find itself all at sea (if one may mix metaphors in describing a very mixed situation) in a melting-pot such as our modern America? May it not be that we are necessarily polyglot, and that to speak American, in any comprehensive sense, is to speak, not English, but something rather more resembling the language of the Swiss tourist: "Donnez-moi some aqua calda, bitte"? In any department of life the Nordic is a sufficiently absurd figment of theory; in music, with its deep obligations to Italians, Germans, Frenchmen, and Jews, and its power of leaping all barriers

of race and of class, he is likely to be both ridiculous and per-
nicious. The nationalistic thread hardly seems capable of leading
us very far, then, in such a labyrinth as we inhabit.

V

But since in art practice is always more important than theory,
the theoretical difficulties of nationalism in America, obvious as
they are, come to seem formidable only when we consider certain practical results of all efforts to apply it to our music. It
seems to be a formula so narrow that it can hardly be applied
without being broken. Thus if we observe carefully the work
of a folk-music setter such as Brockway or Grainger, we find
that he can never quite accept the narrow limits of the idiom
he is using; we notice that he constantly passes beyond the tradition of his material, and enhances its interest by features borrowed from other traditions and wider ones; and if we have a
keen sense of style we feel a resultant incongruity.

The difficulty that all nationalists seem to find in sailing a
course that will avoid shipwreck on the Scylla of incongruity
or the Charybdis of bareness seems to suggest a fatal defect in
their idiom itself. It seems to be so primitive, melodically, harmonically, and structurally, in comparison with other idioms
with which we are all perfectly familiar, that it will neither mix
with them naturally nor long hold our interest without them.

Our sense of restriction in the idiom of folk-song seems, moreover, to be but the index of a deeper dissatisfaction we cannot
but feel in its emotional and intellectual poverty. No doubt its
very charm comes from the contrast of its simplicity with our
complexity; no doubt beings born like us to complexity are apt
to have a rather morbid craving for what they imagine to be
the simple life; but when they get a taste of it they always find
that for them it is not natural but artificial. City people often
daydream of a picnic in the country; but if they actually go on
one they find that much of the charm lies in getting back again
to where they feel at home. Modern music-lovers may enjoy a
folk-song or dance for a change, but for a steady diet they find
a Brahms symphony or a Wagner music-drama more satisfying
than the "Volga Boat-song" or "Barbara Allen." Whatever the

faddists may say, the world of folk music is really too narrow a
habitat for us to feel comfortable in; to live in it is for us unnatural. Says Ernest Newman:

The nationalists isolate a certain genre of expression—the
folk-music of centuries ago—and tell us that only by absorbing
this genre into his tissue can an English composer hope to be
English. That, I claim, is a monstrous fallacy. A modern novelist
who sees the life around him imaginatively and clearly can make
first-rate English art out of what he sees, even if he has never
read a single old English legend or heard a single old English
ballad. The composer has only to do what the novelist does. If
he feels deeply and sincerely about life, and can find beautiful
and convincing expression for what he and the rest of us living
people feel, he will make great English art even though he may
never have heard a folk-song and never have seen an agricul-
tural laborer.

Thus when we examine closely the claims of nationalism it
seems to fail us, at least as a universal formula. Even in England, where the mixture of nations and of races and the confusion of traditions is so much less than here, nationalism is prevented from being a universal panacea by its intrinsic limitations
both of idiom and of emotional and intellectual scope. We seem
therefore to be thrown back upon eclecticism, and obliged to ask
whether there is not, after all, some other kind of eclecticism
than the "featureless" variety. May there not be also an eclecticism of power, of choice, of individuality? May not the distinctiveness achieveable by American composers be a personal rather
than a national distinctiveness? May not such personal distinctiveness be, indeed, the only kind that is genuinely attainable in
an art that has reached such complexity and cosmopolitanism
as modern music?

This view, to be sure, cannot hope to be agreeable to our
American taste for herding, for standardizing, for doing everything in large numbers and en masse. But in art no formula
can be universal, and it is precisely the pretension of nationalism to universality that is its most injurious trait. Nationalism

is excellent as an ingredient, but disastrous as a dogma. The promising way toward a rich and various American music seems much less likely to lie through any system of branding, organizing, and licensing, such as nationalism and all other "isms" are too apt to foster, than through an elastic eclecticism of individual choice.

Originality has been well defined by Van Wyck Brooks as "a capacity to survive and surmount experience after having met and assimilated it." If he is right there must be possible to us as many musical personalties as there are possible combinations and permutations of vital traditions. Therefore, when MacDowell meets and assimilates German Romanticism, when Loeffler meets and assimilates French impressionism, when Powell meets and assimilates Anglo-American folksong, let us not cavil and define, let us rather rejoice and applaud. Were a single one of them to be forcibly "Americanized," music in America would be the poorer. Music in America is the richer for each and all of them; and music in America is a thing far more worth working for than "American music."

HENRY

COWELL was born in Menlo Park, California, in 1897. At
first he simply followed his musical intuitions, which led him
along paths of discovery that anticipated many of the innovations of twentieth-century musical composition. In 1912, for
example, at the age of fifteen, he played one of his own piano
pieces, "The Tides of Manaunaun," in which he used "tone clusters" (groups of adjacent tones struck simultaneously on the
keyboard, requiring, in some cases, use of the entire forearm).
He was persuaded by Charles Seeger (then teaching theory and
composition at the University of California in Berkeley) to take
up the systematic study of counterpoint and harmony, which he
did for several years under Seeger's direction. Later he continued
his studies in New York.

In 1919 he completed the writing of a book, *New Musical
Resources* (not published until 1930), which was the most important theoretical work written in America up to that time.
As Cowell explains his motives for undertaking this work: "My
interest in the theory underlying new materials came about at
first through wishing to explain to myself, as well as to others,
why certain materials I felt impelled to use in composing, and
which I instinctively felt to be legitimate, have genuine scientific
and logical foundation."

Cowell was one of the most prolific and versatile of American
composers. The most important musical innovator between Ives
and Cage, he was also a leading "Americanist" (none of our com-

posers was better acquainted with the grass roots of America's
music), a traditionalist with twenty symphonies to his credit
(he was not afraid to use sonata form when it pleased him to
do so), and a musical globe-trotter who, from his early studies
of ethnic music with Erich M. von Hornbostel in Berlin through
his later travels to the Middle, Near, and Far East, maintained
a keen desire to understand and assimilate a diversity of musical
cultures and to use music as a means of communication among
the peoples of the world.

Cowell died at his home in Shady, New York, on December
10, 1965. At the time of his death he had almost completed his
Twentieth Symphony.

New Musical Resources / (1930)

Contemporary music makes almost universal use of materials
formerly considered unusable. These materials are in some degree acceptable to almost all music-lovers, and there is a tendency
on the part of critics and the sophisticated public to be somewhat bored by new music which uses only old-fashioned means.
In spite of their current use, however, little is known about the
materials of contemporary music, and there are surprisingly
few attempts to organize them into a unified system. Notwithstanding some very interesting works on new problems in music
(such as Redfield's *Music: a Science and an Art*), written for
the most part by scientists rather than musicians, a sytem co-

ordinating the various materials of modern music has not been made public, so far as I know. Schönberg in his *Harmonielehre* carried the conventional study of harmony a step further. He explained many moderately complex harmonies by combining more chromatic passing tones and pointed out some well-known primary overtone relationships; but his work fails to explain music as involved as Schönberg's own compositions. A later theory, as yet unpublished by Schönberg, investigates very thoroughly the possibilities of the twelve-tone scale, which is, however, only one facet of contemporary materials. Eaglefield Hull in his book *Modern Harmony* has made one of the few attempts to give a general explanation of modern phenomena. Hull did not, however, offer any theory as to why the particular materials actually in use should have been found more acceptable than many other means which might have been used in their place. Although Hull's book was written some years ago, his efforts in classifying musical means without giving reasons for their existence are reflected in the attitude of some musicians today. If a student is told that triads are built on intervals of a third, he is not thereby made aware of the entire sytem of conventional harmony. He not only must know why thirds are acceptable materials for building triads, but must study the details of chord-connexion, perhaps for years, to gain a knowledge of their handling. Similarly, to state that a certain chord in modern music is built up in fourths is not a sufficient explanation. A reason for the suitability of fourths as building material must be shown, as well as some idea of the practical problems to be overcome in connecting fourth chords, before any knowledge of such chords is gained.

The purpose of *New Musical Resources* is not to attempt to explain the materials of contemporary music, many of which are not included in its discussion, but to point out the influence the overtone series has exerted on music throughout its history, how many musical materials of all ages are related to it, and how, by various means of applying its principles in many different manners, a large palette of musical materials can be assembled. Some of them are in use, some of them are presaged on contemporary music, and some of them seem to be unused so far. Whether such materials are or are not in use it is not the purpose to discover; rather the purpose is to show the co-ordination of all possible musical materials within a certain overtone radius, regardless of whether they are yet in actual use. The very fact that such materials are built on the overtone series, which is the greatest factor in musical relationships, shows that they probably have potential musical use and value. That many of them remain as yet unused or only very tentatively suggested makes the field which is opened up all the richer.

The result of a study of overtones is to find the importance of relationships in music and to find the measure by which every interval and chord may be related. It is discovered that the sense of consonance, dissonance, and discord is not fixed, so that it must be immovably applied to certain combinations, but is relative. It is also discovered that rhythm and tone, which have been thought to be entirely separate musical fundamentals (and still may be considered so in many ways) are definitely related through overtone ratios. Therefore the theory proposed may be termed a theory of musical relativity.

Incidentally, one of the results of an examination into the application of overtone relationships is to discover a way of logically co-ordinating many seemingly chaotic materials used in contemporary music, so that without that being its purpose, *New Musical Resources* throws an illumination on some difficult problems of "modernism," and shows that much "modern" music is not proceeding blindly. This is not always true, of course, as in many cases it suffers from a lack of knowledge by the composer of the materials used; and there is without question much inconsistency of texture to be found in some contemporary composition.

The aim of any technique is to perfect the means of expression. If a technique serves to dry up and inhibit the expression, it is useless as technique. Leaving the means of expression imperfect, however, does not solve the problem. Hearing innumerable passages in contemporary music which it is evident could be improved by the changing of a few mistaken notes (not to conform to some preconceived standard, but to express more consistently the composer's own idea) makes one wish that there could be more precision in the choice of notes, more intellectual understanding of each particular harmonic connexion. It may be felt that this work is done in the study of conventional harmony. Harmony as it is taught, however, contains discrepancies. Some of its rules are based on underlying science and more inevitable principles, but many other rules, inextricably mixed with the necessary ones, are based on the taste of a former era of music and are subject to change. Perhaps because these empirical rules have little application to problems of contemporary music, there has been on the part of some a reaction against the idea that knowledge of musical materials is necessary. Now, however, it is generally conceded that ignorant daring in the use of new materials results in many childish crudities and is often accompanied by absence of musical invention. It is therefore of interest to make public a system showing the relationship and use of contemporary materials. The aim in suggesting the new materials is not, of course, to have them supersede old ones, but rather to supplement them, as well as adding new resources to the entire tonal palette.

Because the present work is not an attempt to explain the methods of specific composers, no quotations have been taken from actual compositions, but all necessary examples have been specially constructed to illustrate the various points.

A discussion of different sorts of temperament, or tuning, has not been attempted, as it has been assumed that the tones of the overtone series, being unconsciously if not consciously heard whenever a single tone is sounded, are a natural criterion. Therefore all temperaments from this point of view may be considered as an attempt to solve the problem of making some of the overtone relationships practical for musical use. In order to do this it has been necessary to alter the relationships slightly in various ways, by equalizing minute differences, etc. But it seems probable that a keen auditor has suggested to him through his musical imagination the overtone relationship nearest to the very close equivalents of the different modes of temperament, of which some are closer than others to the original series. Differences of temperament, however, and practical methods for making them possible on musical instruments, form a fascinating subject. Divisions of the octave into mathematically equal parts form the basis for the scales in much music. Javanese music divides the octave into five equal parts; Siamese music uses a scale of nine equal divisions of the octave. The whole-tone scale as used by Debussy and others divides the octave into six parts. Our own keyboard instruments divide the octave into twelve parts, and Schönberg bases his new theoretical system on such a division. The quarter-tone scale as proposed by Alois Hába and others would divide the octave into twenty-four equal steps. These divisions are not unrelated to the overtone series, as the intervals they form can be found among overtone relationships. Other systems of temperament more immediately related to the overtone series deal with unequal or diatonic divisions of the octave. Interest in differences of temperament comes largely through consideration of scales. In this work it is suggested that scales as well as other aspects of music are related to the overtone series, which is a scale in its upper reaches, a harmony in its lower reaches, and a basis for rhythmical co-ordination.

It is not the aim of this work to delve into questions of aesthetics, into any philosophical discussion of what is good or bad, what should or should not be done, or what may or may not be done. These are questions which are answered by the dictates of taste, and taste and fashions in taste change. It is my conviction, however, that the finest taste and the perfect use of scientifically co-ordinated materials go together, and that the musical resources outlined add to the possibilities of musical expression and are therefore vital potentialities, rather than merely cold facts.

My interest in the theory underlying new materials came about at first through wishing to explain to myself, as well as to others, why certain materials I felt impelled to use in composition, and which I instinctively felt to be legitimate, have genuine scientific and logical foundation. I therefore made an investigation into the laws of acoustics as applied to musical materials. Some of the results of the investigation convinced me that although my music itself preceded the knowledge of its theoretical explanation, there had been enough unconscious perception so that the means used were not only in accordance with acoustical law, but are perhaps the best way of amalgamating sounds formerly considered discords; namely, by sounding together a number of tones related through the higher reaches of the overtones, in the same spacing in which they occur in the overtone series. Some of the results of this probing into acoustical relationships form the basis for this work.

It will readily be seen that the various fields opened up are merely suggested, and that a separate book would have to be written about each one of the subjects, such as polyharmony, polyrhythm, or tone clusters, to make any detailed application of the principles shown. There are primary subjects other than those treated of here to which the same general method of procedure might be applied, opening up other new fields; and by applying the same process of development to a study of the possibilities of combining the primary elements dealt with in this work, a further extension may be made.

New Musical Resources was first written during 1919, with the literary assistance of Professor Samuel S. Seward, of Stanford University, to whom I am deeply indebted. In this early form it embraced most of the applications given here of the theory of musical relativity. Many of the materials which it predicted would come into music have since been adopted; many materials which were only vaguely suggested in music at the time, and which were pointed out as valid, have since been developed to such an extent that it is difficult to realize with what suspicion they were regarded in 1919. For example, the chapter on dissonant counterpoint was at that time a proposal that such a counterpoint be formulated. Since then Ruggles and Hindemith have been heralded as apostles of dissonant counterpoint, and Schönberg has brought to a clear focus the counterpoint which was a mere suggestion in his Opus 11 and other works of an earlier period. Similar developments have been made in many of the branches treated. Such progress is encouraging and seems to give further proof that the theory as postulated has validity.

GEORGE
GERSHWIN (1898–1937) was born in Brooklyn, New York, the son of Russian-Jewish immigrants (the family name was originally Gershovitz). The family was well enough off to have a maid and a piano, and to afford music lessons for the children. George began his piano-playing on a diet of operatic potpourris, but soon switched to more substantial fare when he began to take lessons from the pianist and composer Charles Hambitzer, who introduced him to the piano literature from Bach to Ravel. To a friend, Hambitzer wrote: "I have a new pupil who will make his mark in music if anybody will. The boy is a genius . . . ." Subsequently Gershwin studied theory and composition with Edward Kilenyi, with Rubin Goldmark, with Henry Cowell (counterpoint), and (from about 1932, when he was at the height of his fame) with Joseph Schillinger. Thus, far from being a popular tunesmith who suddenly decided to turn toward serious music, Gershwin from his earliest years to his last was constantly concerned with improving his knowledge of so-called classical music, and the evidence indicates that he did not feel the dichotomy between popular and serious music that has afflicted so many musicians.

Although much has been written about George Gershwin, the exact nature of his relation to jazz has never been fully explored or documented. The holograph score of *Rhapsody in Blue* bears the inscription (in the composer's handwriting), "For Jazz Band and Piano." In the orchestral score by Ferde Grofé, however, this has been changed to "Piano Solo and Orchestra." And in each subsequent orchestration the rhapsody became more and more "symphonic." What Gershwin did in such works as *Rhapsody in Blue*, the Concerto in F and *An American in Paris*, was to use certain traits of the jazz idiom in a traditionally symphonic manner. This certainly does not make him an "authority" on jazz; nevertheless, what he had to say on the subject is interesting, simply because he was a genius and because he felt that jazz—as he knew and understood it—was vital to his creative purpose.

The Composer in the Machine Age / (1933)

Unquestionably modern musical America has been influenced by modern musical Europe. But it seems to me that modern European composers, in turn, have very largely received their stimulus, their rhythms and impulses from Machine Age America. They have a much older tradition of musical technique which has helped them put into musical terms a little more clearly the thoughts that originated here. They can express themselves more glibly.

The Machine Age has influenced practically everything. I do not mean only music but everything from the arts to finance. The machine has not affected our age in form as much as in tempo, speed and sound. It has affected us in sound whenever composers utilize new instruments to imitate its aspects. In my

An American in Paris I used four taxi horns for musical effect.
George Antheil has used everything, including aeroplane pro-
pellers, door bells, typewriter keys, and so forth. By the use
of the old instruments, too, we are able to obtain modern effects.
Take a composition like Honegger's *Pacific No. 231*, written and
dedicated to a steam engine. It reproduces the whole effect of
a train stopping and starting and it is all done with familiar
instruments.

There is only one important thing in music and that is ideas
and feeling. The various tonalities and sounds mean nothing
unless they grow out of ideas. Not many composers have ideas.
Far more of them know how to use strange instruments which do
not require ideas. Whoever has inspired ideas will write the great
music of our period. We are plowing the ground for that genius
who may be alive or may be born today or tomorrow. If he is
alive, he is recognized to a certain degree, although it is impossible for the public at large to assimilate real greatness quickly.
Take a composer like Bach. In his lifetime, he was recognized
as one of the greatest organists in the world, but he was not
acclaimed as one of the greatest composers of his time until
generations after his death.

I do not think there is any such thing as mechanized musical
composition without feeling, without emotion. Music is one of
the arts which appeals directly through the emotions. Mechanism
and feeling will have to go hand in hand, in the same way that
a skyscraper is at the same time a triumph of the machine and
a tremendous emotional experience, almost breath-taking. Not
merely its height but its mass and proportions are the result of
an emotion, as well as of calculation.

Any discussion of the distinction between presentation and
representation in music resolves itself into an attempt to determine the relative values of abstract music and program music.
It is very difficult for anyone to tell where abstract music starts
and program music finishes. There must have been a picture of
something in the composer's mind. What it was nobody knows,
often not even the composer. But music has a marvellous faculty
of recording a picture in someone else's mind. In my own case,
everybody who has ever listened to *Rhapsody in Blue*—and that

embraces thousands of people—has a story for it but myself. *An American in Paris* is obviously a program piece, although I would say half of it or more is abstract music tied together by a few representative themes. Imitation never gets anyone anywhere. Originality is the only thing that counts. But the originator uses material and ideas that occur around him and pass through him. Out of his experience comes this original creation or work or art, unquestionably influenced by his surroundings which include very largely what we call the Machine Age.

It is difficult to determine what enduring values, esthetically, jazz has contributed, because jazz is a word which has been used for at least five or six different types of music. It is really a conglomeration of many things. It has a little bit of ragtime, the blues, classicism and spirituals. Basically, it is a matter of rhythm. After rhythm in importance come intervals, music intervals which are peculiar to the rhythm. After all, there is nothing new in music. I maintained years ago that there is very little difference in the music of different nations. There is just that little individual touch. One country may prefer a peculiar rhythm or a note like the seventh. This it stresses, and it becomes identified with that nation. In America this preferred rhythm is called jazz. Jazz is music; it uses the same notes that Bach used. When jazz is played in another nation, it is called American. When it is played in another country, it sounds false. Jazz is the result of the energy stored up in America. It is a very energetic kind of music, noisy, boisterous and even vulgar. One thing is certain: jazz has contributed an enduring value to America in the sense that it has expressed ourselves. It is an original American achievement which will endure, not as jazz perhaps, but which will leave its mark on future music in one form or another. The only kinds of music which endure are those which possess form in the universal sense and folk music. All else dies. But unquestionably folk songs are being written and have been written which contain enduring elements of jazz. To be sure, that is only an element; it is not the whole. An entire composition written in jazz could not live.

As for further esthetic developments in musical composition, American composers may in time use quarter notes, but then so will Europe use quarter notes. Eventually our ears will become sensitive to a much finer degree than they were a hundred, fifty or twenty-five years ago. Music deemed ugly then is accepted without question today. It stands to reason therefore, that composers will continue to alter their language. That might lead to anything. They have been writing already in two keys. There is no reason why they will not go further and ask us to recognize quarter or sixteenth notes. Such notes, whether written or not, are used all the time, only we are not conscious of them. In India they use quarter tones and, I believe, consciously.

Music is a phenomenon that to me has a very marked effect on the emotions. It can have various effects. It has the power of moving people to all of the various moods. Through the emotions, it can have a cleansing effect on the mind, a disturbing effect, a drowsy effect, an exciting effect. I do not know to what extent it can finally become a part of the people. I do not think music as we know it now is indispensable although we have music all around us in some form or other. There is music in the wind. People can live more or less satisfactorily without orchestral music, for instance. And who can tell that we would not be better off if we weren't as civilized as we are, if we lacked many of our emotions? But we have them and we are more or less egotistic about them. We think that they are important and that they make us what we are. We think we are an improvement over people of other ages who didn't have them. Music has become a very important part of civilization, and one of the main reasons is that one does not need a formal education to appreciate it. Music can be appreciated by a person who can neither read nor write and it can also be appreciated by people who have the highest form of intelligence. For example, Einstein plays the violin and listens to music. People in the underworld, dope fiends and gun men, invariably are music lovers and, if not, they are affected by it. Music is entering into medicine. Music sets up a certain vibration which unquestionably results in a physical reaction. Eventually the proper vibration for every person will be found and utilized. I like to think of music as an emotional science.

Almost every great composer profoundly influences the age in which he lives. Bach, Beethoven, Wagner, Brahms, Debussy, Stravinsky. They have all re-created something of their time so that millions of people could feel it more forcefully and better understand their time.

The composer, in my estimation, has been helped a great deal by the mechanical reproduction of music. Music is written to be heard, and any instrument that tends to help it to be heard more frequently and by great numbers is advantageous to the person who writes it. Aside from royalties or anything like that, I should think that the theory that music is written to be heard is a good one. To enable millions of people to listen to music by radio or phonograph is helpful to the composer. The composer who writes music for himself and doesn't want it to be heard is generally a bad composer. The first incursion of mechanized reproduction was a stimulus to the composer and the second wave has merely intensified that stimulus. In the past, composers have starved because of lack of performance, lack of being heard. That is impossible today. Schubert could not make any money because he did not have an opportunity through the means of distribution of his day to reach the public. He died at the age of thirty-one and had a certain reputation. If he had lived to be fifty or sixty, unquestionably he would have obtained recognition in his own day. If he were living today, he would be well-off and comfortable.

The radio and the phonograph are harmful to the extent that they bastardize music and give currency to a lot of cheap things. They are not harmful to the composer. The more people listen to music, the more they will be able to criticize it and know when it is good. When we speak of machine-made music, however, we are not speaking of music in the highest sense, because, no matter how much the world becomes a Machine Age, music will have to be created in the same old way. The Machine Age can affect music only in its distribution. Composers must compose in the same way the old composers did. No one has found

a new method in which to write music. We still use the old signatures, the old symbols. The composer has to do every bit of
his work himself. Hand work can never be replaced in the composition of music. If music ever became machine-made in that
sense, it would cease to be an art.

ROY

HARRIS was born in Lincoln County, Oklahoma, on February 12, 1898, of Scotch-Irish descent. When he was five, the family moved to the San Gabriel Valley in southern California. At first he taught himself music, but in California he was able to study composition with Arthur Farwell and Modest Altschuler. An *Andante with Variations* for orchestra, first performed by Howard Hanson at Rochester in 1926, brought him recognition in the East. The following year he went to Paris for further study with Nadia Boulanger.

Serge Koussevitzky took a keen interest in the music of Roy Harris: beginning with the First Symphony (1933), he conducted the premiere of one Harris symphony after another. It was the Third Symphony (1939) which brought Harris wide and enduring fame and he went on to write six more symphonies, including the *Folk Song Symphony* (his fourth), with choral interpolations based on American folk songs, and the Ninth Symphony (1961), inspired by the Constitution of the United States.

Harris has always taken himself very seriously as an American composer; he appears to have assumed a sort of collective responsibility for expressing "the American spirit" in music. He has written extensively on what he regards as the distinguishing traits of American music, which he tends to equate with certain aspects of "national character." In one of his statements he said: "Musical literature never has been and never will be valuable to society as a whole until it is created as an

146

authentic and characteristic culture of and from the people it expresses."

Harris rejects popular music as an expression of the American people because he considers it too frivolous and limited in its emotional range. In connection with his Fifth Symphony (1943), he wrote: "Our people are more than pleasure-loving: We also have qualities of heroic strength—determination—will to struggle—faith in our destiny. We are possessed of a fierce driving power—optimistic, young, rough and ready. . . ." This is what Harris tried to project in much of his music, especially the symphonies.

Problems of American Composers / (1933)

America is vast and elemental; America is desperately struggling to wrest social balance from her omnivorous industrialism. America is rolling plains, wind-swept prairies, gaunt deserts, rugged mountains, forests of giant redwoods and pines, lonely rockbound shores, seas of wheat and corn stretching on to the elastic horizon, cotton and tobacco fields, fruit orchards, little bare mining towns huddled on the sides of mountains, lumber camps, oil fields, and New England mill towns. America is smoking, jostling, clamorous cities of steel and glass and electricity dominating human destinies.

America is a nightmare of feverish struggling, a graveyard of suppressed human impulses; America waits calmly between the Pacific and the Atlantic while the tide of the Mississippi rises and falls with the seasons. Our land waits for us clothed in the elements and the vegetation which rises to meet them; our people, our society, are as spiritually naked as the pastoral Indian society which we conquered.

Wonderful, young, sinewy, timorous, browbeaten, eager, gullible American society, living in a land of grandeur, dignity, and untold beauty, is slowly kneading consistent racial character from' the sifted flour of experience and the sweat of racial destiny. Slowly, surely, there are emerging American types, with characteristic statures, facial expressions, and temperament.

Those of you who have been in Europe know that the characteristic American cannot avoid identification. It makes little difference whether he came from the Western plains or from an Atlantic seaboard city; on the Parisian boulevards or among the Swiss Alps, in the English theaters or in Florentine galleries, he is immediately recognizable as an American. He has no poise, he is searching for something, he is concerned about his destiny and the appraisal of his people and his country, he is willing and eager to discuss homely social philosophy with you, he is naïvely receptive and easily browbeaten, and yet he radiates a fresh vitality and an unlimited reserve of energy; one feels within him a reticent ego which dares not emerge yet. Our climate plus our social, political, and economic customs have produced this characteristic American by the same biological process that characteristic Frenchmen, Germans, and Englishmen were molded from the same Aryan race-stream.

Our subjective moods are naturally being developed to meet the exigencies of our intensely concentrated mechanistic civilization. Our dignity is not pompous, nor are our profoundest feelings suppliant; our gayety is not graceful nor our humor whimsical. Our dignity lies in direct driving force; our deeper feelings are stark and reticent; our gayety is ribald and our humor ironic. These are moods which young indigenous American composers are born and surrounded with, and from these moods come a unique valuation of beauty and a different feeling for rhythm, melody, and form. It is precisely this spontaneous native feeling for distinctly different musical values which makes

the problem of the serious American composer so specially difficult. His moods are not warmed-over moods of eighteenth- and
nineteenth-century European society, nor is his musical material
rearranged and retinted formulas of the standard classics which
our audiences, teachers, and critics, and our imported conductors
and performers have been trained to think of as the only possible music.

   To be more specific: Our rhythmic impulses are fundamentally
different from the rhythmic impulses of Europeans; and from
this unique rhythmic sense are generated different melodic and
form values. Our sense of rhythm is less symmetrical than the
European rhythmic sense. European musicians are trained to
think of rhythm in its largest common denominator, while we
are born with a feeling for its smallest units. That is why the
jazz boys, chained to an unimaginative commercial routine which
serves only crystallized symmetrical dance rhythms, are continually breaking out into superimposed rhythmic variations
which were not written in the music. This asymmetrical balancing of rhythmic phrases is in our blood; it is not in the European blood. Anyone who has heard the contrast between a European dance orchestra and an American dance orchestra playing
in the same dance hall cannot have failed to notice how monotonous the European orchestra sounds. The Hungarian and Spanish gypsies have a vital rhythmic sense, but it is much more
conventional in its metric accents than the native American
feeling for rhythm. When Ravel attempted to incorporate our
rhythmic sense into his violin sonata, it sounded studied; it was
studied, because he did not feel the rhythm in terms of musical
phraseology. We do not employ unconventional rhythms as a
sophistical gesture; we cannot avoid them. To cut them out of
our music would be to gainsay the source of our spontaneous
musical impulses. The rhythms come to us first as musical
phraseology, and then we struggle to define them on paper.
Our struggle is not to invent new rhythms and melodies and
forms; our problem is to put down into translatable symbols
and rhythms and consequent melodies and form those that as-
sert themselves within us. . . .

   And moreover I repeat that the American does not think these rhythms out first as mathematical problems; they come as spontaneous musical ideas. Time and time again I have heard my American associates play rhythmic-melodic phrases which sounded natural and spontaneous but which were very difficult to define on paper. In lecturing to groups I have repeatedly played rhythmic melodies before writing the melody. Invariably some musician in the audience will venture the comment that "it does not look as it sounds." Out of this unique rhythmic sense is developing a different feeling and taste for phrase balancing.

There is nothing strange about this American rhythmic talent. Children skip and walk that way—our conversation would be strained and monotonous without such rhythmic nuances, much like a child's first attempts at reading; nature abounds in these freer rhythms. The strange phenomenon is the power of repetition in accustoming our ears to the labored symmetrical rhythms which predominate in eighteenth- and nineteenth-century European music. Serious European composers have recognized for a long time that all the possible gamut of expression has been wrung out of conventional rhythms and the consequent melodies and form, but they were born with conventional rhythmic impulses, and when they write complicated rhythms they sound as they look on paper, i.e., unnatural. Stravinsky's *Les Noces*, for example, sounds like an imbroglio of rhythmic patterns. To quote Arthur Lourié, an authority on Stravinsky and his friend and champion: ". . . Stravinsky's 'Les Noces' is so constructed as to prevent the hearing of the music itself. Here rhythm is driven to the maximum of its development and actions; melody is totally submerged." Melody can be totally submerged by rhythmic action only when the rhythms are not an organic part of the melodic content and resulting form. His *Le Sacre du Printemps* changes its meter-signature so many times that it is extremely difficult to perform, but underneath it all is a steady reiteration of ultra-conventional rhythmic pulse. In fact the tympani player for the Los Angeles Philharmonic Orchestra told me that he rewrote his whole part into conventional meter signatures. He could not have done that with an authentic American work in which the changing meter signatures were necessary to the spontaneous musical phraseology.

American composers have not as yet developed any predominant type of harmonic idiom, but I have noticed two tendencies that are becoming increasingly prevalent both with our commercial jazz writers and with our more serious composers: (1) the avoidance of definite cadence which can be traced to our unsymmetrically balanced melodies (difficult to harmonize with prepared cadences) and our national aversion to anything final, our hope and search for more satisfying conclusions; (2) the use of modal harmony which probably comes from ennui of the worn-out conventions of the major and minor scales and our adventurous love of the exotic.

I am as confident that a national taste and talent for harmonic balance and nuance is developing as I am sure that we have already developed a national talent for unique rhythmic impulses and the spontaneous melodies and form which come from them. The American composer's problem is not one of inherent talent and authentic musical ideas; it is rather the problem of being assured adequate performances, receptive audiences, intelligent appraisals from commercial critics, and an unprejudiced analytic attitude from teachers and music schools.

The remainder of this article will be given to an exposition of the daily problems which the serious American composer must meet at the present point in our musical development.

The growth of musical culture is manifested in three ways: (1) the understanding and discriminating appreciation of audiences; (2) the development of interpretative musicians; and (3) the production of characteristic native composition. Audiences are the roots of musical culture, interpretative musicians form the professional body of music, and original composition is the final fruit. And musical culture, that strange plant of civilization, develops in much the same way that a tree develops: roots, body, and fruit are interdependent. Obviously there can be no body of interpretative musicians until there is already an audience to feed it; nor can there be a growth in musical composition until composers have the necessary experience of hearing their works performed and appraised by capable and sympathetic interpretative musicians. Such musicians also relate the composer to his audience, and vice versa. Finally, audiences are dependent on interpreters and composers because they form the soil out of which audiences grow. Upon a natural and thorough assimilation of interpretative art and native creative art depends the growth and eventually the life of audiences.

So far American audiences have developed on imported music and imported interpreters. This does not mean that we are unmusical. It means simply that our people have been preoccupied with the building of our economic empire, that cultural pursuits were not pressing issues, and so we had to procure their products from nations which had already passed through the initial stage of civilization. As late as the time of Bach, German courts procured their music and their musicians from France and Italy. Only German church organists, choristers, and composers could grow on German soil, and it was not until the choral-variation forms grew out of the Lutheran church service that Germany really began to develop musically. Similarly American audiences will not grow into anything robust and wholehearted until out of the co-operation of native interpreters and native composers there grows some live, indigenous style and related form. This obviously cannot happen until American audiences recognize that they cannot develop very much more on imported music and interpreters. I do not propose a solution for this first and most important problem, but perhaps at least the issue may be clarified if we retrace the growth of this condition, step by step.

In the beginning it was natural and necessary that we import interpreters and with them their native music; and because America was conceived of as a democratic and capitalistic society, there was no court life; consequently music could be publicly presented only as an economic commodity. It was good business to import a musical personality and watch the eager, excited, socially exploited, and curious American dollars roll in. Barnum was the first big showman. He imported Jenny Lind, Ole Bull, Paderewski, and others. He plastered his artists with a thick coating of "hokum." Some he supplied with private body-guards, others with superhuman attributes. He filled the newspapers with columns of "personality" stories. He auctioned off tickets for the "Swedish Nightingale"; he prospered and set a precedent. The practice of this precedent has been considerably toned down, but with the aid of subtle advertising technique and newspaper circulation it is even more widespread and more penetrating.

There came the development of reproducing machines—records and radio. Each invention has carried such an interest in sheer ingenious mechanical achievement that it has been possible and economically profitable to go through the same stages of musical development again. First in the concert halls, then with the reproducing records, and now with radio the American public has been and still is being led through the same imported musical literature and the same "personality hokum" about the European "maestro" interpreter. Like all good business men, the musical managers, companies, merger trusts, etc., have learned a lucrative formula which they will go on applying over and over again until box-office receipts indicate that it is no longer lucrative.

Then through the combined policies of managers, foreign conductors and performers, newspaper advertisers, commercial critics, music publishers and retailers, graphonola [phonograph] and record manufacturers and retailers, the devisers of the appreciation program in our public schools, and the professional music teachers and schools—the "great American public" has been very efficiently trained to know that it prefers an endless reiteration of the "standard classics"—meaning the best works of eighteenth- and nineteenth-century Europe, especially German instrumental music and Italian opera. The social significance of music is being smothered in commercial dickering, and all the crystallized procedure of incorporated business. Consequently the literature of music itself has become a vehicle for the performer instead of the performer being one of an infinite number of possible vehicles for the music.

This spreading lack of interest in musical literature and growing taste for gala performances and personalities is being understood and capitalized on by managers, conductors, and performers. They are beginning to know that we do not care very much what is presented (with the exception of modern works), but that it must be well performed and with the professional gesture. And our own cultural lethargy fits in well with the European cultural propaganda policy which is understood and accepted by all performers and conductors. For instance, Toscanini knew perfectly well that he would not antagonize American audiences or critics by touring Europe with the New York Philharmonic Orchestra without presenting one single American work. European critics commented on the irregularity of the proceeding, but our own critics accepted it as a matter of course. Toscanini also knew that he would not dare to appear in any European country without presenting works of native composers, and when Ravel publicly denounced him for his theatrical interpretation of *Bolero* he accepted the rebuke as graciously as possible. An American composer who publicly denounced Toscanini at his first 1930 concert in Carnegie Hall for his shameful neglect of American composition would have been cried down and probably jailed as a public nuisance. Until American audiences refuse to be browbeaten by conductors, performers, and critics, until we can accept fine performances and performers as the natural prerequisites of musical culture and become absorbed in the content and meaning of the music itself, American composers cannot hope for much support.

The professional body of interpreters divides naturally into participating interpreters (conductors, orchestral men, and soloists) and appraising interpreters (teachers and critics). Of the participating interpreters, conductors and their orchestras are by far the most important resource of native composers. In the first place, conductors and their orchestras have a closer and more stable relationship to the community which supports them. Touring virtuosi must master a few programs to mechanical perfection. If to this mechanical perfection they can add striking enough personality characteristics, their career is assured, provided it is supported by enough publicity management to maneuver them into the enviable position of being a box-office attraction. They simply tour all over the world repeating the same programs and employing the same publicity leads in each place in much the same way that a vaudeville act tours from one city to another.

Naturally such a touring virtuoso is very chary about including any modern works on his programs. His livelihood depends on steering the safest course from one musical port to the next, and he trims his sails accordingly. His hope is to ride on the popular wave of music which audiences know and unreservedly accept, not to arouse his audience to a critical attentiveness to the music itself.

On the other hand, conductors and their orchestras cannot afford to be too limited in their repertoire. They play to the same public each week for the whole season and their repertoires must be representative. So far the relationship of the American composer to American orchestras and their conductors is not a very fruitful one. In the first place, most of our conductors and orchestral men were born with European temperaments and were surrounded during their most receptive and plastic years with European musical traditions and idioms. They do not readily respond to our serious music. As a general rule they understand and prefer the commercial jazz idiom because it has a very steady rhythmic pulse, its harmonic texture is obvious, its form is elementary, its mood light, and its orchestration effective. Or if a professional gesture of social courtesy is unavoidable, the conductors generally program some American composer whose idiom and moods are frankly post-Wagner or post-Strauss or post-Debussy, one who has learned to capture some of the orchestral effectiveness of those composers.

But conductors do not like the emotional content of our more serious characteristic music; and above all they resent the technical difficulties of its rhythmic patterns and forms. It requires a new receptive approach in which neither the conductor nor his orchestra can rest on their experience. It requires conscientious work; it must be felt, and European conductors and orchestral men rarely have the time, the patience, or the desire to study our music thoroughly enough to feel it. They can play all the literature of the masters from memory; why should they sweat over a young American upstart? Let him get a reputation first! Consequently characteristic American works are side-stepped if possible, and if enough pressure is brought to bear to force their production they are very often given what is professionally known as a "scratch" performance. American audiences have been trained to appraise music by the mechanically perfect performances of Tschaikowsky, Brahms, César Franck, Wagner, Rimsky-Korsakoff, and contemporary Europeans, and they know that Bach and Beethoven are good regardless of performances; when they hear an American work poorly performed they conclude that the work was not good. They do not know that the brasses who were to outline the form of the middle section lost their place—and that all of the men were so uncertain of their entrances that they were afraid to give forth clear clean-cut phrases, that their tones were dull and muddy, and that, placed next to a standard work (which they could play with their eyes shut), the American work inevitably sounded dull and forlorn, faltering and uncertain.

This is an old, old story to many musicians and many patrons and friends of composers, but so far nothing has been done about it; and I believe this condition will not be radically changed until we have a new crop of young American conductors and orchestral men who were born with the American moods and American sense in their blood. Unfortunately the young Americans who thus far are being admitted into our major orchestras are so apt to be impressed with the honor of their opportunity and with the desirability of absorbing the traditions of the seasoned Europeans around them that they often become more rabidly prejudiced than the old routine men are.

This brings us to a consideration of the relationship of American composition to the big music schools and successful teachers. Naturally the objective of teachers and schools is the public success of their pupils, and their pupils are predominately students preparing for public careers either as performers or as teachers. Prospective teachers must learn definite harmonic systems, definite contrapuntal methods, definite crystallized forms to sell again to pupils.

I recall a conversation with a very intelligent teacher who had frankly admitted that in composition each individual circumstance requires its own special solution, that consistency of procedure should be the only rule with respect to vital creative work; but when I criticized the teaching of definite crystallized rules to teachers I was answered somewhat as follows: "What can I do? These people come to me to learn something definite which they can teach to others for a living." This teaching of definite rules about harmony, counterpoint, and form, this academic emphasis on the rules that have been culled from the most obvious formulas of obsolete styles is of course so much dead wood which must be burned out of young students' minds before they can have any intelligent understanding of the nature of American music.

One of the sorest problems which the serious American composers must face is the prevalent incompetence of commercial critics in appraising new works which they have never heard before. There are of course a few exceptions to the rule, but a first-rate critical faculty is as rare as first-rate creative talent and requires as much training. Most commercial critics accepted their positions as an escape from the wear and tear of the profession for which they prepared themselves. Some critics use their responsibility as an opportunity to work off their literary ambitions and naturally concentrate on literary phraseology rather than critical acumen. Very, very few critics were especially prepared in ear-training, musical analysis, and breadth of musical culture. Many of them probably admitted it frankly in the beginning, but their position demands the gesture of authority and they are so coddled by managers and professional artists that they soon lose that first perspective. It is much easier to learn to juggle words in the simulation of authority than it is to develop the authority itself. And even if they were especially gifted and trained to be competent critics, the commercial routine of having to write long articles or virtuosic interpretations of the same genre of music day after day, month after month, season after season, would dull their sensibilities. In fairness it must be added that even if they had the conscious initiative to grow and keep abreast of contemporaneous output, their routine leaves no time or energy for growth. In Europe commercial critics are no problem because no one takes them seriously. Mahler even publicly invited them to stay away from his concerts and refused to give them tickets. But in America critics influence box-office receipts and consequently their ominous power is out of all proportion to their merit.

Finally, we must consider the fruit of musical culture in America. Is it going to matter? Can the flowering promise of so many talented American composers be pollinated by a genial and intelligent social interest in their native characteristic—possibilities divorced from futile comparisons with familiar works of bygone eras? Most important of all, can American composers become socially and economically adjusted? It is my personal conviction that talented American composers will find an economic support more readily than they will achieve a social adjustment. There are many fellowships of recognition being offered for distinguished work, and there is an increasing concern for the economic stability of composers. The Eastman School of Music and the Juilliard Foundation are both publishing serious American works. Then there are the publications, *New Music*, edited by Henry Cowell, and the Cos Cob Press, of which Alma Wertheim is president.

The problem of social adjustment is a very difficult and many-sided one for the serious American composer. I have already shown that American compositions are not presented often enough or well enough to acquaint American audiences with American composers. This one condition alone makes the American composer remote. The prerequisite of all serious composers in all times has always been and will always be that of achieving a subjective calm sufficiently continuous and focused to enable spiritual and mental co-ordination. The solution of this problem depends on their finding and adjusting themselves to a congenial stable environment in which they may develop slowly and naturally. This applies to a nature [*sic*] environment as well as a social environment. Man is so constituted that before he can profit from an intimate contact with nature he must first be at peace with himself, and this peace requires social adjustment. The man who seeks nature as a refuge from society can never absorb the pregnant silences which yield peace, reverence, aspiration, grandeur, and dignity. These moods are too impersonal and complete for the troubled man, they only mock him and send him back to serve his kind. Even if a socially unadjusted individual could temporarily achieve enough detachment

to accept solace from nature, he must always in the end return
to society to fulfill his destiny.

How to serve society as a composer, how to become economically and socially recognized as a worth-contributing citizen,
how to establish durable human contacts with individuals or
groups are harassing problems. The shifting scenes of our social and economic environments are so fluctuating, so crowded
with heterogeneous influences, such a helter-skelter race of commercial jockeying, that it is very difficult to strike any bedrock
economic or human relationships. Our economic system has fostered the productive psychology with such narrow limitations
that no allowance is made for the leisure which is necessary for
productivity in the arts. Utility has become such a raucous slo-
gan of our civilization that intellectual pursuits are generally socially appraised by the commercial value which they get from day
to day. We have become so absorbed in material development
that the intellectual and spiritual achievements by which all
civilizations are eventually appraised are tolerated only if they
serve an immediate commercial end. In this land of football,
baseball, music revue, bridge, and motoring fans, the social significance of music has not yet been realized or felt. In this land
where athletes, air pilots, racing drivers, movie stars and the
sheer accumulation of raw buying-power are revered, it is difficult for a serious composer to avoid the devastating position of
being elbowed by unschooled and thoughtless acquaintances into
an apologetic attitude. The problem of social and economic adjustment is doing more to destroy talented American composers
than any other problem, and of course its solution will come
only when enough American individuals recognize that we cannot buy musical culture any more than we can buy a home environment. Musical literature never has been and never will be
valuable to society as a whole until it is created as an authentic
and characteristic culture of and from the people it expresses.
History reveals that the great music has been produced only by
staunch individuals who sank their roots deeply into the social
soil which they accepted as their own. After a musical literature has been created and traditionalized it becomes the common property of all civilizations. It is added to the cultural store

of human experience as documentary evidence of the emotional gamut and intellectual skill of a people.

America is developing a distinctly different civilization from Europe, Asia, or the Orient, and our percentage of musical creativeness is high. There can be no question of stifling the ultimate musical expression of America. The only question which is under consideration is how soon we as a people will become intelligent enough to lend ourselves willingly and gracefully to the processes of time as they unfold our musical destiny.

FERDINAND "JELLY ROLL" MORTON

MORTON (1885–1941), whose correct name was Ferdinand Joseph La Menthe, was born in Gulfport, Louisiana, and began to play the piano at the age of ten. He was only seventeen when he started to work as a pianist in some of the fancy bordellos of the ill-famed "Storyville" district in New Orleans. As his reputation grew, he appeared in Memphis, St. Louis, Kansas City, and was active for several years in California before moving on to Chicago. Here he won fame as the leader of "Morton's Red Hot Peppers," a group that included such top jazzmen as Kid Ory, Omer Simeon, and Johnny and Baby Dodds. With this group, from 1926 to 1930, he made a series of historic recordings (mostly in Chicago and New York) that included a number of his own compositions.

After this peak of success, his fortunes steadily declined. The late 1930's found him running an obscure night club in Washington, D. C. There he was "rediscovered" by Alan Lomax, who in 1938 brought him to the Library of Congress for a series of autobiographical recordings that were to become a classic of jazz history. Gently prodded by questions from Lomax, "Jelly Roll" talked and played for hour upon hour, at many sessions, revealing himself, in the words of George Avakian, as "a strange mixture of genius, musician, poet, snob and braggart." Later, Lomax transcribed the reminiscences that Jelly Roll had recorded, added some documentation of his own, and published

161

the remarkable book *Mister Jelly Roll* from which the present excerpt is taken.

Soon after this event, Jelly Roll made a series of recordings in New York (1939-40), then went back to California, where he spent his remaining years. During his prosperity he made an ostentatious display of wealth, and in his adversity he lived on memories of his past glory. One of the most controversial figures in jazz, he has been praised and belittled with equal vehemence. Numbering myself among his admirers, I like to quote the words of the English critic Max Jones, who called Jelly Roll Morton "a composer unique in the jazz field." Among his compositions are "Milenburg Joys," "Wolverine Blues," "King Porter Stomp," "Wild Man Blues," "Kansas City Stomps," and "The Pearls."

Jazz Music Comes from New Orleans / (1938)

I might name some of the other great hot men operating around New Orleans at this period and a little later. There was Emmanuel Perez, played strictly ragtime, who was maybe the best trumpet in New Orleans till Freddy Keppard came along. John Robichaud probably had the best band in New Orleans at the time, a strictly all-reading, legitimate bunch. Before him, there was Happy Galloway. Both men had the same type seven-piece orchestra—cornet, clarinet, trombone, drums, mandolin, guitar, and bass. A guy named Payton had a band that played a very

lowdown type of quadrille for the lowclass dance halls. Also a
lot of bad bands that we used to call "spasm" bands, played any
jobs they could get in the streets. They did a lot of ad-libbing
in ragtime style with different solos in succession, not in a regular routine but just as one guy would get tired and let another
musician have the lead.

None of these men made much money—maybe a dollar a night
or a couple of bucks for a funeral, but still they didn't like to
leave New Orleans. They used to say, "This is the best town in
the world. What's the use for me to go any other place?" So the
town was full of the best musicians you ever heard. Even the
rags-bottles-and-bones men would advertise their trade by playing the blues on the wooden mouthpieces of Christmas horns—
yes sir, play more lowdown, dirty blues on those Kress horns
than the rest of the country ever thought of.

All these people played ragtime in a hot style, but man, you
can play hot all you want to, and you still won't be playing
jazz. Hot means something spicy. Ragtime is a certain type of
syncopation and only certain tunes can be played in that idea.
But jazz is a style that can be applied to any type of tune. I
started using the word in 1902 to show people the difference
between jazz and ragtime.

Jazz music came from New Orleans and New Orleans was
inhabited with maybe every race on the face of the globe and,
of course, plenty of French people. Many of the earliest tunes
in New Orleans was from French origin. I'm telling you when
they started playing this little thing they would really whoop it
up—everybody got hot and threw their hats away. . . .

> C'est 'n aut' can-can, payez donc,
> C'est 'n aut' can-can, payez donc. . . .

Then we had Spanish people there. I heard a lot of Spanish
tunes and I tried to play them in correct tempo, but I personally
didn't believe they were really perfected in the tempos. Now
take "La Paloma," which I transformed in New Orleans style.
You leave the left hand just the same. The difference comes

in the right hand—in the syncopation, which gives it an entirely different color that really changes the color from red to blue.

Now in one of my earliest tunes, "New Orleans Blues," you can notice the Spanish tinge. In fact, if you can't manage to put tinges of Spanish in your tunes, you will never be able to get the right seasoning, I call it, for jazz. This "New Orleans Blues" comes from around 1902. I wrote it with the help of Mr. Frank Richards, a great piano player in the ragtime style. All the bands in the city played it at that time.

Most of these ragtime guys, especially those that couldn't play very well, would have the inspiration they were doing okay if they kept increasing the tempo during a piece.[1] I decided that it was a mistake and I must have been right, because everybody grabbed up my style. I thought that accurate tempo would be the right tempo for any tune. Regardless to any tempo you might set, especially if it was meant for a dance tune, you ought to end up in that tempo. So I found that the slow tunes, especially the medium slow tunes, did more for the development of jazz than any other type, due to the fact that you could always hit a note twice in such a tune, when ordinarily you could only hit it once, which gave the music a very good flavor.

About harmony, my theory is never to discard the melody. Always have a melody going some kind of way against a background of perfect harmony with plenty of riffs—meaning figures. A riff is something that gives an orchestra a great background and is the main idea in playing jazz. No jazz piano player can really play good jazz unless they try to give an imitation of a band, that is, by providing a basis of riffs. I've seen riffs blundered up so many times it has given me heart failure, because most of these modern guys don't regard the harmony or the rules of the system of music at all. They just play anything, their main idea being to keep the bass going. They think by keeping the bass going and getting a set rhythm, they are doing the right thing, which is wrong. Of all the pianists today I know

1 Which is a West African way of doing things. Here Jelly imposes the European metronome idea of tempo upon the more fluid African idea of beat just as he imposed rigid and intricate European harmony upon a simpler folk pattern. [Alan Lomax]

of only one that has a tendency to be on the right track and that's Bob Zurke of the Bob Crosby Band. Far as the rest of them, all I can see is ragtime pianists in a very fine form.

Now the riff is what we call a foundation, like something that you walk on. It's standard. But without breaks and without clean breaks and without beautiful ideas in breaks, you don't even need to think about doing anything else, you haven't got a jazz band and you can't play jazz. Even if a tune hasn't got a break in it, it's always necessary to arrange some kind of a spot to make a break.

A break, itself, is like a musical surprise which didn't come in until I originated the idea of jazz as I told you. We New Orleans musicians were always looking for novelty effects to attract the public, and many of the most important things in jazz originated in some guy's crazy idea that we tried out for a laugh or just to surprise the folks.

Most people don't understand the novelty side of jazz. Vibrato —which is all right for one instrument but the worst thing that ever happened when a whole bunch of instruments use it—at the beginning was nothing but an imitation of a jackass hollering. There were many other imitations of animal sounds we used—such as the wah-wahs on trumpets and trombones. Mutes came in with King Oliver, who first just stuck bottles into his trumpet so he could play softer, but then began to use all sorts of mutes to give his instrument a different flavor. And I, myself, by accident, discovered the swats on drums. Out in Los Angeles I had a drummer that hit his snares so loud that one night I gave him a couple of fly swatters for a gag. This drummer fell in with the joke and used them, but they worked so smooth he kept right on using them. So we have "the swats" today—a nice soft way to keep the rhythm going.

A lot of people have a wrong impression of jazz. Somehow it got into the dictionary that jazz was considered a lot of blatant noises and discordant tones, something that would be even harmful to the ears. The fact of it is that every musician in America had the wrong understanding of jazz music. I know many times that I'd be playing against different orchestras and I would notice some of the patrons get near an orchestra and put their hands over their ears. (Of course, I wouldn't permit mine to play that way.) Anyhow, I heard a funny fellow say once: "If that fellow blows any louder, he'll knock my ear drums down." Even Germany and Italy don't want this discordant type of jazz, because of the noise.

Jazz music is to be played sweet, soft, plenty rhythm. When you have your plenty rhythm with your plenty swing, it becomes beautiful. To start with, you can't make crescendos and diminuendos when one is playing triple forte. You got to be able to come down in order to go up. If a glass of water is full, you can't fill it any more; but if you have a half a glass, you have the opportunity to put more water in it. Jazz music is based on the same principles, because jazz is based on strictly music. You have the finest ideas from the greatest operas, symphonies and overtures in jazz music. There is nothing finer than jazz music because it comes from everything of the finest class music. Take the Sextet from *Lucia* and the *Miserery* [*sic*] from *Ill Travadore* [*sic*], that they used to play in the French Opera House, tunes that have always lived in my mind as the great favorites of the opera singers; I transformed a lot of those numbers into jazz time, using different little variations and ideas to masquerade the tunes.

The "Tiger Rag," for instance, I happened to transform from an old quadrille, which was originally in many different tempos. First there was an introduction, "Everybody get your partners!" and the people would be rushing around the hall getting their partners. After a five-minute lapse of time, the next strain would be the waltz strain . . . then another strain that comes right beside the waltz strain in mazooka [mazurka] time. . . .

We had two other strains in two-four time. Then I transformed these strains into the "Tiger Rag," which I also named, from the way I made the "tiger" roar with my elbow. A person said once, "That sounds like a tiger hollering." I said to myself, "That's the name." All this happened back in the early days before the Dixieland Band was ever heard of.

AARON

COPLAND, born in Brooklyn, New York, on November 14, 1900, is one of the most influential American musicians of the twentieth century—as composer, teacher, writer, and lecturer. After four years of study with Rubin Goldmark in New York, he went to Paris in 1921 for three years of further study with Nadia Boulanger. He was the first composer to be awarded a Guggenheim Fellowship (in 1925). Always active in the promotion of new music, he joined Roger Sessions in organizing the Copland-Sessions Concerts for the performance of American music (1928-31) and was a leading spirit in the League of Composers and the International Society for Contemporary Music.

Copland was lecturer on music at the New School for Social Research in New York from 1927 to 1937, and has taught composition each summer at the Berkshire Music Center in Massachusetts. In 1951-52 he gave six lectures as the Charles Eliot Norton Professor of Poetry at Harvard, which were subsequently published in book form as *Music and Imagination* (1952). His earlier books were *What to Listen for in Music* (1939; revised edition, 1957), and *Our New Music* (1941). In 1960 his collected articles were published under the title *Copland on Music*. Two important critical-biographical works about Copland have been published: the first by Arthur Berger (1953), the second by Julia Smith (1955).

As a composer, Copland has been most versatile, his production ranging from highly successful motion picture scores (*Our*

167

Town, The Red Pony, Of Mice and Men) to austere instrumental
compositions, such as the Vitebsk Trio, the Piano Variations, the
Piano Sonata, and the Piano Fantasy, that made difficult demands on the listener. He had his flirtation with jazz in such
works as *Music for the Theatre* (1925) and the Piano Concerto
(1926) ; but he achieved his greatest popularity with the ballet
scores related to American folklore: *Billy the Kid* (1938), *Rodeo*
(1942), and *Appalachian Spring* (1944). His only full-length
opera *The Tender Land* was produced in 1954. Of his three symphonies, the third (1946) is the most widely known. *A Lincoln
Portrait* (1942), for narrator and orchestra, is among his impressive contributions to musical Americana.

Composer From Brooklyn:
An Autobiographical Sketch / (1939)

I was born on a street in Brooklyn that can only be described
as drab. It had none of the garish color of the ghetto, none
of the charm of an old New England thoroughfare, or even the
rawness of a pioneer street. It was simply drab. It probably
resembled most one of the outer districts of lower middle-class
London, except that it was peopled largely by Italians, Irish, and
Negroes. I mention it because it was there that I spent the first
twenty years of my life. Also, because it fills me with mild
wonder each time I realize that a musician was born on that
street.

Music was the last thing anyone would have connected with it.

In fact, no one had ever connected music with my family or with my street. The idea was entirely original with me. And unfortunately the idea occurred to me seriously only at thirteen or thereabouts—which is rather late for a musician to get started.

I don't mean to give the impression that there was no music whatever in our house. My oldest brother played the violin to my sister's accompaniments, and there were passable performances of potpourris from assorted operas. I also remember a considerable amount of ragtime on top of the piano for lighter moments. But these were casual encounters. No one ever talked music to me or took me to a concert. Music as an art was a discovery I made all by myself.

The idea of becoming a composer seems gradually to have dawned upon me some time around 1916, when I was about fifteen years old. Before that I had taken the usual piano lessons, begun at my own insistence some two years previously. My parents were of the opinion that enough money had been invested in the musical training of the four older children with meager results and had no intention of squandering further funds on me. But despite the reasonableness of this argument, my persistence finally won them over. I distinctly remember with what fear and trembling I knocked on the door of Mr. Leopold Wolfsohn's piano studio on Clinton Avenue in Brooklyn, and—once again all by myself—arranged for piano lessons.

The idea of composing came, as I say, several years later. It was Mr. Wolfsohn who helped me to find a harmony teacher when I realized that to be a composer one had to study harmony. At first I had imagined that harmony could be learned by correspondence course, but a few trial lessons cured me of that illusion. So it came about that in the fall of 1917 I began harmony lessons with the late Rubin Goldmark. My new teacher was a nephew of Karl Goldmark, the famous composer of the *Queen of Sheba*. Goldmark had an excellent grasp of the fundamentals of music and knew very well how to impart his ideas. This was a stroke of luck for me. I was spared the flounderings that so many American musicians have suffered through incompetent teaching at the start of their theoretical training.

By the spring of 1918 I had been graduated from high school and was able to devote all my energies to music. It seems curious now that public school played so small a part in my musical training. I neither sang in the school chorus nor played in the school orchestra. Music classes were a kind of joke—we were not even taught to sight-read a single vocal line properly. Perhaps things have changed for the better in that respect. A young person with musical aptitudes would probably find more scope in the regular school curriculum for his or her talents nowadays.

During these formative years I had been gradually uncovering for myself the literature of music. Some instinct seemed to lead me logically from Chopin's waltzes to Haydn's sonatinas to Beethoven's sonatas to Wagner's operas. And from there it was but a step to Hugo Wolf's songs, to Debussy's preludes and to Scriabin's piano poems. In retrospect it all seemed surprisingly orderly. As far as I can remember no one ever told me about "modern music." I apparently happened on it in the natural course of my music explorations. It was Goldmark, a convinced conservative in musical matters, who first actively discouraged this commerce with the "moderns." That was enough to whet any young man's appetite. The fact that the music was in some sense forbidden only increased its attractiveness. Moreover, it was difficult to get. The war had made the importation of new music a luxury; Scriabin and Debussy and Ravel were bringing high prices. By the time I was eighteen I already had something of the reputation of a musical rebel—in Goldmark's eyes at any rate.

As might be expected, my compositions of that period, mostly two-page songs and piano pieces, began to show traces of my musical enthusiasms. It soon was clear that Goldmark derived no pleasure from seeing what seemed to him to be "modernistic experiments." The climax came when I brought for his critical approval a piano piece called "The Cat and the Mouse." He regretfully admitted that he had no criteria by which to judge such music. From that time on my compositional work was divided into two compartments: the pieces that really interested me, that were composed on the side, so to speak, and the conventional student work written in conformity with the "rules."

During these student years I missed very much the companionship of other music students. I had a sense of isolation and of working too much by myself. In America today there are undoubtedly other young musicians who are isolated in big and small communities in a similar fashion.

It was a foregone conclusion twenty years ago that anyone who had serious pretensions as a composer would have to go abroad to finish his studies. Before the war it was taken for granted that "abroad" for composers meant Germany. But I belonged to the postwar generation, and so for me "abroad" inevitably meant Paris. The hitch was that I knew not a living soul in Paris—or in all France, for that matter.

At about that time, I read in a musical journal of the proposed establishment of a music school for Americans to be inaugurated during the summer of 1921 in the Palace at Fontainebleau. I was so quick to respond to this announcement that my name headed the list of enrollments. My plan was to stay on in Paris for the winter after the closing of summer school. This would give me a chance to acclimatize myself to French ways and at the same time to find a suitable teacher with whom to continue my studies.

Paul Vidal of the Paris Conservatory taught us composition at the Fontainebleau School. He turned out to be a French version of Rubin Goldmark, except that he was harder to understand because of the peculiar French patois that he talked. Before summer was very far advanced, rumors began to circulate of the presence of a brilliant harmony teacher, a certain Nadia Boulanger. This news naturally had little interest for me, since I had long finished *my* harmonic studies. It took a considerable amount of persuasion on the part of a fellow student before I consented to "look in" on Mlle. Boulanger's class. On that particular day she was explaining the harmonic structure of one of the scenes from *Boris Godounov*. I had never before witnessed such enthusiasm and such clarity in teaching. I immediately suspected that I had found my teacher.

There were several mental hurdles to get over first, however. No one to my knowledge had ever before thought of studying composition with a woman. This idea was absurd on the face of it. Everyone knows that the world has never produced a first-rate woman composer, so it follows that no woman could possibly hope to teach composition. Moreover, how would it sound to the folks back home? The whole idea was just a bit revolutionary.

Nevertheless, and despite these excellent reasons, I visited Mlle. Boulanger in the fall and asked her to accept me as her pupil. She must have been about thirty-three years old at that time, and, as far as I know, I was her first fullfledged American composition student. I mention this with a certain amount of understandable pride in view of the large number of young American composers who have followed, and are still following, in my footsteps. Two qualities possessed by Mlle. Boulanger make her unique: one is her consuming love for music; and the other is her ability to inspire a pupil with confidence in his own creative powers. Add to this an encyclopedic knowledge of every phase of music past and present, an amazing critical perspicacity, and a full measure of feminine charm and wit. The influence of this remarkable woman on American creative music will some day be written in full.

My one year in Paris was stretched to two and then to three years. It was a fortunate time to be studying music in Paris. All the pent-up energies of the war years were unloosed. Paris was an international proving ground for all the newest tendencies in music. Much of the music that had been written during the dark years of the war was now being heard for the first time. Schoenberg, Stravinsky, Bartók, de Falla were all new names to me. And the younger generation was heard from also—Milhaud, Honegger, Auric, and the other noisy members of the Group of Six. Works by many composers outside France were performed, too—Hindemith, Prokofieff, Szymanowsky, Malipiero, Kodály. It was a rarely stimulating atmosphere in which to carry on one's studies.

Many of these new works were given their *première* at the Concerts Koussevitzky. Every spring and fall Serge Koussevitzky organized and conducted a series of orchestral concerts at the Paris Opera, where a feast of new compositions was offered. I attended these concerts regularly for three years with my friend and roommate Harold Clurman (later to become director of the Group Theatre in New York). The watchword in those days was "originality." The laws of rhythm, of harmony, of construction had all been torn down. Every composer in the vanguard set out to remake these laws according to his own conceptions. And I suppose that I was no exception despite my youth—or possibly because of it.

During my three years in Paris I had composed several Motets for unaccompanied voices, a *Passacaglia* for piano, a song for soprano with the accompaniment of flute and clarinet, a *Rondino* for string quartet, and finally a one-act ballet called *Grohg*, my first essay in the orchestral field. With this baggage under my arm I returned to America in June, 1924.

Looking backward fifteen years, I am rather amazed at my own ignorance of musical conditions in America. I mean, of course, conditions as they affected composers. How a composer managed to get his compositions performed or published and how he was expected to earn his living were equally mysterious. I had left my drab Brooklyn street as a mere student with practically no musical connections. I was returning there in much the same style.

The immediate business in hand, however, was the writing of a symphony for organ and orchestra. Nadia Boulanger was engaged to appear as organ soloist with the old New York Symphony and the Boston Symphony the following winter. Before I left Paris she had had the courage to ask me to supply her with a concerto for her American tour. I, on the other hand, had the temerity to accept the invitation. This, despite the fact that I had written only one work in extended form before then, that I had only a passing acquaintance with the organ as an instrument, and that I had never heard a note of my own orchestration. The symphony was composed that summer while I perfunctorily performed my duties as pianist in a hotel trio at Milford, Pennsylvania.

I returned to New York in the fall to finish the orchestration of the symphony and began to look about me. Without my being aware of it, postwar activities in Europe had affected American musical circles also. Shortly after my departure for France the International Composers' Guild and the League of Composers had begun to familiarize the American public with the output of the new composers of the "left." Like many other composers of so-called "radical" tendencies, I naturally turned to them for support. Through the good offices of Marion Bauer I was invited to play some of my works for the executive board of the League of Composers. The board voted to accept my two piano pieces— "The Cat and the Mouse" and the *Passacaglia*—for performance at their November concert. This was the first performance of any of my compositions in my native land. It was followed in January by the performance of the Symphony for organ and orchestra, with Walter Damrosch as conductor and Nadia Boulanger as soloist.

An unexpected incident occurred at this concert, indicative of the attitude toward "modern music" at that period. When the performance of my symphony was over and the audience had settled itself for the next number on the program, Dr. Damrosch turned round and addressed his public as follows: "If a young man at the age of twenty-three can write a symphony like that, in five years he will be ready to commit murder." Fearing that the elderly ladies in his audience had been shocked by the asperities of the new style in music, Dr. Damrosch found this way of consoling them. That, at any rate, was my interpretation of his little speech.

The performance of the symphony brought me into personal contact with the conductor whose concerts I had admired in Paris. Serge Koussevitzky was serving his first term as conductor of the Boston Symphony that winter. Here was a stroke of extraordinary good fortune for me and for American music generally. For Koussevitzky brought with him from Paris not only his conductorial prowess but also his passion for encouraging whatever he felt to be new and vital in contemporary music. For fifteen years now he has consistently championed young American music while continuing to introduce novelties from Europe. We Americans are all in his debt.

Koussevitzy made no secret of his liking for my symphony. He told me that he had agreed to conduct a chamber orchestra in an all-modern concert for the League of Composers the following winter. It was his idea, agreed to by the League, that I be commissioned to write a new work for that concert. It seemed to me that my first winter in America was turning out better than I had reason to expect.

But one rather important item was being neglected—my financial setup. For lack of a better solution I had decided to make a living by teaching. In the fall I had opened a studio on West Seventy-fourth Street in Manhattan and sent out the usual announcements. Unfortunately the effect of this move was nil. It produced not one pupil. By the time the Symphony had been played in Boston the situation was acute. Something had to be done. It was Paul Rosenfeld who came to the rescue. While still a student in Brooklyn, I had read his appreciations of contemporary music in the Dial. The morning after the performance of the piano pieces at the league concert, he called me up to tell me how much he liked them. (I couldn't have been more surprised if President Coolidge had telephoned me.) It was 1924; money was plentiful and art patrons numerous. Through a mutual friend Rosenfeld was asked if he could not find a musical Maecenas to come to the aid of an indigent young composer. Rosenfeld said he could, and did. Shortly afterward, the Guggenheim Memorial Foundation was established for a preliminary trial year, and I was awarded the first fellowship extended to a composer. This was renewed the following year, and so financial stability was assured until the fall of 1927.

Now I was free to devote my entire energies to the composition of the new work for Koussevitzky's League concert. I was anxious to write a work that would immediately be recognized as American in character. This desire to be "American" was symptomatic of the period. It made me think of my Symphony as too European in inspiration. I had experimented a little with the rhythms of popular music in several earlier compositions, but now I wanted frankly to adapt the jazz idiom and see what I could do with it in a symphonic way. Rosenfeld suggested the MacDowell Colony as a good place to work during the summer months. It was there that I wrote my *Music for the Theatre*, a suite in five parts for small orchestra.

It was also at the MacDowell Colony that I made the acquaintance of another young American composer in embyro,

Roy Harris. I already knew Virgil Thomson and Douglas Moore from my Paris days, and shortly after meeting Harris I came to know Roger Sessions, Walter Piston, and Carlos Chávez. These contacts with kindred spirits among fellow composers led me to take an active interest in the welfare of American composers in general. The first problem to be attacked was the matter of performance. We thought that American compositions were not being performed enough. (They are still not performed enough, it seems to me.) With Roger Sessions I organized a series of concerts under the name of Copland-Sessions Concerts, which functioned from 1928-1931. American music made up the bulk of our programs—that was our one innovation. Later I was active in organizing several festivals of American music at Yaddo, in Saratoga Springs, New York. The serious composers themselves have, more recently, formed the American Composers' Alliance to protect their economic interests in their music.

The jazz element in *Music for the Theatre* was further developed in my next work, a Concerto for piano and orchestra, which I played as soloist with the Boston Symphony in Boston and New York. This proved to be the last of my "experiments" with symphonic jazz. With the Concerto I felt I had done all I could with the idiom, considering its limited emotional scope. True, it was an easy way to be American in musical terms, but all American music could not possibly be confined to two dominant jazz moods: the "blues" and the snappy number. The characteristic rhythmic element of jazz (or swing, to give it its new name), being independent of mood, yet purely indigenous, will undoubtedly continue to be used in serious native music.

In 1929, just before the economic crash, the RCA Victor Company offered an award of $25,000 for a symphonic work. This unprecedented sum obviously implied a composition of major proportions. With this in mind, I began work on a big, one-movement symphony that I had planned to submit for the prize under the title: *Symphonic Ode*. Unfortunately, two weeks before the competition was to close officially, I realized that I could not finish my Ode in time. In despair at having nothing to offer, I seized upon the old ballet *Grohg*, written in Paris, and extracting three of the movements I liked best, called the whole a *Dance Symphony* and sent it in on the final day. The judges found no one work worthy of the full award and so decided to divide it among five of the contestants. My *Dance Symphony* won me $5,000. The *Symphonic Ode* was finished subsequently and performed as one of the works celebrating the fiftieth anniversary of the Boston Symphony.

In retrospect it seems to me that the Ode marks the end of a certain period in my development as a composer. The works that follow it are no longer so grand or so fulsome. The *Piano Variations* (1930), the *Short Symphony* (1933), the *Statements* for orchestra (1935) are more spare in sonority, more lean in texture. They are difficult to perform and difficult for an audience to comprehend.

During these years I began to feel an increasing dissatisfaction with the relations of the music-loving public and the living composer. The old "special" public of the modern music concerts had fallen away, and the conventional concert public continued apathetic or indifferent to anything but the established classics. It seemed to me that we composers were in danger of working in a vacuum. Moreover, an entirely new public for music had grown up around the radio and phonograph. It made no sense to ignore them and to continue writing as if they did not exist. I felt that it was worth the effort to see if I couldn't say what I had to say in the simplest possible terms.

My most recent works, in their separate ways, embody this tendency toward an imposed simplicity. *El Salón México* is an orchestral work based on Mexican tunes; *The Second Hurricane* is an opera for school children of high-school age to perform; *Music for Radio* was written on a commission from the Columbia Broadcasting System especialy for performance on the air; *Billy the Kid* is a ballet written for the Ballet Caravan, which utilized simple cowboy songs as melodic material; *The City, Of Mice and Men* and *Our Town* are scores for the films. The reception accorded these works in the last two or three years encourages me to believe that the American composer is destined to play a more commanding role in the musical future of his own country.

VIRGIL

THOMSON, born in Kansas City, Missouri, on November

25, 1896, studied music at Harvard and in Paris with Nadia
Boulanger. While living in Paris he formed a friendship with
Gertude Stein, who wrote the librettos for his two remarkable
operas, *Four Saints in Three Acts* and *The Mother of Us All*
(produced, respectively, in 1934 and 1947). The latter work, described as "a political fantasy about nineteenth-century America," reveals Thomson's persistent concern with the American
scene, which he has depicted musically in some of its most varied
aspects in such scores as *The River, The Plough that Broke the
Plains, Louisiana Story, Filling Station* (a ballet), and *Symphony on a Hymn Tune.*

Few composers have ever been as consistently articulate in
writing about music as has Virgil Thomson. He has published five
books: *The State of Music* (1939), *The Musical Scene* (1945),
The Art of Judging Music (1948), and *Music Right and Left*
(1951); in the summer of 1965 he finished writing his autobiography—certain to be one of the most fascinating musical
chronicles of our time. For a period of fourteen years (1940-54)
he was music critic of the New York *Herald-Tribune*. Clarity of
style, cogency of thought, catholicity of interests, a keen analytical mentality, and a lively wit characterize his writing.

Of all Thomson's books, *The State of Music* is the most original, the most stimulating, and the most permanently valuable.
Its importance is, I believe, comparable to that of Thorstein

Veblen's *The Theory of the Leisure Class;* and its scope is somewhat similar, for it provides us with a "theory" of the musician
as a social type, as an economic entity, and as a "political animal." Its continued viability is attested by the publication (in
paperback) of a second edition (1962), revised and with additional commentary by the author on changes that have occurred
since the book was first written. These changes are mostly superficial. Fundamentally, Virgil Thomson continues to hold the view
that "one must believe in the arts and give them their head."

How Composers Eat, or Who Does What to Whom and Who Gets Paid / (1939)

It is not necessary here to go into the incomes of musical executants. They have engagements or they don't. If they don't, they
take pupils. If they can't get pupils they starve. If they get tired
of starving they can go on relief. Unemployed musicians of high
ability and experience are shockingly numerous in America. The
development of sound-films and the radio has thrown thousands
of them into technological unemployment. The musicians' union
has a very large relief budget, however, and the W.P.A. formerly
gave musical work to many. Eventually their situation is that
of all artisan wage-earners in crowded crafts. Their large numbers and their powerful union organization have made it advis-
able to handle the problem of large-scale indigence among them
by means of a definite social policy. This policy is operated in
part directly by the union itself (plus some free-lance philan-

thropic organizations like the Musicians' Emergency Relief Committee) and in part by the state and federal governments through unemployment insurance and Social Security.

Composers, being professional men and women and none too well organized either, have not yet found themselves the object of public concern. They do have, however, their little financial problems, I assure you, not the least of which is bare existence.

The poet of thirty works, whenever possible, at something not connected with literature. The composer practically always works at music, unless he can manage to get himself kept. He plays in cafés and concerts. He conducts. He writes criticism. He sings in church choirs. He reads manuscripts for music publishers. He acts as music librarian to institutions. He becomes a professor. He writes books. He lectures on the Appreciation of Music. Only occasionally does he hold down a job that is not connected with music.

A surprisingly large number of composers are men of private fortune. Some of these have it from papa, but the number of those who have married their money is not small. The composer, in fact, is rather in demand as a husband. Boston and New England generally are noted for the high position there allotted to musicians in the social hierarchy and for the number of gifted composers who have in consequence married into flowery beds of ease. I don't know why so many composers marry well, but they do. It is a fact. I don't suppose their sexuality is any more impressive than anybody else's, though certainly, as intellectuals go, the musician yields to none in that domain. After all, if a lady of means really wants an artistic husband, a composer is about the best bet, I imagine. Painters are notoriously unfaithful, and they don't age gracefully. They dry up and sour. Sculptors are of an incredible stupidity. Poets are either too violent or too tame, and terrifyingly expensive. Also, due to the exhausting nature of their early lives, they are likely to be impotent after forty. Pianists and singers are megalomaniacs; conductors worse. Besides, executants don't stay home enough. The composer, of all art-workers in the vineyard, has the prettiest manners and ripens the most satisfactorily. His intellectual and his amorous powers seldom give completely out before his death. His musical powers not uncommonly increase. Anyway, lots of composers marry money, and a few have it already. Private fortune is a not unusual source of income for musicians. It is not as difficult for a rich man to write music as it is for him to write poetry. The class censorship is not so strict. The only trouble about wealth is that spending it takes time. The musician who runs all over town giving lessons and playing accompaniments has often just as much leisure to write music as does the ornamental husband of a well-to-do lady living in five elegant houses.

Many composers are able to live for years on gifts and doles. Include among these all prizes and private commissions. I don't suppose anybody believes nowadays that money one has earned is any more ennobling than money one hasn't. Money is money, and its lack of odor has often been remarked. Gifts sometimes have strings, of course; but so has any job its inconveniences. Equally punctured, I take it, is the superstition formerly current that struggle and poverty are good for the artist, who is a lazy man and who only works when destitute. Quite the contrary, I assure you. Composers work better and faster when they have a bit of comfort. Too much money, with its attendant obligations, is a nuisance to any busy man. But poverty, illness, hunger, and cold never did any good to anybody. And don't let anyone tell you differently.

The number of composers who live on the receipts from their compositions is very small, even in Europe, though on both of the northwestern continents that number is larger in the field of light music than it is in the domain of massive instrumentation and extended forms. We owe it to the composers of light music that we get paid at all for our performing rights, since it is they who have always organized the societies for exacting payment and furnished the funds for fighting infringers in the courts.

Royalties and performing-rights fees are to any composer a sweetly solemn thought. They are comparatively rare, however, in America, since composers, even composers of popular music, are nothing like as powerfully organized there for collecting them as the electrical and banking interests (whose shadow darkens our prospects of profit in all musical usages) are for preventing their being collected. So that when every now and then some composer actually makes enough money off his music to sleep and eat for a while, that is a gala day for the musical art. He feels like a birthday-child, of course, and fancies himself no end. Let him. His distinction carries no security. And he had better keep his hand in at performing and teaching and writing and at all the other little ways he knows of turning a not too dishonest extra penny. He had better seize on the first flush of fame too to "guest-conduct" his own works. This brings in two fees at once, one for his conducting and one for his performing rights. Invariably the composer who has enough composer-income to live on can pick up quite decent supplementary sums, as well as keep his contacts fresh, by not giving up entirely traffic in the by-products of his musical education. [Since this was written both the American Society of Composers, Authors, and Publishers (ASCAP) and Broadcast Music, Inc. (BMI) have developed vastly as collectors and distributors of performance-rights in serious music, while the foundations are commissioning composers.]

I have been running on in this wandering fashion because I wanted to show how flexible is the composer's economic life and how many strings he has to his bow. Briefly, the composer's possible income-sources are:

1. Non-Musical Jobs, or Earned Income from Non-Musical Sources.
2. Unearned Income from All Sources.
    [a.] Money from home
         (x.) His own
         (y.) His wife's
    [b.] Other people's money
         (x.) Personal patronage
              i. Impersonal subsidy
              ii. Commissions
         (y.) Prizes
         (z.) Doles

3. Other Men's Music, or Selling the By-products of His
Musical Education.
[a.] Execution
[b.] Organizing musical performances
[c.] Publishing and editing
[d.] Pedagogy
[e.] Lecturing
[f.] Criticism and musical journalism
[g.] The Appreciation-racket
4. The Just Rewards of His Labor.
[a.] Royalties
(x.) From music published
(y.) From gramophone-recordings
[b.] Performing-rights fees.

Every composer receives the money he lives on from one of
these sources. Most have received money from several. I have
lived on nearly all of them at one time or another.

Between the extremes of being too rich for comfort and being
really too poor, the amount of money composers have doesn't
seem to affect them very much. Photogenic poverty and ostentatious spending are equally repugnant to their habits. The source
of their money has, however, a certain effect on their work. We
have noted that the composer, being a member of the Professional Classes, enjoys all the rights and is subject to the obligations of what is known as Professional Integrity. This does not
mean that he enjoys complete intellectual freedom. He has that
only with regard to the formal, or structural, aspects of his art.
His musical material and style would seem to be a function, at
any given moment, of his chief income-source.

EDGARD

VARÈSE was born in Paris on December 22, 1883, of
Italian and French parentage. He came to the United States at
the end of 1915 and made his home in New York City. Although
he studied music at the Conservatoire National and at the Schola
Cantorum in Paris, it was through his association with Ferruccio
Busoni in Berlin, during six years prior to the outbreak of World
War I, that Varèse received his most decisive formative influences. From Busoni, whose *Aesthetic of a New Music* he read
with enthusiasm, Varèse imbibed the conviction that musical
composition must be based on the complete liberation of sounds,
unshackled by the limitations of the tempered system and of
traditional tonality.

As composer, as conductor, as teacher, and as a great personality in twentieth-century music, Varèse has waged an incessant
battle for creative freedom in music. His own works, mostly instrumental—from *Amériques* (1921) and *Arcana* (1927) for
large orchestra, through the various instrumental combinations
of *Hyperprism* (1923), *Octandre* (1924), *Ionisation* (1932, for
percussion ensemble with two sirens), and *Offrandes* (1922, with
soprano solo), culminating in the "organized sound" techniques
of *Deserts* (1954) and *Poème electronique* (1958)—have consistently explored new domains of musical expression. In *Deserts*
an ensemble of traditional instruments (woodwinds, brasses,
percussion) alternates with interpolations of "organized sound"
on magnetic tape. In *Poème electronique,* as originally conceived

184

and projected at the Philips Pavilion of the Brussels Exposition in 1958, 400 loudspeakers carefully placed along the hyperbolic and parabolic curves of the structure designed by Le Corbusier, caused the sound to sweep in continuous arcs throughout the available space.

Varèse conceives of music as spatial—as moving in space. He had worked out the theoretical basis for such a spatial projection of sound long before electronics made this physically possible. His was the most forward-looking mind in modern music. What he said about freedom for music in 1939 remains in large measure pertinent and valid for the American situation in 1965.

Edgard Varèse died in New York City—which he loved and where he had a large group of devoted disciples—on November 6, 1965.

Freedom for Music / (1939)

There is an institution in New York City whose purpose is the furtherance of modern plastic arts.[1] All of you have heard of it: The Museum of Modern Art. It is unique! It has turned its back on all the gorgeous art of the past in order to make known the new, the disturbing, art of today.

On the occasion of the opening of its new building last month,

1 This essay was originally given as a talk at the University of Southern California, Los Angeles, in 1939. [Ed.]

Mr. Franklin D. Roosevelt made a plea for Freedom and a plea
for Art. All of us must endorse every word that he said and be
grateful that the political head of a nation today recognizes the
vital importance of art and, for art, of freedom.

We, here tonight, are more particularly interested in the art
of music and, of course, also in that freedom which is the essential condition of its development too. Unhappily the conditions
of freedom, necessary for the vigorous growth of music and the
spread of its influence, do not exist today, and I should like you
for a moment to face the facts.

Mr. Roosevelt, emphasizing the importance of spreading the
"opportunity" of getting acquainted with art, highly praised the
plan of the Museum of Modern Art to send traveling exhibitions
all through the country. "The Museum," he says, "can enrich
and invigorate our cultural life by bringing the best modern art
to all the American people."

What he says is very true, but hasn't the music of today also
a cultural value for our country? Why are the modern plastic
arts alone considered essential to the cultural growth of our
country and given every encouragement to increase and flourish
and to make themselves understood, while the music of today,
so-called modern music, is treated like a poor relation? It is obvious that the American of today cannot be culturally affected by
the music of today, since even the music-public, to say nothing
of the great masses, is kept in almost total ignorance of what
living composers have to say.

Mr. Roosevelt praises the democratic form of government for
allowing the artist "freedom." "A world," he says, "turned into
a stereotype, a society converted into a regiment, a life translated into a routine, make it difficult for art or artists to survive."

Certainly no artist who wears the straitjacket of propaganda
can create. Unfortunately it has been the experience of composers in free democracies, that freedom to write as they please
does not bring with it the right to be heard, to say nothing of
the right to live. Our present administration, which has been
a Big Brother to the plastic artist, has done nothing for his
counterpart in music, the composer. Only performers have, as
far as I know, been benefited by the Federal Music Projects.

And in spite of the goodwill of some of the progressive conductors on the project, it is impossible for them to produce really significant modern scores due to the inadequacy of their orchestras or to insufficient rehearsals. And as for material benefits, the Federal Music Budget has entirely ignored the natural needs of the composer who, I assure you, enjoys eating just as much as a violinist, a drummer, or even a conductor!

Now, why not a Modern Music Instituiton which would do for living music what the Museum of Modern Art does for living plastic arts? The difficulties, to be sure, are much greater and too obvious to dwell upon. Nevertheless, one very simple solution occurs to me: that each of the major symphonic orchestra organizations in this country establish a department of Modern Music with, at its head, an associate conductor—preferably young, young in spirit at any rate—or to put it in another way, a conductor who is living, not in the eighteenth or nineteenth, but in the twentieth century! I rather think that the first orchestra to instigate such a revolutionary scheme would find itself benefited by a whole new set of subscribers to support it.

So much for Modern Music's hope for freedom to be heard!

I think that music stands in need of other fundamental liberations. And I feel sure that they would be quickly realized if only the need for them were clearly recognized. I believe that, because the nature of music is not fully understood, music has not gone forward with the other arts today; instead it turns around and around like a squirrel in a cage.

The philosophers of the Middle Ages separated the liberal arts into two branches: the trivium or the arts of reason as applied to language—grammar, rhetoric, and dialectic; and the quadrivium or the arts of pure reason—which today we would call the sciences. It was among the latter that music had its place in the company of mathematics, geometry, and astronomy.

Today music is more apt to be rated with the arts of the trivium. It seems to me, at least, that too much emphasis is placed on what might be called the grammar of music.

At different times and in different places music has been considered either as an art or as a science. In reality music partakes of both. Jean Wronsky and Camille Durutte in their treatise on harmony at the end of the last century, were obliged to coin new words when they assigned music its place as an "Art-Science" and defined it as the "corporealization of the intelligence that is in sounds." Most people would rather think of music solely as an art. But when you listen to music do you ever stop to realize that you are being subjected to a physical phenomenon? Not until the air between the listener's ear and the instrument has been disturbed does music occur. Do you realize that every time a printed score is brought to life it has to be re-created through the different sound machines, called "musical instruments," which make up our orchestras and which are subject to the same laws of physics as any other machine? In order to anticipate the result, a composer must understand the mechanics of the instruments and must know just as much as possible about acoustics. We are all familiar with the term "paper music"—music that can be read but that fails to say anything in sound. But music must live in sound. On the other hand the possession of a perfectly pitched ear is only of relative importance to a composer; what a composer must have, must have been born with, is what I call the "inner ear," the ear of imagination. The inner ear is the composer's Pole Star.

In a moment I shall come back to the question of music as an art-science. But first let us look at music as it is more popularly considered, as an art, and inquire: what is composition?

Brahms says that composition is the "organizing of disparate elements." But what is the situation of the would-be creator today, shaken by the powerful impulses and rhythms of this age! How is he to accomplish this "organizing" in order to express himself and his epoch? Where is he to find those "disparate elements"? Are they to be found in the books he studies in his various courses in harmony, composition, and orchestration? Are they in the great works of the great masters he pores over with love and admiration and which, with all his might, he means to emulate? Unfortunately too many composers have been lead to believe that these elements can be found as easily as that. And this undoubtedly accounts for one of the most deplorable trends of music today: the impotent return to the formulas of the past which has been called "neoclassicism." But what would a Bach have thought of a neo-Bach; a Mozart of someone who "returned to" Mozart? And I am quite sure that if Debussy returned to the world today, after hearing the Debussyists, he would change his name!

Professor Eric Temple Bell, in a book called *The Search for Truth*, says: "Reverence for the past no doubt is a virtue that has had its uses, but if we are to go forward the reverent approach to old difficulties is the wrong one!"

I should say that in music the "reverent approach" has done a great deal of harm: it has kept would-be composers from composing their own works; it has even kept would-be appreciators from really appreciating! And, it has created the music critic!

The very basis of creative work is irreverence! The very basis of creative work is experimentation, bold experimentation. You have only to turn to the revered past for the corroboration of my contention.

Music critics have always minimized the changes of the past and represented those of the present either as ridiculous, childish, and laughable or as dangerous, revolutionary, criminal, according to temperament or temporary digestive indisposition. But they have all defined the development of music in the past as "evolution." And the conservative musician, whether listener, performer, or composer, either through laziness, self-interest, or incompetence, is sure to agree with D. C. Parker who in his indictment of "modernism" bluntly states: "Pioneers and experimentors are seldom first-rate creators"! Mr. Parker undoubtedly never heard of Bach—Bach the experimeter, who tuned the clavichord to the tempered system for the first time and who devised such surprising new fugal patterns; or Beethoven with his experiments in dissonances, his new key-relationships, his polyharmonies, his off-beat accents, abolition of the transitional phrase . . . and so on.

Messrs. Weber and Spohr may not live very long as creators but they will certainly have their curious place in history for the imbecilities they have written about Beethoven. Chopin, too, was bitterly attacked in his day for his impossible innovations. During the time that I was conducting the concerts of modern music of the International Composers' Guild in New York, while

other critics were telling the New York public that these modern composers were writing for no other reason than to poke
fun at the critics, a veteran New York critic who is also a scholar
with enviable files full of musical curiosities, Lawrence Gilman,
took the trouble to dig up the following: "He is indefatigable,
almost inexhaustible in his ear-splitting dissonances, forced tran-
sitions, ugly distortions of melody and rhythm. Everything that
is impossible to think of is raked up to produce the effect of
originality." And Gilman goes on to explain: "No, gentle reader,
that is not the comment of an exasperated reviewer of 1924 discussing the performance of Mr. Edgard Varèse's *Octandre* at a
recent concert of the International Composers' Guild. It was
written by [Ludwig] Rellstab, once an eminent Berlin music
critic, concerning Chopin."

I think we would conform more nearly to the facts in our possession if we totally disagreed with Mr. Parker and stated just
as categorically that there had never been a creator of lasting
importance who has not also been an innovator. The links in the
chain of tradition are formed by men who have all been revolu-
tionists! To the student of music I should say that the great
examples of the past should serve as springboards for him to
leap free, into his own future.

In every domain of art a work that corresponds to the need of
its day carries a message of social and cultural value. Preceding
ages show us that changes in art occur because societies and
artists have new needs. New aspirations emanate from every
epoch. The artist being always of his own time is influenced by
it, and in turn, is an influence. It is the artist who crystalizes
his age, who fixes his age in history. Contrary to the general
notion, the artist is never ahead of his own time, but is simply
the only one who is not way behind his times.

We all think it very sensible that tools that have become out-
moded should be replaced by the very newest thing in "efficiency." We do not think that the horse plow is still adequate for the
needs of today. We are quite satisfied that Boulder Dam expresses us better than the Egyptian pyramids. But in music we
composers are forced to use, in the realization of our works, instruments that have not changed for two centuries. String in-

struments reached their climax of perfection in the eighteenth century and should by now be as obsolete for the transportation of our music as stage coaches for the transportation of our bodies. And although for convenience and profit in our daily lives we have found something better than the hand pump, we still blow with effort into wind instruments. And the arbitrary, tempered system to which we still cling is not capable of setting down even as much as our obsolete instruments are capable of playing. Now in conclusion let me come back to the subject of music as an art-science.

The raw material of music is sound. That is what the "reverent approach" has made most people forget—even composers. Today when science is equipped to help the composer realize what was never before possible—all that Beethoven dreamed, all that Berlioz gropingly imagined possible—the composer continues to be obsessed by traditions which are nothing but the limitations of his predecessors. Composers like anyone else today are delighted to use the many gadgets continually put on the market for our daily comfort. But when they hear sounds that no violins, wind instruments, or percussions of the orchestra can produce, it does not occur to them to demand those sounds of science. Yet science is even now equipped to give them everything they may require.

Personally, for my conceptions, I need an entirely new medium of expression: a sound-producing machine (not a sound-reproducing one). Today it is possible to build such a machine with only a certain amount of additional research.

If you are curious to know what such a machine could do that the orchestra with its man-powered instruments cannot do, I shall try briefly to tell you: whatever I write, whatever my message, it will reach the listener unadulterated by "interpretation." It will work something like this: after a composer has set down his score on paper by means of a new graphic, similar in principle to a seismographic or oscilographic notation, he will then, with the collaboration of a sound engineer, transfer the score directly to this electric machine. After that anyone will be able to press a button to release the music exactly as the composer wrote it—exactly like opening a book.

And here are the advantages I anticipate from such a machine: liberation from the arbitrary, paralyzing, tempered system; the possibility of obtaining any number of cycles or if still desired, subdivisions of the octave, and consequently the formation of any desired scale; unsuspected range in low and high registers; new harmonic splendors obtainable from the use of subharmonic combinations now impossible; the possibility of obtaining any differentiation of timbre, of sound-combinations, new dynamics far beyond the present human-powered orchestra; a sense of sound-projection in space by means of the emission of sound in any part or in many parts of the hall as may be required by the score; cross rhythms unrelated to each other, treated simultaneously, or to use the old word, "counterpuntally," since the machine would be able to beat any number of desired notes, any subdivision of them, omission or fraction of them—all these in a given unit of measure or time which is humanly impossible to attain.

In closing, I want to read to you something that Romain Rolland in his *Jean Christophe* said—it must be almost thirty years ago now—but which remains pertinent today. Jean Christophe, the hero of the novel, was a prototype of the modern composer and was modeled on different composers whom Romain Rolland knew—among others, myself.

The difficulty began when he [Jean Christophe] tried to cast his ideas in the ordinary musical forms: he made the discovery that none of the ancient molds were suited to them; if he wished to fix his visions with fidelity he had to begin by forgetting all the music he had heard, all that he had written, to make a clean slate of all the formalism he had learned, of traditional technique, to throw away those crutches of impotency, that bed, all prepared for the laziness of those who, fleeing the fatigue of thinking for themselves, lie down in other men's thoughts.

HARRY

PARTCH was born in Oakland, California, in 1901, and was reared in Arizona. Self-taught in music, his aims as a composer have been pursued with entire independence of the established musical system, both technically and institutionally. He designed his own musical instruments, invented his own notational system, and developed his own theory of music. He has worked toward an integration of music and speech in a new kind of musical theater, not based on conventional singing but on microtonal inflections of the vocal line. His first achievement in this direction was the musical drama *King Œdipus* (based on the William Butler Yeats version of Sophocles), produced at Mills College (Oakland, California) in 1952. This work was completed while Partch was the recipient of a Guggenheim fellowship.

Since Partch's musical system necessitates the division of the octave into forty-three tones (instead of the twelve tones of the tempered scale), he had to invent and construct special instruments to perform his music. His basic instrument was the "chromelodeon," a reed organ with forty-three tones to the octave scale spreading over three-and-one-half keyboard octaves. In some cases, such as the viola and the Hawaiian guitar, he adapted conventional instruments to his microtonal scale.

Partch continued to develop his conception of an "integrated" musical theater—combining instrumental music, song, speech, dance, and mime—in *The Bewitched* (1956, described as a "dance

193

drama") and *Revelation in the Court-house Square* (1961), the latter a modern version of *The Bacchae* of Euripides.

Grants-in-aid from the University of Wisconsin enabled Partch to write his book *Genesis of a Music* (1949), in which he finds some historical precedents for his theory of "corporeal music" —a concept that he contrasts with "abstract music" (i.e., music that seeks its own autonomous structure). This volume includes a chapter on "American Musical Tendencies," from which the most pertinent passages have been excerpted for the following selection.

American Musical Tendencies / (1949)

The fundamental stimuli that are the reasons for the music of these United States are intriguing to ponder. First, does Abstraction continue to guide us in the uniting of words and music? Have the Germanic traditions in the abstract, enhanced in coming to us by way of the well-known English devotion to them, taken full possession of our educational and creative endeavors in music? Is there any evidence of a drift away from the general assumption that music, to merit comparison with the "best," must be *Abstract*? Does popular music, either in tendencies or intrinsic characteristics, offer any hope of relief from the inequities in the usages of "serious" music? Can our American leanings in the "big business" of the concert system come to any good end? Finally, will the American genius for perverting

a spark of individual imagination into a commodity for nationwide distribution permit us—ever—to hope for a significant evolution in American music? These questions suggest a few of the
drives; there are others.

. . . . . .

From one standpoint the twentieth century is a fair historical
duplicate of the eleventh. At that time the standard and approved ecclesiastical expression failed to satisfy an earthly this-
time-and-this-place musical hunger; result—the troubadours. Today, and especially in America, the approved Abstraction is
a full musical fare for only a small percentage of our people, and
the resulting hunger is satisfied by anything that breaks the formal barriers in the direction of Corporeality—hillbilly, cowboy,
and popular music, which, whatever its deficiencies, owes nothing to scholastic and academic Europeanisms.

The devitalized tricks of "serious" singing, if they belong anywhere, certainly do not belong here. Examples are: (1) the ubiquitous rolled r's, an articulation common in European tongues
but alien to America; (2) precise attacks and precise release
(like the tones of an organ), as opposed to the gliding tones so
characteristic of American speech, the portamento of "faulty
attack" and "faulty release"; and (3) the affected stylization of
"refined" English. Many of our folk and popular singers unconsciously tend to preserve word form and drama. Frequently their
manner is simple. Frequently they "explode" consonants, and
sustain such consonants as l, m, n, and z rather than the vowels
preceding them. Frequently they personify a directness of word
appeal, characteristic of this age and this land, and characterized
by suggestions of actual times, actual localities, actual identities,
and actual human situations—all of which is the very antithesis
of the Abstract concept.

By mere control of the lips, mouth, tongue, palate, glottis, and
diaphragm under emotional stimulus, the human voice is ready
to express all the feelings and attitudes which the cumulative
centuries have symbolized in words and poured into the dictionary—from joyful spite to tragic ecstasy, from ecstatic melancholy to hedonistic fatuity, from furtive beatitude to boisterous
grotesquerie, from portentous lechery to obdurate athanasia—

prescience, felicity, urbanity, hauteur, surfeit, magniloquence, enravishment, execration, abnegation, anguish, riot, debauch, hope, joy, death, grief, effluent life, and a lot more.

This bottle of cosmic vintage is the endowment of all of us. Do the freedom-fearing music schools of Europe and America train singers to give us even a little draught of these vocal potentials? They concoct one special brand of their own, put it in an atomizer in the singers' throats, and send it in a sweet sickening stream over the proscenium and the kilocycles; it anoints the hair, it titillates the brows, it mizzles on the temples, and this wretchedest of intellectual infamies in the name of music—mark the term!—is called "musical tone."

. . . . . .

Both the musical idea of Abstraction and the temperament which genuinely prefers it find themselves in sterile company. . . . I am trying to hope that we are not entering an era where the only men of significance in music will be those facile at quoting Bach and Beethoven, Brahms and Tchaikowsky. . . . If we are entering such an age it is already dead, and I can think of no epitaph more fitting than this: "They did not like modern music." . . .

What of the immediate future? The consistent development of our present musical attitudes would seem to call for even larger masses of performers, even greater volume, greater speed in tones tumbling over themselves on instruments, and away from the individual and the individual's subtlety. . . .

The situation in music is actually only one of the more obvious aspects of general paralysis of individuality. What is the situation from the more fundamental—the sociological—viewpoint? It begins in the cradle. The late Scudder Mekeel, who was in the forefront of the battle to free the American personality from the tyranny of race prejudice, asserts that "by the very way in which we train our children, we make certain that they can never really carry individualism very far, or take full advantage of being themselves. This is the crux of our particular system of social control."[1]

1 "Race Relations," *Mental Hygiene*, XXIX (April, 1945), 185.

Where is the "Bill of Rights"—in the age of skyliners and electronically amplified symphony orchestras—to forestall destruction of individuality in the individual? Is our "particular system" of musical control any less rigorous?

Ennui over the Waves

It has been said that because today more people hear Beethoven in twenty-four hours (on the radio) than heard him in his whole lifetime, the people have music. Momentarily disregarding the question of the quality of emanation from the radio, we can say: yes, and a citizen doubtless sees more policemen now in twenty-four hours than Beethoven saw in his whole lifetime. The people hear more music, and *ipso facto* they are more musical? The people have more law, and *ipso facto* they are more lawful?

The analogue is not so absurd. If we are to make of this age one that is at all comparable to that of ancient Greece or the Italian Renaissance, it will be through a surge of real individuality, stimulating ideas, and a resolution to execute them faithfully. Hearing more music—ninety-nine percent of which is not Beethoven but the equivalent of radio vibrations of frankfurters —accomplishes just one thing: ennui in the eardrum.

Beethoven is a value that may be expected to persist because he has had value for generations of human beings. The point is not the value of Beethoven, but whether in our schools of serious music we shall confine ourselves to finer and finer degrees of perfection in the "interpretation" of past treasures, and whether we shall go on devouring or unconsciously absorbing vibrating frankfurters to that point of melomaniacal satiety at which our appetite vanishes, or whether some few of us will chuck the music school, turn off the radio, and go into the kitchen and cook ourselves a nourishing meal. . . .

That ninety-nine percent [of music] which—a thousand to one—will be heard at a given moment on the radio, is not Beethoven but an industrialized development of something which small groups of musically leaderless people spontaneously cooked up a few generations ago, and which—without the familiar American knack for "giving the people what they want"—might have evolved into a charming, colloquial, and provincial particle of American culture.

Radio's use of Abstract music, conceived with all the "independent" intentions in the world, as background and "incidental" music in a thoroughly dependent application, and the purists' protests against this use are but further evidence of a widespread unconscious reaction against Abstraction. It almost seems that the curve, which began with a Corporeal genesis in the West, then saw the Corporeal mechanics used to establish an Abstract musical philosophy, is now beginning to come full circle with an application of the Abstract mechanics in a Corporeal musical idea. But the circle will not be complete until the Corporeal idea is accepted consciously, along with conscious efforts to make it a significant declaration.

That intermittent extraneity which the radio and movies call "incidental" is of course not a significant declaration. But even the worst of it, even that which is obviously born of outside pressure and inward weariness, suffers, not so much because of bad intrinsic quality as because of the subservient, sense-changing, punctuating role it is cast in. It is no integral part of the moment's drama; with tiresome repetition of device it "prepares" the moment, or "comments" on it, or connects it to another; or it is obliged to accompany a weak moment to save the situation from sheer cliché.

The "singing commercial," however obnoxious its sentiment or the product it sells, is meticulously prepared; it suffers from lack of imagination less often, and in mechanics of presentation it has much more to offer. If, from a musical standpoint, a better solution for "incidental" music were instituted, many times more work would be required for each program, and therefore so much could not be programmed so often to "entertain" so many—the oft-repeated alibi for democratic mediocrity. The time is rapidly coming when we must either decide to do something about this "incidental" situation which, along with the juke box and other influences, is turning us into a nation of amusiacs, or admit, frankly, that our kind of democracy means selling music short.

. . . . . .

The Enchanted Land

At this point questions loom on every side. What is the connection, if any, between a blind love of tradition in music and personality paralysis? What is the connection, if any, between the tendency toward exploitation and a widespread taste for the banal-mediocre? between social-political illiberalism and a widespread taste for the banal-mediocre?

One experience is not much, but when it operates without advance reputation it invites honesty—it combats no fear of *ex cathedra* or *ex neighbor* opinion. (There can be no fear of *ex cathedra* opinion when the subject is *extra cathedra*.) When as subject it is unknown to everyone, and everyone realizes that it is, no one is under any pressure to say anything except what he really thinks.

Honesty on one subject has a long way of horning honesty on other subjects into open air, and of stimulating opinions and attitudes of a general nature. The suggestion is consequently made, on the foundation of experience, that the interconnections aforementioned do exist—and significantly.

The courses corrective? They are at least two. Perhaps it is possible to teach a man to find both his superior self and his child-creative self under bemedalled diploma wrappings, but the psychologist James H. Leuba has different ideas: "To seek to mold the character by proposing ideals, imparting knowledge, providing rewards and punishment, is often an appalling waste of effort."[2] And he suggests that the time may not be far distant "when years of labored and unreliable efforts by the direct method indicated above will be replaced by a shorter and more reliable indirect method acting upon the body."

Whether it is achieved through a biochemical action on the body or through bio-spiritual action on the mind, there is—veritably—a universality which is ultimately attainable without reducing the entire world to the minus centigrade of the average swing band. In the world of perception beyond knowledge—here is the enchanted land! But perception cannot be manifested without opportunity: the opportunity to hear, to create, and to

2 Leuba, *God or Man* (New York: Henry Holt & Co., 1933), 92.

be heard. And opportunity simply does not appear where there is little sensitivity in powerful places, and where seemingly endless frankfurters vibrate through the brain accompanied only by the drone bass of a profit motive. It is the people interested in music who confer on individuals the privilege of becoming powers in music. Consequently, it is up to us to see that more of the powers in music are leaders also.

Without aspiring to those ambitious ideas expressed by the fashionable words "timeless" and "immortal," we can do much to exert an influence worthy of our obligation to help point a way, and we need not be too despondent. There is a German proverb which denies the proverbial impertinence of proverbs when it says, literally: "What is not can yet become."

. . . . . .

The desideratum for which I am pleading is a congenial milieu for the music of creators who do not fit into the Abstractionist framework of "serious" music, composers who want their words to sound not like mellifluous melody but like words, and their words to have only their natural span of enunciation. For them the Abstractionist technicians are not to be trusted.

ARTHUR
BERGER was born in New York City in 1912. After graduating from New York University he enrolled in the Longy School of Music in Boston and also studied composition with Walter Piston at Harvard, where he obtained his M.A. in 1936. As recipient of a Paine Fellowship from Harvard he went to Paris for further study with Nadia Boulanger and Darius Milhaud (1937-39). Prior to this he had come under the influence of Cowell and Copland; but in the 1940's he became an avowed "disciple" of Stravinsky, in the sense of endeavoring to emulate certain "universal" qualities that he professed to find in the works of that composer's middle period.

For ten years (1943-53) Berger was active as a music critic in New York, first for the New York *Sun* and later for the New York *Herald-Tribune*. In 1953 he published a book on Aaron Copland, a composer whom he greatly admires. In that same year he became a member of the musical faculty of Brandeis University. He is a member of the editorial board of the important periodical *Perspectives of New Music* and has contributed significant articles to this and other publications.

Berger's first important composition was the Quartet in C Major for Woodwinds (1941), which indicates how soon he had outgrown his early atonalism. His *Ideas of Order* for orchestra (1952), commissioned by Dimitri Mitropoulos, was his first full-scale symphonic work. It was followed by *Polyphony for Orchestra* in 1956, which makes use of twelve-tone technique. Ber-

201

ger had first employed twelve-tone writing, in fairly strict fashion, in Chamber Music for 13 Players, written in the same year
but not performed until 1960, when Robert Craft conducted it in
Los Angeles. Berger has written many other chamber music
works, including the String Quartet of 1958 and a series of duos
for various instruments, among which the Duo for Oboe and
Clarinet (1952) is particularly notable.

Since Berger's article, "Stravinsky and The Younger American Composers," was published (1954), most of the composers
he writes about have gone in other directions (and so has Stravinsky himself, for that matter!); but the existence of a group
of "Stravinsky disciples" in the United States (first characterized as such by Copland in 1947) is a historical fact that is very
much a part of the American musical scene.

Stravinsky and the Younger American Composers / (1954)

Among the brief "Appreciations" of Stravinsky that comprise
a section of the book *Stravinsky in the Theatre*, published some
five years ago (Minna Lederman, editor), there is one by Aaron
Copland in which he writes: "Among our younger generation it
is easy to discover a Stravinsky school: Shapero, Haieff, Berger
Lessard, Foss, Fine." Copland was commenting on the capacity
of this master to "influence two succeeding generations in ways
diametrically opposed," and the younger Americans he cites represent, naturally, those who "rallied to the new cause" of what

has been saddled with the unfortunate rubric (or so it seems to me) of "neo-classicism."

If he were writing today I doubt that Copland would have limited himself to these six. Charles Jones, Talma, Dahl, Smit and DesMarais are additional names to this growing circle that come at once to my mind. Nor am I sure there are not others, since this is not a group strictly defined by its members or pamphleteers. If the term "group" is applicable to the subject at hand, there are groups within the group. Essentially I am writing about separate figures who admire the example set by a dominating master of the century, and a common cause has brought them together in friendships, exchange of ideas and severe mutual criticism.

I may be doing an injustice in calling attention to this common cause. Twelve-tone composers enjoy a certain immunity from the accusation of being servile followers. Their method is taken to be abstract and impersonal, something that may be adapted to individual ends. But though the principles embodied in Stravinsky's music may be abstracted and adapted in a somewhat similar fashion (though not as a concrete system), his dominating personality is likely to be invoked in the mind of the critic or listener whenever these principles are applied elsewhere. Twelve-tone method in a new work by a young composer is generally acknowledged as a matter of vocabulary or technique. The critic then proceeds to an evaluation that depends on whether or not he accepts the methods. But if the young composer has profited in any substantial degree from the contributions made by Stravinsky between, roughly, 1920 and 1950, the onus of unwarranted borrowing is almost sure to be placed on him. After a première of a work of my own, for example, I was presented by the press with the verdict that if any "name were not attached one might easily guess it to be one of (Stravinsky's) smaller ballet scores." While I regret the critic's failure to grasp the qualities that I should like to believe are my personal contributions (though I cannot say whether they are successful or not), I feel highly complimented that my craftsmanship should have been in any way mistakable for Stravinsky's.

That is, of course, an extreme instance. But even when Stravinsky's name is brought in less obtrusively for description, a criticism is already implied. Nothing is gained when the term "neo-classicist" replaces his name. If it shares with the phrase, "twelve-tone composer," the advantage of being impersonal and impartial, it carries implications of pseudo-classicism, academicism, conservatism.

It is a curious paradox that on the subject of Stravinsky's own music we so often read pronouncements like this: "Bits of Handel, Gounod, Wagner, Bellini, Delibes, Johann Strauss and fragments of a dozen other of Stravinsky's predecessors out of different centuries float to the surface, disappear, reappear. The music is without coherence, without integrity of style." But if, in what we may now call his "middle" period, he made no contribution of his own, if he was a mere cataloguer of old formulae, how is it possible to detect so readily his manner of this period in the works of younger men?

I can only conclude that the unfortunate attitude towards Stravinsky's musical progeny is motivated by the same factors that are responsible for the critical disapproval he himself receives. Among these factors I might mention a preconceived notion as to how music ought to evolve (onward, that is to say, in a straight line from Wagner and Strauss) and an inability for many listeners to apprehend a new work in its totality, with the result that they are weighed down with disembodied materials and superficial symptoms. Stravinsky's disciples, even those with fully developed personalities, are stigmatized for their debt to him by critics who disavow him in the first place, while almost any conservatory student is allowed to get by though he may lean in the most flagrant fashions upon Bartók or Prokofieff.

Disapproval of new music is far from unexpected, and some of it may be just. But criticism can scarcely be heeded when it fails to show any signs of discriminating one personality from another within a school that makes no secret of its common allegiance. Merely drawing attention to the allegiance resembles the reproach levelled at Brahms because of the suggestions of Beethoven in his music—a reproach that he is reported to have dismissed promptly with the remark, "Any ass can see that." It would seem far more to the point to attempt to determine the differences among the composers of the Stravinsky school—differences that, to one observing from within, appear far too substantial to be figments of a prejudiced participant.

If it is difficult to recognize the traditional element in works that seem very radical at first, it may be equally difficult to recognize what is new in works that are not radical in idiom. At one time Copland was described as the "Brooklyn Stravinsky," which may seem an odd characterization for anyone who manifested strong personality almost from the start. Twenty-five years from today it may also seem odd that the individuality of Stravinsky's more recent disciples was not appreciated. But I should not be willing to risk a wager on this, nor do I think it is enormously important. In general the cultivation of personality is not the ardent and almost conscious pursuit nowadays that it was for composers who grew up closer to the influence of that intensified quest for novelty that came as an aftermath of *Le Sacre*. The challenge to our newer generations is to consolidate our country's vast new resources and to rehabilitate solid structures after years of sheer effect for its own sake. It is in these areas that Stravinsky has set remarkable examples. Personal elements exist among his newer disciples, but they will be harder to fathom than those that existed among his disciples in earlier generations. On the other hand, there are many different approaches in the current school, there is no regimentation.

Not only is cultivation of personality in the "old-fashioned" sense of, say, twenty-five or fifty years ago not a major consideration of the new Stravinsky school, but, along the same lines, it is also indifferent to developing the American characteristics that occupied Copland's attention. There is a feeling we have entered another of the periods of internationalism that recur from time to time in music's history. I suspect this may be a source of disappointment to Copland after his spade-work. But he may find consolation in the fact that most of the younger composers who are devoted to Stravinsky are devoted to him, too. This may be because his own debt to the Stravinsky of such works as the Octet places him in the family and because, in or out of this family, his own stature on the American scene casts a sizeable shadow as inescapable to many Americans as Stravinsky's. Certain works of the forties by members of the Stravinsky school might have been very different were it not for Copland's contribution. Of these I might mention Shapero's *Sonata for Piano Four Hands*, Lukas Foss's *The Prairie* (a cantata), Irving Fine's *Music for Piano*, Louise Talma's *Piano Sonata*, and Leo Smit's earlier piano pieces and ballet music.

It was Nadia Boulanger, no doubt, who was a key figure in solidifying the kinship between Copland and Stravinsky, and my account of the parentage of our school would be very incomplete, indeed, if she were not mentioned. Copland started the procession of American composers to Paris to study with her, and it was following the example of Copland and such of his fellow-composers as Walter Piston that the majority of our school similarly came into contact with her and shared her enthusiasm for Stravinsky—all of us but Dahl, Foss, Jones and Smit.

My own interest in Stravinsky's works of the decade from 1925 to 1935 was aroused before I went to Paris, while I was a graduate student at Harvard University in the mid-thirties. The works were just becoming known in America. At Harvard they found a congenial atmosphere for study and the Boston Symphony provided rare opportunity to hear some of them at a time when they were pretty much ignored elsewhere. When I returned to Harvard in 1941, I met Shapero, then an undergraduate. His early works, under Krenek's guidance, had taken a turn in a twelve-tone direction. I seem to have been instrumental in changing that direction (though I do not doubt he would have reached the same conclusion on his own) and then it was that the Stravinsky school mentioned by Copland above established a nucleus.

The origin and early flowering of the school in and around Harvard prompted some people to talk of it in the early days as a "Harvard" or "Boston" group. Even when we look back today, Boston seems to be the centre from which its various arteries flow. Several members are either natives of the Boston region (Shapero, Fine) or have spent long periods there (Foss, Des-Marais, myself) and the godparents, Stravinsky, Copland and

Boulanger, have gravitated there from time to time, leaving a profound impression with their lectures and teaching at Harvard and Radcliffe. The Boston Symphony's summer school at Tanglewood, where Copland, Fine and Foss have taught, may be considered a Boston annex. As a faculty member, Dahl established contact with the centre. But his entrance was relatively recent. Prior to that, the nucleus of Shapero and myself was augmented by Fine, another Harvard man, and each of us individually met Alexei Haieff who, an inhabitant of New York since 1932, had been born in Russia and thus brought with him a certain authenticity as a Stravinsky heir. Foss entered the circle after years of devotion to Hindemith and Smit entered it unabashedly as a disciple of Shapero. Boulanger seems to have been responsible for Louise Talma, John Lessard and Paul Des-Marais. Jones has been somewhat aloof from the group or school as such, his affinity stemming, rather, from personal contact with Stravinsky, while at the same time he remains faithful to Milhaud.

Though musical illustrations are important to a musical discussion, passages out of context will not do much to illuminate the present subject. Stravinsky's own allusions to Bach or Mozart do not convey the essence of his restatement of classical principles. They are accidents or materials that happen to fit a medium in which new qualities are achieved with diatonic materials. I could cite characteristic Stravinskian twists of melody that recur in the music of his disciples (the ascent of a major third, for example, followed by the descending major seventh: Do-Mi-Fa). But such tune detection is common enough, and besides, it does not tell us much. Devices like these are material elements in the music of the Stravinsky school in much the same way that a Bachian pattern is a material element in Stravinsky's own music. "The artist is a receptacle for emotions from all over the place," Picasso once remarked, "from the sky, from the earth, from a scrap of paper, from a passing shape, from a spider's web. . . . Where things are concerned there are no class distinctions. We must pick out what is good for us where we find it. . . . when I am shown a portfolio of old drawings, for instance, I have no qualms about taking anything I want from them."

If you admire someone and feel you may benefit from his well-organized ways and character you may find yourself adopting some of his superficial traits when you model yourself on him. But these are not your end. They are ancillary to your activity of probing the fundamental man, and if they are good traits there is no reason why you should not adopt them. Future musicologists, studying the works of Stravinsky, and, perhaps, his school, will be able to make a legitimate study out of tracking down these traits to their sources. This is not my concern.

The sheer exploitation of diatonic principles, however much they may be subjected to new ends, suggests to some people that classical composers are being evoked even when there is no such intention. It is their historical conditioning that makes them want to place any diatonic music in a chronological position anterior to chromaticism. Also, there is a tendency to consider all diatonic composers of our time as being united under one banner and the chromaticists under another. This division ignores the elusive internal attributes of Stravinsky's music that are not present in the music of his most prominent contemporaries, though they share his general character as a diatonicist.

Such a categorical division is further perturbing to an enlightened disciple of Stravinsky, since it leaves room for including the academician on his side. The academician, who often carries the tag of "neo-classicist" more suitably than Stravinsky or his disciples, is devoted to classical principles (if he has not succumbed to conservatoire Romanticism) because he has led a sheltered life in the conservatoire where he closed his ears to the stormy musical proceedings of the first decades of this century. Stravinsky's American disciples, with few exceptions, were acutely aware of those proceedings and went through periods of being directly influenced by them. Even when they had reacted against them they never quite cast them off, which obviously invests their music with the quality of having tasted of the fruit.

Still, members of the Stravinsky school are sometimes regarded in somewhat the same indulgent way as the pedant. Listeners set themselves up as the arbiters who are to determine the precise degree of novelty the artist requires in his idiom to produce a unique work. But this is really *his* problem, not theirs. His choice of techniques whose modes of development are so well established that they threaten to carry him along familiar channels may simply make it more difficult to succeed. But they do not make it impossible, unless, of course, he is content with mere exercises which, in the words of the American aesthetician, D. W. Prall, are only "works of art in the derivative sense, reproductions, with slight and sometimes even unconscious modification, of compositions or of structural units familiar to artists and often familiar enough to laymen." Thus, "instead of taking their origin in an artist's own peculiar purpose, the purpose that defines activity as artistic, their function is the exhibition of a structure of a given sort, the exemplification of a definition that has been given by the works of others."

Any member of a school that has special concern with tradition must heed well the warning implied by such a statement. Yet I admit it is a statement not easily reconcilable with the following one that Shapero has made: "As the composer continues to work exercises in imitation of models he will be surprised to find that along with the thousand subtleties of technique he will absorb from his masters, he will discover the personal materials of his own art." But Shapero is, in a way, the most problematic representative of the whole movement. His forceful creative gifts have been acknowledged, yet he is apt lately to dally so precariously on the borderline between conservatoire practice and a fully-fledged composer's flair and scope that he tends to upset our traditional concepts of what makes good art. In turning from his early twelve-tone training, Shapero was obviously motivated by Stravinsky's reinstatement of classical principles and especially by the great Symphony in C. But the disciple carried the implications of this reinstatement to a more literal point than the master. Like certain nineteenth-century composers, Shapero is acutely aware of the looming figure of Beethoven, in such works as the *Symphony for Classical Orchestra* and the two lengthy sets of piano variations.

His conformity is not unmixed with a strain of defiance. His is not the kind of conventional music that makes it easy for performers. He seems to be letting us know that he knows we think he ought to be writing in a more obviously contemporary idiom but that he feels he can derive new qualities out of what he is doing and that he has the right to attempt big works of the kind the traditional symphonists achieved. That he has developed some personal traits, though Beethoven and Stravinsky may have inspired them, becomes apparent when we recognize them as Shapero's own in the music of his disciple, Smit. Both Shapero and Smit have enormous musical facility, and it may be this that they mistake at times for creativity. Or they will set up as their aim some vast proportions dictated by late classical models and obviously have to force themselves in some instances to fill them. But Shapero has admirable control over tonal functions and structure, and in somewhat the same way that he came by this control through Stravinsky, Smit is striving to come by it through Shapero.

Fine seems to be attracted to Stravinsky for his lyricism and delicate sonority more than by matters of tonal function and structure. Virgil Thomson regards Fine as an American Sauguet. According to Thomson, Sauguet represents "neo-Romanticism" —the revival of the intimate romanticism that prevailed among composers like Schumann, before the advent of Wagnerian grandiosity. This trend Thomson characterizes as follows: "Spontaneity of sentiment is the thing sought. Internationalism is the general temper. Elegance is the real preoccupation." There is, I think, in this "internationalism" a strong French ingredient, and Fine, without specifically suggesting Sauguet or Poulenc, has a Gallic quality. His music falls very pleasantly on the ears, and has taste and polished detail. A few years ago it occurred to Fine that amiability was becoming too steady a diet with him and that some relief was in order. To this end he set himself the task of writing a twelve-tone string quartet (1952) which turned out to be an impresisve work, perhaps his best to date. Since that work he has been flirting with tone-rows, and it will be interesting to see what direction his future will take.[1] It was,

1 Fine died in 1962. [Ed.]

I think, Fine's espousal of the twelve-tone idea that prompted
Talma to adopt it. Her piano études employ the row effectively
as a vehicle for demonstrating a variety of keyboard touches.
She has an excellent grasp of piano style and this was a very
apt medium for her talents.

It was not, as far as I can judge, Stravinsky's recent concern
with tone-rows that motivated Fine and Talma. That they should
think of using twelve-tone devices at all is, of course, related
to the whole general rapprochement between the Stravinsky and
twelve-tone schools and the growing acceptance of twelve-tone
music. Certainly, works such as Copland's *Piano Quartet* of 1950,
which was a part of this broad trend, were factors in preparing
the ground for Fine to write a twelve-tone quartet. But the frag-
mentation, permutation and wide leaps that fascinate Stravinsky,
whose rows have often been diatonic or constituted, at least,
of less than twelve tones, are of a variety that seems to have
been suggested by Webern. These devices are not particularly
evident in the twelve-tone works of Fine and Talma, who have
absorbed the row-technique into their customary manner.

I doubt if the Stravinsky school would have flourished any the
less in America if he had not settled here. As Americans we still
feel closer to Copland, in a way, and look to Stravinsky for timeless principles. But Haieff, as I have already indicated, by virtue of his Russian origin, could attach himself to the master as
uninhibitedly as Stravinsky himself, when a youth, had attached
himself to Rimsky-Korsakoff. He has legitimately taken certain
Stravinskian devices and made them his own. The listener may
be aware of their origin, but he must also grant the transformation they have undergone. Haieff's youthfulness and non-
chalance are quite distinct from Stravinsky's peculiar tautness
and breathtaking dynamism. There is an element that may be
characterized as an almost Chaplinesque dry humor at times,
and this seems to point to "Les Six" more than to Stravinsky.
Haieff, it has been said by an unusually perceptive observer,
"delights in playful manipulation of his musical materials, and
has a special fondness for sudden interruptions of the musical
flow with abrupt silences or unexpected leaps or brief back-
trackings." Now it may occur to one that these words are ap-

plicable to Stravinsky, too. But no one would deny that Haieff has by nature been able to venture closer to the letter of the master than the rest of us. At the same time, those who know his music realize that the words are applicable to him in a rather special sense.

Haieff's orchestra is no mere coating for materials independently conceived, and in this he has clearly learned the lesson of his master well. Counterpoints and rhythmic figures seem to originate in the process of instrumentation. Instrumental lines return to one another just when they seem to be going precariously astray; and figures are strikingly divided between pairs in a single timbre. It may be this fascination with the orchestra that has stunted his growth in other spheres, so that looking forward to a new work of his we may predict it in a few too many ways.

Foss and Dahl (both born in Germany) reached the Stravinsky school through the devious channel of mid-European orientation. Foss started composing at seven and, discovering at fourteen the attractive qualities of the music of Hindemith (with whom he studied several years later), he turned out suprisingly convincing pastiches in this German composer's style in 1938, when he (Foss) was sixteen. They were promptly published by the influential house of G. Schirmer. I offer these details so that it may be known how much temptation there was for him to take an easy way out. He was accepted early as a composer (though he received his share of critical disapproval) and he might equally have made a distinguished career as pianist or conductor. (His steadfastness has been contrasted with Leonard Bernstein's pursuit after celebrity. Ten years ago Fine spoke of them as "twin prodigies, the fair-haired boys of the American scene.")

But Foss was willing to search. The painful task of freeing himself from Hindemith's autocratic domination was accomplished with breast-beating Americanism that was also to convince us of his passion for his adopted country. The gesture was well intended, but the attitude forced. When I was first aware of references to him as a member of the Stravinsky school I thought this was a case of dividing up the musical world into the two camps I spoke of above. (In such a broad division he could, of course, not be placed on the side of the adherents of

Bartók or Schoenberg.) But the discovery of Stravinsky's significance seems really to have been important for him; and the new influence has been absorbed into those that had already exerted themselves upon him. It is Stravinsky in his religious or lofty Hellenic attitude that appeals to Foss, and it suits him better than the attitude of American folklore. Perhaps we expect too much from Foss in view of his precocity. But he somehow tends to disappoint us, though he always displays the real composer's craft. It may be he is too cognizant of our expectation. For if he were less so he might not, in such a work as his *Parable of Death* (employing a Rilke text) have felt impelled to reach out prematurely for the nobility of a Bach Passion.

Stravinsky's influence, as I have said, was absorbed by the other influences in the music of Foss. But Dahl broke sharply with his past. A comparison of his Woodwind Quintet of 1942 with his *Concerto a Tre* of 1947 leaves no doubt that the change was beneficial for him. His undisciplined post-Romantic chromaticism and loose form gave way to finer textures and better organized wholes. I recommend his charming trio of 1947 (the *Concerto*) to listeners, but I must admit that too little of his music has been heard on the Eastern seaboard for me to have formed any substantial idea of his essential nature.

The order in which I have discussed the composers implies no value judgment of them. I have merely been working from the centre outwards according to the view I have, as a founding member, of their ties with the "school" as such. I have already mentioned Jones' aloofness, and this is only one aspect of his general detachment from the music world, his quiet pursuit of his own creative purpose. It is very difficult for me to connect his present manner with what I recall as having been a post-conservatoire manner in his music of the period around 1940, when we were both teaching at Mills College in California. The analyst who sets himself the task of determining the Stravinskian ingredient of Jones' more recent works may notice the spacious sonority, the cold and mordant textures of diatonic dissonance and a liking for the sonata formula. Copland has also left an impression on Jones. But it is not easy to account for the total effect, since Jones has neatly dove-tailed so many ele-

ments of his experience—among them, the free, independent
counterpoint of Milhaud that gives the music a certain general
obscurity even though its materials are often simple enough.
His devotion to his sincerest aims is to be admired, and it is both
a deplorable and perplexing condition that he receives so little
attention in America even in advanced musical circles.

It is typical of Jones that he never sounded a fanfare when
he entered the ranks of Stravinsky's adherents nor did he passionately declare it his salvation. Perhaps his own thoughts on
his music would help us arrive at a certain definition of its
nature. Or better, it would be nice if there were some dedicated
student of his scores who was willing to work on them to wrench
their secret from them.

Of Lessard and DesMarais, the young men with short composing careers, I think it best for me to say merely that they
bear watching since I am not aware of any mature profile of
their own in their music as yet. They enjoy the bliss of having
come by a belief in Stravinsky directly and pretty much without
a struggle at an early stage through Boulanger's influence. The
rest of us, however, though we may have been caught up first
in currents that no longer seem right for us, may find comfort
in a certain confidence that it was not arbitrarily or by accident
or without consciousness of other possibilities of choice that we
found our way.

I have placed almost a dozen American creative musicians in
a vulnerable spot, since a debt to the composer of the *Symphony
of Psalms, Persephone,* and the Symphony in C is regarded as
a transgression, and openly avowing it may be more shocking
still. But artistic evolution need not proceed according to the
same standards. After being confronted so long with composers
who violently denounced their predecessors and presented their
own calling card in every minuscule musical detail, critics have
been conditioned to expect the same procedure. They forget that
Mozart made no secret of how much he owed to Haydn, and that
Bach candidly reproduced various styles of his contemporaries.
The same critics who fail to penetrate the logic of an original

new idiom will bemoan the absence of this originality when an original set of relations, rather than a new idiom, is the means of conveying unique feeling or ideas. Criticism would be very easy indeed if this uniqueness were but a matter of idiom. As the English humanist, T. E. Hulme, long ago cautioned us, it is important to determine whether the artist has had a "grip" over himself to prevent him from "falling into the conventional curves of ingrained technique. . . ." This may involve an intimacy that may only be acquired with the expenditure of time and effort. But who is eager to take such trouble when there is involved the risk of not being able to predict whether a new work will be significant enough to warrant so much attention?

GUNTHER
SCHULLER was born in New York City in 1925. He studied theory and counterpoint at the Manhattan School of Music, but his proficiency on the French horn led to his joining the Cincinnati Symphony and later the orchestra of the Metropolitan Opera House, in both cases as first horn player. After 1959 he devoted himself to composing, conducting, writing, lecturing, and teaching. In 1960 he received the Brandeis University Creative Arts Award and the National Institute of Arts and Letters Award.

Schuller has been very active in the promotion of contemporary music and has taken a particular interest in modern jazz, manifested especially through his association with John Lewis and the Modern Jazz Quartet. Together with Lewis he founded the Society for Jazz and Classical Music. One of his main interests has been to bring together musicians from the fields of jazz and of classical music, in both composition and performance. To the type of music resulting from the combined efforts of these two groups he has given the name, "Third Stream Music." Typical of his own compositions along this line are the Concertino for Jazz Quartet and Orchestra (1959) and *Variants on a Theme of Thelonius Monk* (1960), for chamber ensemble.

Among Schuller's more important orchestral works are the Concerto for Cello and Orchestra (1945), Concerto for Horn and Orchestra (1943–44), Fantasia Concertante for Three Trombones and Orchestra (1947), *Seven Studies on a Theme of Paul*

Klee (1959), Symphony for Brass and Percussion (1949–50), and Concerto for Piano and Orchestra (1962). He has also written a quantity of chamber music and some vocal music.

During the 1962–63 season in New York, Schuller organized and conducted a series of concerts devoted to "Twentieth-Century Innovations." He also prepared a series of 150 radio programs for Station WBAI on "Contemporary Music in Evolution." He has written extensively on contemporary music, including jazz, and is the author of a book, *Horn Technique* (1962).

In 1965, Schuller succeeded Copland as professor of composition at the Berkshire Music Center in Tanglewood, Massachusetts.

The Future of Form in Jazz / (1956)

If there is one aspect of present-day modern jazz that differentiates it from the jazz of even five years ago, it is its preoccupation with new musical forms. Jazz today, with its greatly enriched language, seems to feel the need for organization at a more extended level. Few musicians seem to find complete satisfaction in the procedure so prevalent even a few years ago of wedging a group of generally unrelated "blowing" solos and several choruses of "fours" between an opening and closing theme.

At a time, therefore, when one hears and reads terms such as "extended form" and "free form" almost every day, and because there seems to be very little agreement as to what is meant by these expressions, it might be interesting to examine these new tendencies, to see where they may be leading modern jazz, and to investigate what role composition is beginning to play in a music whose greatest contribution has been a renaissance of the art of improvisation.

I suppose the question will be raised: why new or extended forms? Why not continue with the same conventions and forms we associate with the main tradition of jazz? Obviously an art form which is to remain a legitimate expression of its times must grow and develop. As jazz becomes more and more a music to be *listened* to, it will automatically reach out for more complex ideas, a wider range of expression. Obviously, too, more complex harmonies and techniques require more complex musical forms to support the increased load of this superstructure. The long-playing record, moreover, has emancipated jazz from its previous three-minute limitation, and the *forming* of tonal material on a larger scale has thus automatically become a main concern of the younger generation.

It would be dangerous, however, if the jazz musician were to be satisfied with complacently reaching over into the classical field and there borrowing forms upon which to *graft* his music. The well-known classical forms—such as sonata or fugue, for instance—arose out of and were directly related to specific existing conditions, musical as well as social: and their effectiveness in most cases has been greatly diminished to the extent that these conditions have changed.

For example, the sonata form, originally based upon the dominant-tonic relationship which governed diatonic music, obviously no longer applies to an atonal work. This has been amply proven by the discrepancy between musical material and form in many Schoenberg works, and by the progress made in this respect by Anton Webern and the young generation of composers following in his footsteps. It has become increasingly clear that "form" need not be a confining mold into which the tonal materials are poured, but rather that the forming process can be *directly* related to the musical material employed in a specific instance. In other words, form evolves *out* of the material itself and is not imposed upon it. We must learn to think of form as a verb rather than a noun.

Experience, moreover, has shown us that the borrowing of a baroque form such as the fugue—the most widely used non-jazz form at the moment—very rarely produces the happiest results. Even when successful, it is certainly not the ultimate solution to the problem of evolving new forms in jazz, mainly because jazz is a player's art, and the old classical and baroque forms are definitely related to the art of composing (Bach's ability to improvise complete fugues notwithstanding). Used in jazz these classic forms can, at best, produce only specific and limited results, but cannot open the way to a new musical order. Jazz, it seems to me, is strong and rich enough to find within its own domain forms much more indigenous to its own essential nature.

The idea of extending or enlarging musical form is not a new one in jazz. By the middle thirties Duke Ellington, the masterly precursor of so many innovations in common use today, had already made two attempts to break beyond the confines of the ten-inch disk with his *Creole Rhapsody* of 1931 and the twelve-minute *Reminiscing in Tempo*.

The latter work, written in 1935, took up four ten-inch sides, but the Columbia label blithely continued to call it a "fox-trot." Its length, its advanced harmonic changes, its unusual asymmetrically coupled fourteen- and ten-bar phrases aroused angry reactions and cries of "arty," "pretentious" and "not jazz." In retrospect we find that it is a poem of quiet melancholy, evoking that special nostalgia which so consistently distinguishes early Ellington from most of his contemporaries; and we see that it was a small, weak step forward to expand form in jazz. Ellington was simply trying to do two things: (1) to break away from the conventional phrase patterns based upon multiples of four measures (in *Creole Rhapsody* he had already experimented with a sixteen-bar phrase made up of a pattern of 5 plus 5 plus 4 plus 2); (2) to organize his musical material in a slightly more complex form, at the same time integrating solos within that form so that the entire work would produce a unified whole. The least ambitious but perhaps the most inspired of his large-scale works, *Reminiscing in Tempo*, opened up a new vista on the jazz horizon.

And yet Ellington—in those days always years ahead of his colleagues—was to wait a decade to see his early experiments emulated by other musicians. Perhaps the intense commercialism of the swing-era with its emphasis on polish (and too often slickness) led jazz temporarily in other directions; or maybe it was simply that jazz had reached a period of consolidation and gestation. Be that as it may, a new style began to crystallize in the early forties under the influence of Parker and Gillespie, a style which already embodied in an embryonic stage the considerable strides jazz has made in the last fifteen years.

It is impossible within the limits of this discussion to examine all the achievements that have led jazz to its present status. The genius of Charlie Parker, the important contributions made by the Miles Davis Capitol recordings, and the success of the Modern Jazz Quartet in popularizing a musical concept that combines classical organization with conventional jazz traditions—all these have already become a matter of history and require no further emphasis here.

More recently, serious contributions to the freeing of form have been made by an ever-increasing number of musicians. Among them (without attempting a complete listing) are: Teddy Charles (although he says most of what he and Hall Overton are doing is not jazz), Buddy Collette, Giuffre, Gryce, La Porta, John Lewis, Macero, Mingus, the Phil Nimmons group in Toronto, George Russell, the Sandole brothers, Tony Scott, and many others.

A closer look, however, at some outstanding representative examples may help to give a clearer idea of what solutions in the search for new forms have been found.

One of the most interesting uses of form has been developed by Charlie Mingus with what he calls "extended form." I think some of the confusion regarding this term arises from the fact that "extended form" can mean simply *that*—extending form in a general way—but also can mean a more specific idea as envisioned by Mingus. For him it means taking one part of a chord pattern, perhaps only one measure, and extending it indefinitely by repetition until the soloist or the "composer" feels that the development of the piece requires moving on to another idea. Actually, this procedure does not represent a new form as such, since it is simply a stretching or magnifying of a standard pattern. Its liberating possibilities, however, are considerable, as exemplified by Mingus' finest efforts in this direction, *Pithecanthropus Erectus* and *Love Chant* (Atlantic 12-inch LP 1237).

Jimmy Giuffre made a giant step forward with his *Tangents in Jazz*, the full implications of which may not be assimilated for years. Aside from his remarkable musical gift, his concern for clarity and logic, his economical means and direct approach indicate that Giuffre is already one of the most influential innovators in present-day jazz. Excellent examples of his concern for formal clarity, with actually extremely simple means, are his written pieces like *Side Pipers, Sheepherder* and the moving *Down Home* with its Ellingtonish mood of quiet intensity (Atlantic 12-inch LP 1238).

Down Home makes me think of another earlier masterpiece with the same combination of formal perfection and mature musical sensitivity, namely John Lewis' *Django* (Prestige).

What can be done in terms of integrating musical substance with form is also beautifully illustrated by recent recordings of André Hodeir in France. In two albums, not released as yet in this country, Hodeir not only incorporates some of the most recent compositional techniques of European twelve-tone writing, but also indicates through them ways in which original forms can be derived from the very core of a musical idea.

Suffice it to cite one especially felicitous example, *On a Blues*. Beneath an evenly sustained tenor solo of some length there appears, at first imperceptibly, a riff, which gradually increases dynamically and orchestrationally until it has over-powered and absorbed the improvised solo. The riff, moreover, is not simply repeated in its original form, but undergoes a gradual transformation, at first by means of changing registers, then by inversion, still later by increasingly complex harmonization, and finally through a kind of harmonic and rhythmic condensation of the original riff into a new shape. This building line of intensity, both dynamically and structurally, gives the piece a unique driving force and makes it swing beautifully.

Another remarkable instance of total musical organization (without sacrificing the essential vitality and spirit of jazz) is George Russell's *Lydian M-1* (Atlantic 12-inch LP 1229), a swinging piece that moves with relentless drive and "quiet fury," to quote Teddy Charles. In a way which is rare in jazz, the entire piece grows tonally and formalistically out of a nucleus of thematic material which in turn is based on a principle which the composer calls the "Lydian concept of tonal organization."

An eighth-note figure of considerable length dominates the opening, and from this as we shall see, emanates almost all that is to follow. This figure consists at first of a single repeated note divided into a 3/4 pattern (against an underlying 4/4 rhythm set up by the drums), then breaks out into an ascending arpeggio-like pattern which sounds all the notes of the modal scale that determines the tonality of the work. As the thematic line continues, it descends gradually via a series of asymmetrically grouped rhythmic patterns (constantly shifting combinations of 3/8's and 2/8's) to its original starting point, but now grouped on a 3/2 pattern. (The emphasis on ternary rhythms is obvious.) This pattern extended over sixteen measures provides a sort of running commentary to chordal aggregates in the "horns," again derived from the thematic material by combining vertically (harmonically) what had previously been stated horizontally (melodically). Four bars of the original repeated-note figure provide a bridge to a sort of second aspect of the main theme, this time characterized by a blue-note motive which, however, still relates back to the original underlying modal scale.

During the course of the composition, unity is achieved through reference to this reservoir of material: a 3/2 pattern by the rhythm section contrasts vividly with a trumpet solo in quarter-note triplets; or chordal accompaniments retain the modality of the opening by being derived through transposition almost entirely from the blue-note motive; a recurring chord progression that frames the three improvised solos is based on the modal scale; and so on.

Above all, the over-all form of the piece is a direct natural product of its own tonal material, giving the whole a feeling of rightness and completeness which marks the work of art.

Now this high degree of integration—which should appeal to anyone admiring order and logic—is considered by many jazz musicians to be too inhibiting. They claim it limits their "freedom of expression" and they consider such music outside the realm of jazz. There is violent disagreement on this point—not without reason. It is a difficult point, usually beclouded by subjectivism and the intrusion of the ego, and it needs to be discussed.

The assumption that restrictions upon intuitive creativity (such as improvisation) are inhibiting is, I think, not tenable, as is demonstrated by all successful art. A great masterpiece, for example, grows out of the interacting stimulus of the constant friction between freedom and constraint, between emotion and intellect.

Charlie Parker seems to have known this. But he also sensed that his work would have been stimulated to even greater heights by the freedom inherent in a context more complex. The chord patterns of his day began to bore him; he said he knew every way they could be played. Many of his solos were so loaded—even over-loaded—with musical complexities and razor-sharp subtleties that the implications of a more complex over-all structural level seem incontrovertible. That he did not live to realize the implications of his own style is one of the tragedies of recent music history.

In this connection, there is another point which needs to be aired. It is very much in vogue these days for jazz musicians to "put down" the classical or "legit" way of playing. They scorn the playing of written music (and therefore also composing) and exalt improvisation beyond all reasonable justification.

This is a delicate subject since it touches the very core of a musician's personality, and his reasons for being a musician. The subject thus always arouses a defensive and subjective reaction—on either side. I think, however, certain *objective* facts can be stated regarding this controversy which may help set things right.

Many jazz musicians claim that the classical musician's playing lacks spontaneity, that it has become dulled by repetition and by the very act of *re*producing music rather than by creating it. Only those musicians who have actually played in a first-rate symphony or opera orchestra under an inspired conductor can know to what height of collective spontaneity an orchestra can rise. After fifteen years of playing in such organizations, I can personally attest to this most positively. Admittedly it *is* rare, since it depends on many factors. But it does occur, and, I think, with more or less the same degee of frequency with which it occurs in jazz.

Listening to several sets on an average night by an average group at Birdland or at an all-night private session will bear this out. How often does a group *really* swing or *really* communicate at an artistic level? (After all, getting "knocked-out" by the beat of an average rhythm section is not yet communication at a very high level. I may respond to it—and I generally do—but that does not by itself make what I'm hearing great music.)

Moreover, is the batting average of a quartet playing "How High the Moon" for the umpteenth time any higher than a symphony orchestra doing its annual performance of the Beethoven "Eroica"? I humbly suggest that the average jazz musician is not in a position to answer that question since he has seldom, if ever, been to a symphony concert, and even more rarely has he caught one of those inspired performances. Furthermore, the Parkers, Gillespies, and Lester Youngs exist in the classical world too, only their names are Lipatti, Szigeti, and Gieseking, and *they are indeed just as rare.* Obviously, I do not mean musicians who can improvise like those first three, but soloists who are as highly trained and sensitive in their job of *spontaneously re-creating* a masterpiece as those jazz-greats are in creating.

The illusion of spontaneous re-creation is a factual possibility, as we all know from great acting performances in the theatre. At its highest level, it is an art as rare and as fine as improvisation at *its* highest level—no better, no worse; just different. If re-creating another man's music authentically and illuminatingly were all that easy, then every jazz trumpet player could play the trumpet part from *The Rite of Spring*. Obviously what needs to be reiterated is that both ways of playing are highly specialized and require a different combination of skills.

Improvisation is the heart of jazz and I, for one, will always be happy to wait for that 5 percent which constitutes inspired improvising, but is the average jazz musician prepared to look for that 5 percent in classical music?

As for the purists who feel that the pieces under discussion here—and all those works that seem to be gravitating toward classical or composed music—do not qualify as jazz, one can only say that a music as vital and far-reaching as jazz will develop and deepen in an ever-widening circle of alternating penetration and absorption, of giving and taking.

Actually it matters little what this music is called; the important thing is that it is created and that it represents the thoughts and ways of life of its times. Let the academicians worry about what to label it. Seen in this light, the future of this music—jazz or not—is an exciting one. And a fascinating one, because exactly what shape this future will take will not become entirely clear until the next Charlie Parker arrives on the scene.

JOHN

CAGE, born in Los Angeles, California, in 1912, has long been the most controversial musical figure in the United States. Since 1950 his reputation and influence have become worldwide. The publication in 1961 of his collected lectures and articles, under the significant title *Silence*, confirmed his position as one of the leading musical theorists and aesthetic thinkers of our times. An exponent of "chance" music, he has been deeply influenced by Far Eastern philosophy and aesthetics, most notably by Zen Bhuddism and by the Chinese *I Ching*, or Book of Changes.

Cage's teachers in composition were Arnold Schoenberg and the latter's American pupil, Adolph Weiss; but Cage soon abandoned all attempts to work within the twelve-tone method of composition. He profited much more from his contacts with Henry Cowell, whose lectures in comparative musicology stimulated his interest in non-Western musical systems and cultures. He also profited from Cowell's early technical innovations, particularly in the new sound effects that Cowell drew from the piano. Cage himself invented the "prepared piano," which is simply an ordinary grand piano whose strings have been muted by the insertion of miscellaneous small objects, such as nuts, bolts, screws, hairpins, bits of wood or metal, etc.

Around 1950, Cage decided to eliminate preconceived "ideas of order" in his music. To achieve this, he used chance operations in composing the *Music of Changes* for piano (1951), so that the structure of the work became *indeterminate*. Among other "chance" compositions of Cage are *Imaginary Landscape IV* for twelve radios, Music for Piano, and Concert for Piano and Orchestra (1957-58). His aim in all these works is the "composing of sounds within a universe predicated upon the sounds themselves rather than upon the mind which envisages their coming into being." He is concerned with "composition as process" rather than as the means of producing a specific object. In his own words, his later compositions "are not preconceived objects, and to approach them as objects is to utterly miss the point."

In the following essay, Cage explains why he accepts the term "experimental," and what it means for him.

Experimental Music / (1957)

Formerly, whenever anyone said the music I presented was experimental, I objected. It seemed to me that composers knew what they were doing, and that the experiments that had been made had taken place prior to the finished works, just as sketches are made before paintings, and rehearsals precede performances. But giving the matter further thought, I realized that there is ordinarily an essential difference between making a piece of music and hearing one. A composer knows his work as a woodsman knows a path he has traced and retraced, while a listener is confronted by the same work as one is in the woods by a plant he has never seen before.

Now, on the other hand, times have changed; music has changed; and I no longer object to the word experimental. I use it in fact to describe all the music that especially interests me and to which I am devoted, whether someone else wrote it or I myself did. What has happened is that I have become a listener, and the music has become something to hear. Many people, of course, have given up saying "experimental" about this new music. Instead, they move either to a halfway point and say "controversial," or depart to a greater distance and question whether this "music" is music at all.

For in this new music nothing takes place but sounds: those that are notated and those that are not. Those that are not notated appear in the written music as silences, opening the doors of the music to the sounds that happen to be in the environment. This openness exists in the fields of modern sculpture and architecture. The glass houses of Mies van der Rohe reflect their environment presenting to the eye images of clouds, trees, or grass, according to the situation. And while looking at the constructions in wire of the sculptor, Richard Lippold, it is inevitable that one will see other things, and people, too, if they happen to be there at the same time, through the network of wires. There is no such thing as an empty space or an empty time. There is always something to see, something to hear. In fact, try as we may to make a silence, we cannot. For certain engineering purposes, it is desirable to have as silent a situation as possible. Such a room is called an anechoic chamber, its six walls made of special material, a room without echoes. I entered one at Harvard University several years ago and heard two sounds, one high and one low. On describing them to the engineer in charge, he informed me that the high one was my nervous system in operation, the low one my blood in circulation. Until I die there will be sounds. And they will continue following my death. One need not fear about the future of music.

But this fearlessness only follows if, at the parting of the ways, where it is realized that sounds occur whether intended or not, one turns in the direction of those he does not intend.

This turning is psychological and seems at first to be a giving up of everything that belongs to humanity, for a musician, the giving up of music. This psychological turning leads to the world of nature, where, gradually or suddenly, one sees that humanity and nature, not separate, are in this world together, that nothing was lost when everything was given away. In fact, everything is gained. In musical terms, any sounds may occur in any combination and in any continuity.

And it is a striking coincidence that just now the technical means to produce such a free-ranging music are available. When the Allies entered Germany towards the end of World War II, it was discovered that improvements had been made in recording sounds magnetically such that tape had become suitable for the high fidelity recording of music. First in France, with the work of Pierre Schaeffer, later here, in Germany, in Italy, and in Japan, and, perhaps, without my knowing it, in other places, magnetic tape was used not simply to record performances of music, but to make a new music possible only because of it. Given a minimum of two tape recorders and a disc recorder, the following processes are possible: (1) a single recording of any sound may be made; (2) a rerecording may be made, in the course of which, by means of filters and circuits, any or all of the physical characteristics of a given recorded sound may be altered; (3) electronic mixing (combining on a third machine sounds issuing from two others) permits the presentation of any number of sounds in combination; (4) ordinary splicing permits the juxtaposition of any sounds, and when it includes unconventional cuts, it, like rerecording, brings about alterations of any or all of the original physical characteristics. The situation made available by these means is essentially a total sound-space, the limits of which are ear-determined only, the positions of a particular sound in this space being the result of five determinants: frequency or pitch, amplitude or loudness, overtone structure or timbre, duration, and morphology (how the sound begins, goes on and dies away). By the alteration of any one of these determinants, the position of the sound in sound-space changes. Any sound at any point in this total sound-space can move to become a sound at any other point. But advantage of these possibilities can only be taken if one is willing to change radically one's musical habits. That is, one may take advantage of the appearance of images without visible transition in distant places, which is a way of saying television, if one is willing to stay at home instead of going to a theater. Or one may fly if one is willing to give up walking.

Musical habits include scales, modes, theories of counterpoint and harmony, and the study of the timbres, singly and in combination of a limited number of sound-producing mechanisms. In mathematical terms these all concern discrete steps. They resemble walking, and, in the case of pitches, on steppingstones twelve in number. This cautious stepping is not characteristic of the magnetic tape possibilities which are revealing to us that musical action or existence can be at any point or along any line or curve or whatever or constellation in total sound-space, that we are, in fact, technically equipped to transform our contemporary awareness of nature's manner of operation into art.

Again there is a parting of the ways. One has a choice. If he does not wish to give up his attempts to control sound, he may complicate his musical technic towards an approximation of the new possibilities and awareness. (I use the word, approximation, because a measuring mind can never finally measure nature.) Or, as before, one may give up the desire to control sound, clear his mind of music, and set about discovering means to let sounds be themselves, rather than vehicles for man-made theories or expressions of human sentiments.

This project will seem fearsome to many, but on examination it gives no cause for alarm. Hearing sounds which are just sounds immediately sets the theorizing mind to theorizing, and the emotions of human beings are continually aroused by encounters with nature. Does not a mountain unintentionally evoke in us a sense of wonder? otters along a stream a sense of mirth? night in the woods a sense of fear? Do not rain falling and mists rising up suggest the love binding heaven and earth? Is not decaying flesh loathesome? Does not the death of someone we love bring sorrow? And is there a greater hero than the least plant that grows? What is more angry than the flash of lightning and the sound of thunder? These responses to nature are mine and will not necessarily correspond with another's. Emotion takes place in the person who has it. And sounds, when allowed to be themselves, do not require that those who hear them do so unfeelingly. The opposite is what is meant by response ability.

New music: new listening. Not an attempt to understand something that is being said, for, if something were being said, the sounds would be given the shapes of words. Just an attention to the activity of sounds.

Those involved with the composition of experimental music find ways and means to remove themselves from the activities of sounds they make. Some employ chance operations, derived from sources as ancient as the Chinese Book of Changes,[1] or as modern as the Tables of Random Numbers used also by physicists in research. Or, analogous to the Rorschach Tests of psychoanalysis, the interpretation of imperfections in the paper upon which one is writing may provide a music free from one's memory and imagination. Geometrical means employing spatial superimpositions at variance with the ultimate performance in time may be used. The total field of possibilities may be roughly divided and the actual sounds within these divisions indicated as to a number but left to the performer or to the splicer to choose. In this latter case, the composer resembles the maker of a camera who allows someone else to take the picture.

---

1 "In order to understand what such a book [the Chinese Book of Changes] is all about, it is imperative to cast off certain prejudices of the Western mind. It is a curious fact that such a gifted and intelligent people as the Chinese has never developed what we call science. Our science, however, is based upon the principle of causality, and causality is considered to be an axiomatic truth. But a great change in our standpoint is setting in. What Kant's *Critique of Pure Reason* failed to do, is being accomplished by modern physics. The axioms of causality are being shaken to their foundations: we know now that what we term natural laws are merely statistical truths and thus must necessarily allow for exceptions. We have not sufficiently taken into account as yet that we need the laboratory with its incisive restrictions in order to demonstrate the invariable validity of natural law. If we leave things to nature, we see a very different picture; every process is partially or totally interfered with by chance, so much so that under natural circumstances a course of events absolutely conforming to specific laws is almost an exception." This passage appears on Page ii of the foreword by C. G. Jung to the I Ching [Chinese Book of Changes], trans. by Richard Wilhelm into German, rendered into English by Cary F. Baynes (Bollingen Series XIX; New York: Pantheon Books, 1950).

Whether one uses tape or writes for conventional instruments, the present musical situation has changed from what it was before tape came into being. This also need not arouse alarm, for the coming into being of something new does not by that fact deprive what was of its proper place. Each thing has its own place, never takes the place of something else, and the more things there are, as is said, the merrier.

But several effects of tape on experimental music may be mentioned. Since so many inches of tape equal so many seconds of time, it has become more and more usual that notation is in space rather than in symbols of quarter, half, and sixteenth notes, and so on. Thus, where on a page a note is will correspond to when in a time it is to occur. A stopwatch is used to facilitate a performance; and a rhythm results which is a far cry from horse's hooves and other regular beats.

Also it has been impossible with the playing of several separate tapes at once to achieve perfect synchronization. This fact has led some towards the manufacture of multiple-tracked tapes and machines with a corresponding number of heads. While others, those who have accepted the sounds they do not intend, now realize that the score, the requiring that many parts be played in a particular togetherness, is not an accurate representation of how things are. These now compose parts but not scores, and the parts may be combined in any unthought ways. This means that each performance of such a piece of music is unique, as interesting to its composer as to others listening. It is easy to see again the parallel with nature, for even with leaves of the same tree, no two are exactly alike. The parallel with art is the sculpture with moving parts, the mobile.

It goes without saying that dissonances and noises are welcome in this new music. But so is the dominant seventh chord if it happens to put in an appearance.

Rehearsals have shown that this new music, whether for tape or instruments, is more clearly heard when the several loudspeakers or performers are separated in space rather than grouped closely together. For this music is not concerned with harmoniousness as generally understood, where the quality of harmony results from a blending of several elements. Here we are concerned with the coexistence of dissimilars and the central points where fusion occurs are many: the ears of the listeners wherever they are. This disharmony, to paraphrase Bergson's statement about disorder, is simply a harmony to which many are unaccustomed.

Where do we go from here? Towards theater. That art more than music resembles nature. We have eyes as well as ears and it is our business while we are alive to use them.

And what is the purpose of writing music? One is, of course, not dealing with purposes but dealing with sounds. Or the answer must take the form of paradox: a purposeful purposelessness or a purposeless play. This play, however, is an affirmation of life—not an attempt to bring order out of chaos nor to suggest improvements in creation, but simply a way of waking up to the very life we're living, which is so excellent once one gets one's mind and one's desires out of its way and lets it act of its own accord.

MILTON
BABBITT was born in Philadelphia in 1916, but was raised in Jackson, Mississippi, where he displayed an equal aptitude for mathematics and for music. When he matriculated at New York University in 1931, his major interests were mathematics and logic; but the discovery of the music of Schoenberg and Webern reawakened his interest in music, and he switched to that field for his academic major. He studied composition in New York with Marion Bauer and Philip James and at Princeton, where he undertook graduate studies, with Roger Sessions. He obtained his M.A. degree at Princeton in 1942, having served as instructor there from 1938. He remained on the faculty of Princeton University and in 1961 was appointed to be one of the four directors of the Columbia-Princeton Center for Electronic Music (the other directors were Sessions, Otto Luening, and Vladimir Ussachevsky).

Babbitt first became interested in electronic music about 1959. His *Composition for Synthesizer* (1961) was "the first extended musical composition produced entirely on the RCA Electronic Sound Synthesizer" at Columbia University. His *Vision and Prayer* (1961), with texts by Dylan Thomas, was written for soprano and synthesized accompaniment.

During the 1940's, Babbitt wrote a number of twelve-tone works, such as Three Compositions for Piano and the Composition for Four Instruments, which are believed to contain the earliest application of serial techniques to all the "parameters" of a musical composition (such as rhythm, timbre, dynamics, instrumentation, in addition to pitch).

Through his highly technical articles and lectures, which draw heavily upon his mathematical knowledge, Babbitt has made himself a leading theorist of the post-Webern movement in America. In the following article he writes in a lighter mood, but probes a vital problem for the contemporary composer: that of communicating with an audience.

Who Cares if You Listen? / (1958)

This article might have been entitled "The Composer as Specialist" or, alternatively, and perhaps less contentiously, "The Composer as Anachronism." For I am concerned with stating an attitude towards the indisputable facts of the status and condition of the composer of what we will, for the moment, designate as "serious," "advanced," contemporary music. This composer expends an enormous amount of time and energy—and, usually, considerable money—on the creation of a commodity which has little, no, or negative commodity value. He is, in essence, a "vanity" composer. The general public is largely unaware of and uninterested in his music. The majority of performers shun it and resent it. Consequently, the music is little performed, and then primarily at poorly attended concerts before an audience consisting in the main of fellow professionals. At best, the music would appear to be for, of, and by specialists.

Towards this condition of musical and societal "isolation" a variety of attitudes has been expressed, usually with the purpose of assigning blame, often to the music itself, occasionally to critics or performers, and very occasionally to the public. But to assign blame is to imply that this isolation is unnecessary and undesirable. It is my contention that, on the contrary, this condition is not only inevitable, but potentially advantageous for the composer and his music. From my point of view, the composer would do well to consider means of realizing, consolidating, and extending the advantage.

The unprecedented divergence between contemporary serious music and its listeners, on the one hand, and traditional music and its following on the other, is not accidental and—most probably—not transitory. Rather, it is a result of a half-century of revolution in musical thought, a revolution whose nature and consequences can be compared only with, and in many respects are closely analogous to, those of the mid-nineteenth-century revolution in mathematics and the twentieth-century revolution in theoretical physics. The immediate and profound effect has been the necessity for the informed musician to re-examine and probe the very foundations of his art. He has been obliged to recognize the possibility, and actuality, of alternatives to what were once regarded as musical absolutes. He lives no longer in a unitary musical universe of "common practice," but in a variety of universes of diverse practice.

This fall from musical innocence is, understandably, as disquieting to some as it is challenging to others, but in any event the process is irreversible; and the music that reflects the full impact of this revolution is, in many significant respects, a truly "new" music. Apart from the often highly sophisticated and complex constructive methods of any one composition, or group of compositions, the very minimal properties characterizing this body of music are the sources of its "difficulty," "unintelligibility" and—isolation. In indicating the most general of these properties, I shall make reference to no specific works, since I wish to avoid the independent issue of evaluation. The reader is at liberty to supply his own instances; if he cannot (and, granted the condition under discussion, this is a very real possibility), let him be assured that such music does exist.

First. This music employs a tonal vocabulary which is more "efficient" than that of the music of the past, or its derivatives. This is not necessarily a virtue in itself, but it does make possible a greatly increased number of pitch simultaneities, successions, and relationships. This increase in efficiency necessarily reduces the "redundancy" of the language, and as a result the intelligible communication of the work demands increased accuracy from the transmitter (the performer) and activity from the receiver (the listener). Incidentally, it is this circumstance, among others, that has created the need for purely electronic media of "performance." More importantly for us, it makes ever heavier demands upon the training of the listener's perceptual capacities.

Second. Along with this increase of meaningful pitch materials, the number of functions associated with each component of the musical event also has been multiplied. In the simplest possible terms, each such "atomic" event is located in a five-dimensional musical space determined by pitch-class, register, dynamics, duration, and timbre. These five components not only together define the single event, but, in the course of a work, the successive values of each component create an individually coherent structure, frequently in parallel with the corresponding structures created by each of the other components. Inability to perceive and remember precisely the values of any of these components results in a dislocation of the event in the work's musical space, an alteration of its relation to all other events in the work, and—thus—a falsification of the composition's total structure. For example, an incorrectly performed or perceived dynamic value results in destruction of the work's dynamic pattern, but also in false identification of other components of the event (of which this dynamic value is a part) with corresponding components of other events, so creating incorrect pitch, registral, timbral, and durational associations. It is this high degree of "determinacy" that most strikingly differentiates such music from, for example, a popular song. A popular song is only very partially determined, since it would appear to retain its germane characteristics under considerable alteration of register, rhythmic texture, dynamics, harmonic structure, timbre, and other qualities.

The preliminary differentiation of musical categories by means of this reasonable and usable criterion of "degree of determinacy" offends those who take it to be a definition of qualitative categories, which—of course— it need not always be. Curiously, their demurrers usually take the familiar form of some such "democratic" counterdefinition as: "There is no such thing as 'serious' and 'popular' music. There is only 'good' and 'bad' music." As a public service, let me offer those who still patiently await the revelation of the criteria of Absolute Good an alternative criterion which possesses, at least, the virtue of immediate and infallible applicability: "There is no such thing as 'serious' and 'popular' music. There is only music whose title begins with the letter 'X' and music whose title does not."

Third. Musical compositions of the kind under discussion possess a high degree of contextuality and autonomy. That is, the structural characteristics of a given work are less representative of a general class of characteristics than they are unique to the individual work itself. Particularly, principles of relatedness, upon which depends immediate coherence of continuity, are more likely to evolve in the course of the work than to be derived from generalized assumptions. Here again greater and new demands are made upon the perceptual and conceptual abilities of the listener.

Fourth, and finally. Although in many fundamental respects this music is "new," it often also represents a vast extension of the methods of the other musics, derived from a considered and extensive knowledge of their dynamic principles. For, concommitant with the "revolution in music," perhaps even an integral aspect thereof, has been the development of analytical theory, concerned with the systematic formulation of such principles to the end of greater efficiency, economy, and understanding. Compositions so rooted necessarily ask comparable knowledge and experience from the listener. Like all communication, this music presupposes a suitably equipped receptor. I am aware that "tradition" has it that the lay listener, by virtue of some undefined, transcendental faculty, always is able to arrive at a musical judgment absolute in its wisdom if not always permanent in its validity. I regret my inability to accord this declaration of faith the respect due its advanced age.

Deviation from this tradition is bound to dismiss the contemporary music of which I have been talking into "isolation." Nor do I see how or why the situation should be otherwise. Why should the layman be other than bored and puzzled by what he is unable to understand, music or anything else? It is only the translation of this boredom and puzzlement into resentment and denunciation that seems to me indefensible. After all, the public does have its own music, its ubiquitous music: music to eat by, to read by, to dance by, and to be impressed by. Why refuse to recognize the possibility that contemporary music has reached a stage long since attained by other forms of activity? The time has passed when the normally well-educated man without special preparation can understand the most advanced work in, for example, mathematics, philosophy, and physics. Advanced music, to the extent that it reflects the knowledge and originality of the informed composer, scarcely can be expected to appear more intelligible than these arts and sciences to the person whose musical education usually has been even less extensive than his background in other fields. But to this, a double standard is invoked, with the words "music is music," implying also that "music is *just* music." Why not, then, equate the activities of the radio repairman with those of the theoretical physicist, on the basis of the dictum that "physics is physics"? It is not difficult to find statements like the following from the New York *Times* of September 8, 1957: "The scientific level of the conference is so high . . . that there are in the world only 120 mathematicians specializing in the field who could contribute." Specialized music on the other hand, far from signifying "height" of musical level, has been charged with "decadence," even as evidence of an insidious "conspiracy."

It often has been remarked that only in politics and the "arts" does the layman regard himself as an expert, with the right to have his opinion heard. In the realm of politics, he knows that this right, in the form of a vote, is guaranteed by fiat. Com-

parably, in the realm of public music, the concertgoer is secure
in the knowledge that the amenities of concert-going protect his
firmly stated: "I didn't like it" from further scrutiny. Imagine,
if you can, a layman chancing upon a lecture on "Pointwise Periodic Homeomorphisms." At the conclusion, he announces: "I
didn't like it." Social conventions being what they are in such
circles, someone might dare inquire: "Why not?" Under duress,
our layman discloses precise reasons for his failure to enjoy himself; he found the hall chilly, the lecturer's voice unpleasant, and
he was suffering the digestive aftermath of a poor dinner. His
interlocutor understandably disqualifies these reasons as irrelevant to the content and value of the lecture, and the development
of mathematics is left undisturbed. If the concertgoer is at all
versed in the ways of musical lifemanship, he also will offer reasons for his "I didn't like it"—in the form of assertions that
the work in question is "inexpressive," "undramatic," "lacking
in poetry," etc., etc., tapping that store of vacuous equivalents
hallowed by time for: "I don't like it, and I cannot or will not
state why." The concertgoer's critical authority is established
beyond the possibility of further inquiry. Certainly he is not responsible for the circumstance that musical discourse is a never-
never land of semantic confusion, the last resting place of all
those verbal and formal fallacies, those hoary dualisms that have
been banished from rational discourse. Perhaps he has read,
in a widely consulted and respected book on the history of music,
the following: "to call him (Tchaikovsky) the 'modern Russian
Beethoven' is rootless, Beethoven being patently neither modern
nor Russian. . . ." Or, the following, by an eminent "non-ana-
lytic" philosopher: "The music of Lourié is an ontological music.
. . . It is born in the singular roots of being, the nearest possible
juncture of the soul and the spirit. . . ." How unexceptional the
verbal peccadilloes of the average concertgoer appear beside
these masterful models. Or, perhaps, in search of "real" authority, he has acquired his critical vocabulary from the pronouncements of officially "eminent" composers, whose eminence, in turn,
is founded largely upon just such assertions as the concertgoer
has learned to regurgitate. This cycle is of slight moment in a
world where circularity is one of the norms of criticism. Com-

posers (and performers), wittingly or unwittingly assuming the
character of "talented children" and "inspired idiots," generally
ascribed to them, are singularly adept at the conversion of personal tastes into general principles. Music they do not like is
"not music," composers whose music they do like are "not composers."

In search of what to think and how to say it, the layman may
turn to newspapers and magazines. Here he finds conclusive evidence for the proposition that "music is music." The science
editor of such publications contents himself with straightforward
reporting, usually news of the "factual" sciences; books and articles not intended for popular consumption are not reviewed.
Whatever the reason, such matters are left to professional journals. The music critic admits no comparable differentiation. He
may feel, with some justice, that music which presents itself
in the market place of the concert hall automatically offers itself
to public approval or disapproval. He may feel, again, with some
justice, that to omit the expected criticism of the "advanced"
work would be to do the composer an injustice in his assumed
quest for, if nothing else, public notice and "professional recognition." The critic, at least to this extent, is himself a victim of
the leveling of categories.

Here, then, are some of the factors determining the climate
of the public world of music. Perhaps we should not have overlooked those pockets of "power" where prizes, awards, and commissions are dispensed, where music is adjudged guilty, not only
without the right to be confronted by its accuser, but without
the right to be confronted by the accusations. Or those well-
meaning souls who exhort the public "just to *listen* to more contemporary music," apparently on the theory that familiarity
breeds passive acceptance. Of those, often the same well-meaning
souls, who remind the composer of his "obligation to the public," while the public's obligation to the composer is fulfilled,
manifestly, by mere physical presence in the concert hall or
before a loudspeaker or—more authoritatively—by committing
to memory the numbers of phonograph records and amplifier
models. Or the intricate social world within this musical world,

where the salon becomes bazaar, and music itself becomes an ingredient of verbal canapés for cocktail conversation.

I say all this not to present a picture of a virtuous music in a sinful world, but to point up the problems of a special music in an alien and inapposite world. And so, I dare suggest that the composer would do himself and his music an immediate and eventual service by total, resolute, and voluntary withdrawal from this public world to one of private performance and electronic media, with its very real possibility of complete elimination of the public and social aspects of musical composition. By so doing, the separation between the domains would be defined beyond any possibility of confusion of categories, and the composer would be free to pursue a private life of professional achievement, as opposed to a public life of unprofessional compromise and exhibitionism.

But how, it may be asked, will this serve to secure the means of survival for the composer and his music? One answer is that after all such a private life is what the university provides the scholar and the scientist. It is only proper that the university, which—significantly enough—his provided so many contemporary composers with their professonal training and general education, should provide a home for the "complex," "difficult, and "problematical" in music. Indeed, the process has begun; and if it appears to proceed too slowly, I take consolation in the knowledge that in this respect, too, music seems to be in historically retarded parallel with now sacrosanct fields of endeavor. In E. T. Bell's *Men of Mathematics*, we read: "In the eighteenth century the universities were not the principal centers of research in Europe. They might have become such sooner than they did but for the classical tradition and its understandable hostility to science. Mathematics was close enough to antiquity to be respectable, but physics, being more recent, was suspect. Further, a mathematician in a university of the time would have been expected to put much of his effort on elementary teaching; his research, if any, would have been an unprofitable luxury. . . ." A simple substitution of "musical composition" for "research," of "academic" for "classical," of "music" for "physics," and of "composer" for "mathematician," provides a strikingly accurate picture of the current situation. And as long as the confusion I have described continues to exist, how can the university and its community assume other than that the composer welcomes and courts public competition with the historically certified products of the past, and the commercially petrified products of the present?

Perhaps for the same reason, the various institutes of advanced research and the large majority of foundations have disregarded this music's need for means of survival. I do not wish to appear to obscure the obvious differences between musical composition and scholarly research, although it can be contended that these differences are no more fundamental than the differences among the various fields of study. I do question whether these differences, by their nature, justify the denial to music's development of assistance granted these other fields. Immediate "practical" applicability (which may be said to have its musical analogue in "immediate extensibility of a compositional technique") is certainly not a necessary condition for the support of scientific research. And if it be contended that such research is so supported because in the past it has yielded eventual applications, one can counter with, for example, the music of Anton Webern, which during the composer's lifetime was regarded (to the very limited extent that it was regarded at all) as the ultimate in hermetic, specialized, and idiosyncratic composition; today, some dozen years after the composer's death, his complete works have been recorded by a major record company, primarily —I suspect—as a result of the enormous influence this music has had on the postwar, nonpopular, musical world. I doubt that scientific research is any more secure against predictions of ultimate significance than is musical composition. Finally, if it be contended that research, even in its least "practical" phases, contributes to the sum of knowledge in the particular realm, what possibly can contribute more to our knowledge of music than a genuinely original composition?

Granting to music the position accorded other arts and sciences promises the sole substantial means of survival for the music I have been describing. Admittedly, if this music is not supported, the whistling repertory of the man in the street will be little affected, the concert-going activity of the conspicuous consumer of musical culture will be little disturbed. But music will cease to evolve, and in that important sense, will cease to live.

ELLIOTT

CARTER, born in New York City in 1908, studied composition at Harvard with Piston, Davison, Hill, and Holst, and in Paris with Nadia Boulanger. Labeled an "élite composer" by *Time* magazine (May 28, 1956), his approach to music is intellectual and reflects the exceptional scope and solidity of his cultural background. Early works, such as the First Symphony (1942), *A Holiday Overture* (1944), and the ballet scores for *Pocahontas* (1939) and *The Minotaur* (1947), gained the respect of the *cognoscenti*; but it was with compositions such as the Sonata for Piano and Cello (1948) and the First and Second String Quartets (1951 and 1959), that Carter achieved international stature as one of the most important composers of his generation.

His reputation was further strengthened by the Variations for Orchestra (1953-55), which present a new concept of the variation form, and by the Double Concerto for harpsichord and piano with two chamber orchestras (1961), based on the "confrontation of diversified action-patterns" in the musical texture. A fastidious and critical worker, he lavishes much time on each composition, seeking to combine new approaches and techniques with the traditional forms of Western music. He is not interested in repetition or imitation of what has already been done. As he once said, "I want to invent something I haven't heard before."

Although Carter has taught at various colleges and universities from time to time, his main occupation has always been writing music. Yet his writings *about* music, while secondary to his main creative interests, reveal the qualities of intellectual depth and analytical perception that characterize all his thought. The present essay was originally written at the request of the Editor for a special issue of the periodical *Buenos Aires Musical* dedicated to contemporary music of the United States; it appeared then in a Spanish translation, and this is its first publication in English.

A Further Step / (1958)

At present a new situation seems to be taking shape in the field of musical composition. Many young and a few older composers are being driven by what appears to be an imperious need to find a new principle of musical structure. Up to now, twentieth-century composers have explored new domains of harmony and their implications and have tried experiments with rhythm, timbre, and sonority; but for the most part they have employed these new materials in familiar contexts, and often produced expressive or formal effects similar to those found in older music. But today—as befits an art whose formative dimension is time—the techniques of continuity and contrast, of qualities and types of motion, of the formation and development of a musical idea or event, and in general the various kinds of cause and effect patterns that can be suggested in musical flow, occupy the attention of composers more than harmony or other matters all of which now become simply details in a larger kind of concern.

In this view, no item, no unifying principle or method of continuity is self-evident or considered a given part of musical process, but all are considered in the light of the whole and included or worked over so as to be able to fit the general scheme. Such a re-examination of musical discourse seems inevitable now, and a necessary culmination of all the different efforts of composers in our century. The intention is somewhat similar to the emancipation of musical discourse that took place during the time of Bach's sons and the Mannheim School, although today's is much more thoroughgoing. As in the products of that period, preceding the present transformation there were many suggestions of change in the previous time.

The first formulation of this recent direction was made by Debussy in his letters and articles, in which he made it plain that he was seeking a new and fresher musical psychology that did not use such classical devices as development and sequence. His ideas are, of course, wonderfully carried out in the later works, although within a limited frame. The influence of his point of view was widespread, leaving its effect on Stravinsky, particularly in the work dedicated to Debussy's memory, the Symphonies of Wind Instruments, and in the remarkable Symphony in Three Movements, a work that gives a first impression of being a loose construction of short condensed ideas but with familiarity reveals a tight organization of inner relationships that provides an entirely new solution for the problem of large-scale continuity.

In Vienna the influence of Debussy's ideas fell on fertile ground, as shown particularly in the works written there before the adoption of the twelve-tone method, such as Schoenberg's Five Orchestral Pieces and *Pierrot Lunaire*, Alban Berg's Four Pieces for Clarinet and Piano and Three Orchestral Pieces, and Webern's *Bagatelles*. These and other works of the time give a glimpse of a new universe of emancipated discourse, unfortunately quickly abandoned when Schoenberg returned to the classical musical shapes upon adopting the twelve-tone system.

Similar explorations can be found in some of the music of

Sibelius and Janáček, in the early works of Chávez and Lourié, and to a lesser extent in Charles Ives and Roy Harris, as well as in a number of scarcely remembered Americans and in some Russians from before the time of Stalin. This trend remained secondary, emerging only from time to time, as in Schoenberg's String Trio, Opus 45 (1946), a work that is significant for its combination of the twelve-tone method with the emancipated discourse of his earlier period. Even today, this development is not clearly discerned by critics, who confound it with stylistic trends that have at times come to grips with the problem as "serial technique," "pointillism," or "expressionism." Clearly, none of these is necessarily associated with the other, nor are they mutually exclusive since each comes from a different category of description.

While it is not the point of this article to maintain the very dubious notion that artistic quality appears only in the musically advanced works, still it must be pointed out that new directions and ideas in art exercise in our day an increasing influence, even on conservatives. One of the present problems among musicians is that of keeping abreast of the time, since the musical world like any other professional world of today is in a very rapid state of change. The purpose here is simply to try to establish a general description of the direction which many different trends seem to be taking today, to consider a few of the many reasons for this, and to speculate on the problems of artistic quality and intelligibility that these new departures seem to raise. One of the most interesting and perplexing of these problems is that of the extent to which our judgment of "musicality," or of the possibility of important communication that a work contains, depends on the carrying over of pre-established patterns, both of attitude and of method, from familiar works that unquestionably have these qualities.

When listening to the recent works of Stravinsky, such as *Agon* or the *Canticum Sacrum*, or Copland's new Piano Fantasy, there can be no doubt in the mind of the listener accustomed to new music that these works make the kind of impression that more immediately accessible music never can. They may now be perplexing to many of the musical public because of their unusual sound and unfamiliar ideas and procedures; but to those listeners for whom modernity holds no terrors, they are on the same high level as many works of the older concert repertory. Hence they will, sooner or later, unquestionably become accessible to the larger public. At first hearing, we are struck by their artistic power and unity of vision, all the more remarkable as having been achieved by integrating very conflicting currents of feeling, thought and technique, and by using this integration in a positive way to communicate a musical experience of commanding importance. Just as in the classics of the repertory, there are many levels of different pre-established techniques in these works. There is first of all the personal vision of the composer and his high standards of integration and of musical interest, which in turn are part of his sense of professional responsibility. There is the personal musical point of view that involves using a musical commentary on other styles as a feature of one's own expression. Then there are the many stylistic and formal features, small and large, that have become part of the composer's vocabulary over the years—a mixture of digested techniques drawn from other music, with predilections and inventions of his own. Lastly, in these particular works there is the use of twelve-tone technique (comparatively new in both composers), which Stravinsky and Copland have turned to their own uses. As in the case of the classics, a new work is made out of the materials of all these pre-established elements, each of them the result of slow, painstaking musical evolution.

A more trivial example may illustrate one kind of improvisation, at least, and its relation to pre-established techniques. Many of the older generation of French organists have developed an extraordinary ability to improvise on a given theme and occasionally give public demonstrations of their prowess, asking the public for the notes of a theme. At one of these sessions a particularly tortuous twelve-tone series was presented by a group of music students. With hardly a moment's hesitation the organist pulled out his stops and embarked on a half hour of variations, a *passacaglia* and fugue with many incidental canons; all quite audibly connected to the given theme, but all in the standard post-Franckian style with its romantic altered chords, its modulating sequences—and winding up, of course, with an apotheosis of the theme against a background of rapid arpeggiation. The power of this highly developed, scholastic, pre-established world of musical devices was so great that it could meet any musical problem with a ready-made solution of great intricacy and refinement. There was, of course, no pretense that this was great music; it was intended simply as a demonstration of skill—much the same kind of skill (but with an added element of genius) that Bach must have revealed to Frederick the Great. But in Bach's time, and especially in his later life, many more elements of general technique and of his own were "given" as part of his musical vocabulary. But fifty years ago such was not the case, and it was unlikely that an improviser could do more than astonish his listeners with a display of remarkable musical ingenuity based on a whole group of academic or commercial routines. In fact, one might almost say that improvisation itself, if it is to be interesting to the listener, must have a whole set of pat, standardized, prearranged techniques, even though devised by the performer. Thus in improvisation as we know it today, especially in much popular music, the weight of pre-established routine is often great enough to carry the music forward like a well-oiled machine without reacting to any communication from the outside.

These two examples of different uses of pre-established compositional methods—the recent works of Stravinsky and Copland which reveal a living and meaningful sensitivity to the mutual interaction of details and whole and to differences of qualities and styles based on a thorough reworking of the inherited musical language; and the improvisation of the French organist that ticks away like a complicated clock, insensitive to the human meaning of its minutes and hours—should serve to clarify the new direction away from pre-established techniques which this article is attempting to describe. This new direction may be labeled "emancipated musical discourse" after the "emancipation of dissonance" which Schoenberg coined for the new trends in harmony.

One cannot escape the feeling that this new direction is a reaction to the extraordinary increase of interest in the past and the remote, bringing to what was once a product of Romantic nostalgia (and still is, perhaps) modern scientific precision and modern techniques. The bewildering wealth of all history and of all cultures has suddenly been made easily available through phonograph recordings and publications, and our temperaments do not permit us to dismiss older styles as most of the composers of earlier periods would have done. On the contrary, as everyone knows, the interest in older music even of rather obscure and not too interesting composers is on the whole greater than in that of contemporaries—a situation that would have profoundly shocked any of the older composers whose music is now being exhumed.

This vast array of information, of methods and ideas, increases the composer's range of possibilities so enormously that one of his greatest problems now is to make choices, to decide what to discard and what to keep for his own use. Even the most erudite composers of the past did not have so much to learn and so much to choose from. Therefore it becomes imperative for a composer to limit his range so that he can concentrate his efforts. This need for choice explains why young composers have relied on one dominating figure after another—following Stravinsky and others in neoclassicism, or Schoenberg in expressionism. In this matter the twelve-tone system has been particularly helpful, since it allows considerable latitude while limiting the composer's choices and giving these choices a kind of hierarchy of relationships. Once you have chosen the twelve-tone row, you have chosen a method of harmony and a collection of motives that are all interrelated. This is an enormous advantage, for it helps to put the composer in that situation of focused freedom that finds its counterpart in all species of musical training, from learning to play an instrument to writing an opera.

The resurrection of this vast world of forgotten music and the bringing into the living room of music from all parts of the world as it sounds is such a recent development that it is still intellectually and artistically undigested—quite unlike the situation in literature and the fine arts where the opening up of the horizons of the past and of the remote took place some time ago and several generations of critics and historians have had time to discover stimulating facts and to elaborate valuable ideas.

Musicology has hardly passed the cataloguing stage, and so far has provided very little intellectual or aesthetic stimulus. However, the activity of musicology which has, in America and elsewhere, raised music to a university discipline brings with it scientific attitudes—among them the analogy of the composer to a scientist in a laboratory who works for years on some piece of obscure research which will be brought to light only when popularized by a professional popularizer, or when some imaginative scientist uses his data as part of a comprehensive theory of large application. Whether this attitude is healthy, when applied to the public art of music, remains to be proved. Likewise the amassing of vast amounts of information about all branches of this art tends also to draw it away from the general public, since there is so much to know that the public simply becomes discouraged.

For the composer, in spite of all, does write for a public. One might very well wonder *what* public, if it were not for the fact that the public is constantly changing, and one of the forces exerted upon it is that of the very works of music themselves. For now we can see that strong, commanding works of art, no matter how strange they seem on their first appearance, sooner or later reach the public. Their intrinsic quality acts as a centripetal force that first educates the musical profession and finally the public to understand. In the context of this article, the question to be asked at this point is whether the familiar, delayed public acceptance that has greeted so many contemporary works will not be delayed forever if works in the new advanced style eliminate too many of the pre-established techniques in their efforts to obtain complete consistency and very close coordination of all their elements. The effort of striking out along the new path, which was described at the beginning of this article, could result in complete hermeticism. How far along this road toward hermeticism one can go is perplexing to us today when we see the poems of Mallarmé and Valéry in our children's high-school French book.

It is not an easy or a comfortable thing for a musician trained in the traditional techniques to break away from them—particularly from those discussed here which are so fundamental. One might suppose that a person without traditional training might be able to approach the problem more freshly. Yet in spite of the fact that musical training is still not at all adapted to deal even with the most familiar modern techniques, experience so far has shown that the results of practically all untrained musicians are either so chaotic or so pedestrian as to be without interest. Usually such people, like many listeners with little musical experience, are overwhelmed by the sheerly physical qualities of sound and can do little more than make a display of surprising sound effects like a display of fireworks, which pay slight attention to organization, since this seems meaningless to them. A knowledge and feeling for the high standards of coherence and meaning which the musical tradition has brought to great subtlety is probably much more important than many musicians of advanced tendencies have thought. What is needed is a restudying of existing music and the elaboration of a more significant kind of music theory that is more widely applicable. This inevitably goes with the point of view discussed here and is found reflected likewise in many places. The musicians of the United States have produced a number of important books, articles, and teachings in this field, which are revolutionizing the thinking of the present student generation of composers.

In Europe, the search for emancipated musical discourse has been much more closely associated with the twelve-tone system than in the United States. There it has taken its departure from Webern's pointillist works and has applied serial methods to other dimensions besides that of pitch. As a method of discovering new possibilities of momentary and unexpected sound effects, this exercise is useful. At its best it resembles the turning of a musical kaleidoscope that shuffles at random fragments of sound which may or may not fall into interesting patterns—the burden of reading meaning and of finding interest in these rests with the listener and not the composer. The real problem of such music-puzzles is illustrated simply by the verbal palindrome ("able was I ere I saw Elba") which has to obey both a strict patterning of letters and has to make sense into the bargain. A palindrome of random letters is a bit pointless, in itself. Although musical meaning is not quite so easy to establish, still up to the end of

Webern's life this double standard of order and of meaning applied to all such types of musical ingenuity, with the exception perhaps of certain medieval and early Renaissance works. But the recent European school seems to have become occupied with pattern alone, hoping somehow that interest and meaning would emerge. Even on their own admission, this has not always been the case. This ordering according to the random application of number systems seems wasteful because it produces so many useless possibilities, like the monkeys at typewriters.

In the United States, the tendency has been to start with a co-ordinating principle having to do with techniques of listening or to begin with our experience of time and not some arbitrary numerological formula. Examples of emancipated discourse in America are beginning to be more numerous. Some of the abstract works of Copland and especially the recent works of Roger Sessions, such as his Third Symphony, and those of the writer of this article, strive for this principle using any system or musical procedure that seems suitable. Others, like Milton Babbitt, use the twelve-tone system emphasizing its co-ordinative possibilities rather than its disintegrative ones as the Europeans do. Certainly audible musical order that can be distinguished, remembered, and followed is a necessary condition for this new adventure.

WILLIAM
FLANAGAN who was born in Detroit, Michigan, on August 14, 1926, concentratèd on the study of journalism during the two years that he attended the University of Detroit. His main interest then veered toward musical composition, and he went to the Eastman School of Music in Rochester, New York, where his principal teacher was Bernard Rogers. Later he studied with Arthur Berger, David Diamond, and Aaron Copland. He served as music critic for the New York *Herald-Tribune* from 1957 to 1960 and has written many articles and reviews for such publications as *Partisan Review, The Musical Quarterly, Tempo,* and *Musical America.*

Although he has written some orchestral works (*A Concert Ode,* 1951; *Notations for Large Orchestra,* 1960) and some chamber music (*Chaconne* for violin and piano, *Divertimento* for string quartet), as well as a Sonata for Piano (1950), Flanagan is particularly concerned with vocal music, ranging from the solo song to opera. He has written two song cycles: *The Weeping Pleiades* (poems by A. E. Housman) and *Time's Long Ago* (poems by Herman Melville); a dramatic cantata, *The Lady of Tearful Regret,* after a text by Edward Albee; *Chapter from Ecclesiastes* (1963) for mixed chorus and string quartet; and an opera, *Bartleby* (1960), based on the story by Melville. He has also composed incidental music for three plays by Albee: *The Death of Bessie Smith, The Sandbox,* and *The Ballad of the Sad Cafe* (adapted from the novel by Carson McCullers). In 1963

he was commissioned by Julius Rudel and the New York City
Opera Company to compose an opera with a libretto by Albee,
tentatively titled *The Ice Age* (this commission was made possible by a grant from the Ford Foundation).

The following essay was written, at the request of the Editor,
for a special edition of *Buenos Aires Musical* devoted to music
in the United States; the original English version appears for
the first time here.

The Younger Generation / (1958)

Any discussion of the activities, interests, and potentialities of
the younger generation of composers in the United States is
straight off complicated by our general confusion over what the
word "young" means in this context. Composers hereabouts are
mostly thought to be young until they approach the age of forty.
Howard Taubman, music editor of the New York *Times*, established twenty through thirty-five as the "young" age group in
a series of useful articles he published in that newspaper during
the summer of 1957. But while he conceded that there was some
blurring around the upper number, the project worked out curiously: composers of forty—perhaps even older, in some cases—
appeared on the list of talented "young" composers that was
featured with the final article of the series. At the same time,
many of the "established," "older" composers called upon to suggest names for the list were, for a fact, younger and, in some

cases, less "established" than a few of the composers they named. Similarly, we have in the United States composers like Harold Shapero and Lukas Foss, both of whom are between thirty-five and forty, who have been prominent figures on the local scene for ten years or better and are, as such, rarely thought of in connection with the younger generation. On the other hand, many composers of this age—or very little under it—seem, by virtue of their status and musical outlook, to fit perfectly into the "younger" category.

The conclusion is apparent enough; chronological age is, in the composing field, an unreliable determinant. For the purposes of the forthcoming, then, I shall confine myself to that generation of composers whose training or earliest emergence took place during the years following World War II. As a group, as a generation of manners, they are easy to spot regardless of chronological age because, as one of their number, I can testify to their strange sense of isolation, evident state of uncertainty, patent lack of unity and common cause. Their ages are roughly between twenty-five and thirty-five; I shall sidestep discussion of those younger because virtually none of them has had sufficient recognition in the form of either publication or performance for even minimal acquaintance with their work. The day when a man like Serge Koussevitzky fostered the reputation of United States composers in their early or middle twenties is, for the moment, at least, past.

While I can think of no one—save, perhaps, the composer William Schuman—who has more than *hinted* it, it is widely held that the United States has failed to produce a new generation of composers to rival the vitality, originality—raw talent, if you will—that was so characteristic of men like Roy Harris and Aaron Copland during the twenties, or David Diamond and William Schuman during the thirties. Of the present younger generation, only Peter Mennin and Leon Kirchner have produced music that is accepted and performed on the highest professional level and, at the same time, is respected by the profession at large. Ned Rorem and Carlisle Floyd both stand on the border of genuine recognition, but the music is in each case widely considered to be devoid of intellectual interest. There are perhaps a few more exceptions that could be considered, but the recognition average is extraordinarily low in comparison to previous generations of composers in this country. The remainder of us is either totally obscure or has gained the sort of intramural acceptance that is local in range and comes from smaller performances by contemporary music societies or, perhaps, a listing in the long-playing catalogue.

Our primary difficulty—whether it be the result of the music we write, lack of the sort of talent that makes a "name composer," our fantastically increasing numbers, or a reactionary policy on the part of conductors and orchestra management—rests with our failure to achieve consistent performance with the major symphony orchestras. None of this country's older, established generation (save a couple who have gained fame through opera *not* produced by the Metropolitan Opera Company) has achieved status without this level of performance. But opera is the growing rage in the United States—even contemporary opera; some young composers have turned to its composition with a kind of desperate gusto, and it is in this field that the new generation has made its strongest stand for recognition in the last five years or so. The medium, however, is not one to attract young composers working in advanced styles.

A composite picture of what the younger men are up to in this country is all but impossible. As a music critic, located in New York City, I hear as much new music as anyone. But Taubman's list of composers alarmed us all with the suggestion that on the West Coast and the country wide there are young composers of first-class ability whom we in the East had not so much as heard of. It would require, then, one's full time and a generous expense account to keep pace with even a portion of them. Still, it seems unlikely that compositional trends are substantially more or less astonishing anywhere than those to be found in the major centers of the East. These are the Juilliard School of Music, Columbia University and the New York area in general; Harvard University, nearby Brandeis University and the Boston area in general; the Eastman School of Music in Rochester, New York; and Princeton University, eastern headquarters of advanced atonal and twelve-tone composition.

Before approaching the numerous, confusing, often conflicting stylistic biases of our young, something of their psychology should be provided for a background. This current generation is, for one thing, in a unique position for any group of American composers: it has—reject or no—a relatively brief but very real tradition to account to. The United States composers who rose during the twenties and thirties were, in the improved sense that we look upon our musical creators today, our first "real" composers. The men who preceded them—like MacDowell, Griffes, Henry Hadley—were not considered to be important cultural entities and their work, apart from the exceptions that proved the rule, was almost entirely a contentedly resigned reflection of exact Germano-European tradition. The twenties brought an end to this: Roger Sessions, Aaron Copland, Walter Piston, Roy Harris, Virgil Thomson, and the rest came to take their place in what was to become our first school of American "master" composers, a school that has provided a "usable past" for the composers that have since come. But the generation of the thirties emerged so rapidly and coexistently as to grow up almost along side of the older men rather than behind them. It was instead the generation that came into being after World War II that was the first to face the responsibility of the usable tradition that the older composers had fostered. Piston's influence as a teacher has been more notable than his influence as a composer. Virgil Thomson, on the other hand, is quite a different case: his stylistic manners are so special that any composer, young or old, would be foolish to allow anything more than the aesthetic of simplicity that lies behind them to touch his music. Sessions' musical influence has increased in recent years with the postwar vogue for atonality. But Copland and Harris are separate matters, and thereby hangs a tale that must be told if we are to see young composers in the United States with accurate perspective. For it was the nationalistic aesthetic of both Copland and Harris, along with that of the belatedly discovered Charles Ives, that became so hearty an influence among composers of this country in the thirties and early forties. And the strange fact is that even so brief an era of endeavor has been all but totally abnegated by the new composers.

Copland, as far back as the twenties, had worked to fuse jazz materials into the harmonic and formal syntax of concert music. Like George Gershwin, he failed: Gershwin, because he was unable to concentrate jazz elements into a significant formal cast; Copland because he utilized jazz after the example of the Paris composers—like Stravinsky and Milhaud—and thereby produced a music more French than American. While Virgil Thomson had, for a surprising fact, begun to explore regional folk materials even before Copland, it was the latter who carried the research to its fullest fruition through the smooth assimilation of Latin American rhythms, New England Protestant hymnody, and cowboy folklore into concert music of first-rate distinction.

But Copland and Thomson were not the only nationalistically inclined composers of the era and *they,* moreover, were thought by many to be somewhat corrupted by the sophistications of their French training. To many, Roy Harris, the "composer from the West," was the first assertion of a purely "American" national genius. Harris, far from being sophisticated, had never quite been tamed by formal training and was, for that matter, a primitive of sorts. He remains, nonetheless, one of the most extraordinarily original talents the United States has ever produced. His music was at one time played more, attacked and condemned more, and praised more than any other native composer's. After the last war, however, his vogue diminished as he rather haughtily cultivated a self-conscious set of neo-Baroque mannerisms and even set about to systematize his highly personal approach to harmony for the purposes of teaching his students how—I *suppose* it amounts to this—to sound like Roy Harris.

Copland and Harris are, in all probablity, the United States composers whose work has been most drawn on by the young. As a very young undergraduate student at the Eastman School of Music in the middle forties, I recall the vitality of the Harris influence on composers like Peter Mennin and virtually every young composer in the school. And one has only to mention names like Leonard Bernstein and Lukas Foss to emphasize the power of Copland's music during the middle forties. But from all available evidence, the younger generation of 1958 has turned its eyes uneasily away from these sources to experimental and quasi-experimental techniques born on the European continent.

The first trend away from the composers discussed above, and others of their persuasion, dates back to the early and middle forties when Stravinsky's neoclassicism took its steely hold on composers like Arthur Berger, Irving Fine, Harold Shapero and Alexei Haieff. Men younger than even these composers were at the time—like Lukas Foss and Leo Smit, both of whom had been Coplandites—began to work, not in an internationalist neo-classic style, but after Stravinsky's example of "reevaluating tradition,"[1] and with quite precise reference to his musical language. The "spiritual home" of the Stravinskyites, then and now, is Harvard University and its immediate geographical environment. Brandeis University, a relatively new educational establishment, is in the neighborhood and has a stunning musical faculty manned by Berger, Fine, Shapero. Harvard University's star composer-teacher is Walter Piston, a "first generation" figure whose stern, international neoclassicism—in recent years somewhat "humanized"—supports the younger group of Stravinskyites with something like parental sympathy.[2] Men of the present writer's generation to be found in the area such as Daniel Pinkham, Douglas Allanbrook, Paul DesMarais—are all contingent to one degree or another to the Stravinskian school.

Harvard's opposite number is Princeton University, where Roger Sessions, an atonalish, twelve-tone-toward, "first generation" composer of splendid integrity and enormous stature, oversees a younger group of composers, some of whom, in the wave of its postwar revival, have embraced the most advanced dodecaphony with virtually religious fervor. Milton Babbitt, a youngish and brilliant teacher-practitioner of the twelve-tone method, is a rising influence among our new composers who bend in this direction—not only at Princeton, but in New York and elsewhere. He was the rage of the Berkshire Music Center this past summer where his lectures dazzled even those intelligent mu-

1 Neoclassicism, as such, seems to me to be a frame of mind, an attitude, and not necessarily a "style" like Stravinsky's. I shall then, use the word "Stravinskianism" or "Stravinskyite" in direct allusion to this *particular* brand of neoclassicism.
2 Piston retired in 1960. [Ed.]

sicians who were unable to penetrate or, basically, *understand* their unduly complicated technical syntax.

These two styles, European in discovery and international in practice, are the ones that young composers in the United States think and talk about most—both for and against. As of the present, Stravinskianism is on the wane as a pure, neoclassic style; the assimilation of neoclassic practice and Schoenbergian serial techniques, once considered irreconcilable, is the latest trend among the Stravinskyites, after the example, I imagine, of the master himself. Even a composer like Copland, most of whose concert pieces have been severely diatonic and tonal, produced a Piano Fantasy in 1957 that was involved with the tonal application of dodecaphonic principles. It is perhaps significant that, for all the present handshaking and mutual admiration between the two camps, there has been no consolidating trend in reverse.

Perhaps, in attempting to indicate the *primary* influence on the young, I have applied too heavy a hand. While these are dominant, some young composers are susceptible to—or, if they should choose to be, are at least within easy reach of—other advanced techniques. We have, for one, our own version of France's *Musique Concrète* and its chief exponents—neither of whom is young—are Otto Leuning and Vladimir Ussachevsky, both of Columbia University. Their experiments with tape recording never fail to attract the attention of young composers and they have inevitably caused much talk. The experiment has no real followers, however; one wonders nonetheless if this would be the case if the necessary electronic equipment were less expensive.

The experimentalist John Cage, now forty-six, persists on the scene in New York, and a large audience of his followers recently gathered in the city's Town Hall to witness an entire evening dedicated to his works. His earlier experiments only affected sound, as such: the "prepared" piano, an investigation which involved putting nuts, bolts, and other hardware on the strings of the instruments, gave us unusual instrumental alterations to think about, but Cage composed nothing more than pandiatonic, quasi-oriental ditties for them. He once "composed" a piece for normal piano which contained no materials but time-measured silence and, I assume, he offered it to the public in perfect seriousness. He has also composed a piece where the conductor cues "musicians" who have at their disposal only ordinary radios carrying only ordinary broadcasting sounds. Add to the list pieces where a pianist, for example, may play any chord or combination of notes he pleases at a given and indicated place in the score.

But, no matter how peculiar and, perhaps, foolish these pieces may seem in description, an intelligent principle lies behind them. It is one of *depersonalizing* sound, freeing it from its historical commitment to logical arrangement, formal design, and personal expressivity that the usual composer imposes upon it. Cage is, in the last analysis, questioning the classic definition of music, which he has every right to do. His only well-known follower who is of my generation is Morton Feldman, a young composer with ideas that result in music often more fantastic than Cage's own.

One could continue somewhat further with a description of the experimental materials that are available for a young composer in this country. Henry Brant, at forty-five, chooses to write experimental pieces where conventional instruments are placed in unusual locations about the concert hall to test acoustical effects. Like Cage's early work with the prepared piano, the music Brant writes for these experiments is at its core as conventional as it can be and, as such, fails to sustain the geographical fantasy of the experiment. On the other hand, a new movement in serious jazz, which brings to mind the names of young men like Jimmy Giuffre, Teo Macero, and Gunther Schuller, is a considerably more promising trend for composers to observe with interest.

All of these forces—ebbing Stravinskianism, advanced dodecaphony, mutual assimilation of the two, and the less impacting directions I have noted—are the musical styles that have been confusing (perhaps), fascinating (certainly) and troubling the youngest generation of composers in the United States. I use the word "troubling" advisedly. For anything that I may say to suggest the contrary, I am no musical reactionary. But every available indication points to the fact that our newest generation is writing, and will continue to write, the most esoteric music that can be found anywhere in the world today, outside, perhaps, that of the Leibowitz and Boulez followers in France. Quite apart from music itself, this situation poses human problems. For this is not the Left Bank of Paris, but the industrial civilization of the United States. This direction may very well prove to be a deadening cul-de-sac that will produce a generation of Ivory Tower misanthropes. Even the most daring, audience-be-damned composer in the United States has at least a subconscious propensity for professional recognition. And the bright, young men of my generation, while fully aware of the fact that a composer's life in our environment is an unrewarding one, have the living evidence—in men like Barber, Copland, Thomson, Blitzstein—that there indeed is such a thing as an honored, recognized, even successful composer in the United States. It is difficult to believe that their headlong plunge away from at least a competitive pursuit of these satisfactions can lead to anything but fearful frustration for any but the most objectively self-appraising and level headed of their number.

If I seem to draw too severe a picture of young American composers, let me hasten to add that there are, as my readers might well have guessed, exceptions to the trend. I have been severe only because I wish to emphasize the fact that what I have previously described in this article seems to me to be the most general characteristic of our time. Our young esoterics, what is more, are the composers most discussed among composing and noncomposing intellectuals. But let me hasten to add that our generation is not without its pure neoclassicists, post-nationalists and neo-Romantics. We have, naturally, some composers who have *not* rejected the background of music composed by Thomson, Harris, Copland, Blitzstein, William Schuman and, now, Walter Piston. Leonard Bernstein, whose recent fortieth birthday and international celebrity clearly separates him from the "young," is much in debt to both Copland and Blitzstein for the successful works he has composed for the concert hall, ballet, and in the field of our rapidly advancing commercial lyric theater. A recent Broadway musical by Bernstein, *West Side Story*, for all its financial success, is a stage piece that has advanced to a point where it simply cannot be separated from the field of "serious" music. And Ned Rorem, Jack Beeson, Peter Mennin, William Bergsma, Hall Overton, Ezra Laderman, Lester Trimble, and Lawrence Rosenthal are all gifted and intelligent composers who, to one degree or another, accept the last three generations of American music as at least a partial point of departure. Copland, for example, has had a strong influence on my own work. In my student days, every piece I wrote manifestly bore the mark of his style. This is generally regarded to be less the case now, and I have found that I, at least, can move my own way with the recent past of American music as a point of departure. Not in terms of nationalistic folklore, perhaps, but through a frame of reference engendered by the very special tone and mood that I associate with our musical tradition of the thirties and forties.

Although I am constantly surprised by how little it is noted, there are a number of young composers—composers who are moving more quickly toward public status than those of any other group—whose ties are loosely attached to Mount Kisco, New York, place of the country home of Samuel Barber and Gian-Carlo Menotti. While Menotti has long taught composition at the Curtis Institute in Philadelphia, it is only recently that a clearly defined group of young composers—all of whom are more or less interested in opera—has become known. They include young men like Lee Hoiby, Marc Bucci, Stanley Hollingsworth, and Charles Turner. As a group, they are characterized by a certain detachment from the usual circles that composers move and are heard in. (This was also true of Barber and Menotti as young composers.) And their work, as such, is uncommitted to any twentieth-century musical cause save the *fact* of Barber and Menotti, who, in turn, for the most part show little allegiance to twentieth-century music but, instead, to eclectic post-Romanticism.

Still, Turner has two or three orchestral pieces that have been performed by a number of leading symphony orchestras with success; and the other composers have enjoyed first-class, professional mountings of their operatic works. All, except Turner, who is a bit older, are between thirty and thirty-five. They are exceptions among others of their generation in that the opportunities I have described have been granted to no more than a handful of young composers. One wonders, as a result, if it is not by such music that our generation will show its face to the world at large—untypical as it may be.

If, as a spokesman for the younger generation of composers in the United States, I have drawn a picture of chaos, I can only suggest that I have done so because chaotic seems to be its state. But it is not chaos born of strife or, for that matter, terribly strong conviction. When rival neoclassic and dodecaphonic schools found that they had common cause, all semblance of healthy animosity disappeared. No one says anymore that twelve-tone music defies the auditory and imaginative possibilities of the ear and the mind; and no one shouts that Stravinsky is an intellectual copycat, beating the dead horse of tradition.

But for all the chaos, theorizing, pretentiousness and mumbo-jumbo—daring, as it were, the world to so much as *try* to understand its work—our new generation is venturesome and even defiant in its refusal to cotton to the sociological and critical pressure that would wish it otherwise. Its future—even its prevailing disposition—is a disquieting question mark. Another decade may clear the air, give us some clarification as to what—if anything—we have contributed.

ROGER

SESSIONS, who was born in Brooklyn, New York on December 28, 1896, occupies a unique place in American music—the intellectual mentor of what might be called the "academic wing" of the advanced movement in contemporary composition. He matriculated at Harvard at the age of fourteen and after graduating went on to study composition with Horatio Parker at Yale. But the teacher who exercised the deepest influence on him was Ernest Bloch, whom he accompanied to Cleveland in 1921. Two years later, Sessions composed his first important work, the incidental music for a performance of Andreyev's play *The Black Maskers*, given at Smith College, Northampton, Massachusetts (where he had taught from 1917 to 1921).

The next eight years were spent in Europe, chiefly in Berlin, Florence, and Rome: he was the recipient of the American Prix de Rome of 1928. While in Europe he wrote his First Symphony (1927) and the First Piano Sonata (1930). From 1935 to 1945 he was on the faculty of Princeton University; he then went to the University of California in Berkeley, but in 1953 returned to Princeton as the William S. Conant Professor of Music. In 1961 he became one of the four co-directors of the Columbia-Princeton Electronic Music Center.

Among the compositions of Sessions are four symphonies, two string quartets, two piano sonatas, a concerto for piano and or-

267

chestra, an Anglican Mass for unison chorus and organ, *Idyll of Theocritus* for soprano and orchestra, and two operas: *The Trial of Lucullus* (1947) and *Montezuma* (produced in Berlin on April 19, 1964). A highly articulate writer on music, he has published several books: *The Musical Experience of Composer, Performer, Listener* (1950), *Harmonic Practice* (1951), and *Reflections on the Musical Life in the United States* (1956). He also contributed a thoughtful essay to the volume *The Intent of the Artist*, edited by Augusto Centeno (1941).

The following essay is an aftermath of the Princeton Seminar in Advanced Musical Studies held during the summer of 1959. The general topic of the seminar was "Problems of Modern Music."

Problems and Issues Facing the Composer Today / (1960)

The premises behind such an undertaking as was attempted in last summer's Princeton Seminar in Advanced Musical Studies were of course based on the obvious changes in orientation and outlook that are taking place—and have for many years been taking place—in the minds, attitudes, and intentions of the composers, performers, and even listeners of our day. It is hardly necessary to point out in these pages that change is inevitable at any period whatever in the development of an art. The history of the art is itself primarily an account of such changes and an attempt to fathom both their wide-ranging causes and their equally far-reaching effects, and to formulate terms in which these can be adequately grasped. The History of Art likewise seeks and provides criteria by which the main periods of change may be compared with one another in character and extent.

The history of Western music reveals at least two phases, and possibly three, that may well have seemed to those who observed them as contemporaries to shake the art of music to its depths and to raise questions of the most fundamental kind—questions, that is, not only as to the character and trend of current developments, but as to the function, the significance, and even ultimate nature of music itself. The beginnings of polyphony, the late sixteenth and early seventeenth century, and possibly the thirteenth and fourteenth—if this be not indeed considered as a late phase of the first-named—were such phases. They were periods of apparent crisis, during which long-established values were brought into deep question and challenged both on the most profound and the most superficial levels; "experimental" periods in the sense that many things were tried which soon proved abortive, while others, soon discarded, seemed to find justification at a much later date; but periods of intense creativity not only by virtue of the music of genius that survived them, but because they tapped new veins, uncovering the resources out of which the music of the following three or four centuries was to be built. In each period the musical transformation was coeval with a far-reaching transformation in Western society, and undoubtedly related to it, though the exact nature of this relationship seems—at least to this writer—far more difficult to penetrate and to clarify than it is frequently assumed to be.

The period in which we live has at the very least much in common with these earlier ones. For well over a hundred years each successive generation has seemed to many of its members to contain within itself the seeds of the imminent destruction, not only of a great musical tradition, but possibly of music itself. Though this had happened at earlier periods also, it has happened at a steadily increasing tempo since, roughly, the death of Beethoven. Each generation has, to be sure, at length become assimilated, by and large, to the "main stream"; the "revolutions" have in each case been discovered eventually to be not so revolutionary after all, and the revolutionaries of one generation have become symbols of conservatism and eventually clubs with which to beat their revolutionary successors of the next. But, with each succeeding phase, this has come about a little more slowly, and there is no doubt an easily discernible reason for this. It is true that in our time the situation of all the arts, and in all of their phases, has been rendered far more complex, first through the development of mass media, and the consequent immeasurable expansion of the more-or-less interested public, and secondly through various economic factors, including not only the decline of private patronage and the consequent and inevitable increase in commercialization, but drastically rising costs in virtually every phase of musical production. It is, however, no less true that, precisely at this moment of economic and, if you will, social crisis in the arts, the inner dynamic of music itself should be leading to developments of which the eventual result can at best be only dimly sensed.

One symptom—or result—of this, of course, may be seen in the increasing articulateness of musicians themselves in regard to their own artistic principles. Since the early years of the nineteenth century, composers have felt more and more inclined to express themselves in print regarding music and all of its phases. In the case of earlier composers—Mozart and Beethoven, for instance—one must rely on correspondence, on reminiscences, and on a few sibylline and perhaps problematic quotations that have become traditional, and no doubt often distorted, if one wants to discover their working principles beyond the evidence of the music itself. From Carl Maria von Weber on, however, composers have devoted considerable effort and energy to criticism, later to theory, and more recently still to teaching. This is certainly due in very large part to the fact that, in a period of artistic upheaval, creative artists find themselves first of all sharply aware of their own relationship to their traditional inheritance and to the directions in which they feel impelled to extend or even to reject it. Secondly, they find themselves, in a period in which the formulated notions regarding musical esthetics, mu-

sical theory, and musical syntax have long since lost the vitality
they once possessed, impelled or even obliged to arrive at what
are at least working formulations of their own. If they are not
to remain in relative solitude they are also likely to communicate these formulations. Since the cultural pessimism of our
time abhors solitude—once considered a decidedly honorable
state for an artist—and demands "news" at almost any price,
they may even find themselves virtually compelled to do so.

One has only to open practically any European periodical devoted to living music in order to become aware of the intellectual
ferment that characterizes the musical life of today. One will find
there, as one finds in fact on all hands, serious and often acute
discussion of every phase, from generalized esthetic attitudes to
the most precise and esoteric matters, and on a level that the
conscientious artist of mature age, or the ambitious one of more
tender years, cannot wholly ignore except at the price of an inherent lack of adventurousness which in itself bodes somewhat
ill for his achievement as an artist. I, of course, do not mean to
imply by this that he is bound to accept all or even any of the
ideas he will find urged upon him. If he is genuinely adventurous
he will accept anything whatever only strictly on his own terms.
But he will find himself, certainly, challenged at every point, and
obliged to find his own answer to the challenges thus presented
to him; and if he is young and gifted he will welcome these challenges as a test of his creative conviction, if not as a source of
direct stimulation along the lines of his own expression. At the
very least, he will have the opportunity to become more aware
of his own musical nature, and at the best he will learn to be
untiring in his effort to avail himself of that opportunity, and
to pursue his own creative efforts accordingly.

That the situation as I have described it contains its own
peculiar pitfalls is, of course, obvious. I am not referring to the
comment one frequently hears to the effect that a period in which
musicians think and talk so much about their art must necessarily be a sterile one. As a matter of fact the present-day habit
of drawing broad inferences of such a kind—apparently plausi-
ble but inherently farfetched—is one against which we should
guard ourselves in the name of elementary logic. It is not my

purpose here, however, to propose value judgments on contemporary music, but merely to comment on facts and phenomena as they exist. But the least one can do is to point out that contemporary music, and in fact any music whatever, is to be judged in terms of music itself, not of circumstances with which no clear connection can be convincingly demonstrated. One cannot insist too strongly or too frequently that, in the arts generally and in music in particular, it is only productions that really count, and that only in these—music, written or performed—are to be found the criteria by which ideas about music as well as music itself, must finally stand or fall: not the converse. This is a refrain that will recur repeatedly in the course of this discussion, as indeed it must in the course of any valid discussion of music.

The generic pitfall at which I have hinted is precisely this one. In an age in which theoretical speculation in either the esthetic or the technical sphere has assumed the importance it has in our own, there is always the danger that it may be overvalued, and assumed to furnish criteria in itself, and not regarded simply as a means that may prove useful in helping composers to achieve the artistic results they are seeking—in the realization, that is, of a genuine musical vision. Again, one finds oneself obliged to emphasize that the primary function of the composer is to possess, develop, and with the utmost intensity to realize his own particular vision—a vision which, if it is genuinely vital, will be found to contain both general and specifically personal elements; and that theory and esthetics can have validity for him only in so far as they can find roots in this vision. Otherwise they can represent only a flight away from music, or at a very dubious best, a crutch on which a faltering musical impulse can find some measure of support.

It is in fact fairly easy to recognize the pitfalls characteristic of those past musical periods with which we are most familiar. To a certain extent they are mirrored in the way in which these periods are regarded by the succeeding generations, which rebel against them. The characteristic pitfall of the nineteenth century was undoubtedly that of literary association and the manner of overemphasis—sentimental, violent, or pretentious—just as that of the eighteenth was a certain type of elegant and formal conventionality. Our own particular brand of emptiness is perhaps beginning to emerge in a variety of clichés, derived both from so-called neoclassicism and from serialism in its earlier as well as its later phases. In each case we are dealing with a manner that has become generalized through lack of substance, and not with ideas in any positive sense. What is necessary, if the pitfalls are to be avoided, is that composers in the first place should always retain the courage of their own artistic vision, that teachers should emphasize the supremacy of real musical imagination, and that listeners, of whatever category, should, by holding themselves open to whatever genuine and even unexpected experience music can bring, learn to discriminate between what is authentic and what is fictitious.

Thus far I have spoken at length of a general situation in the musical world, and of some of the questions that situation raises as such, without attempting to deal with the situation itself, its background, or its nature, other than to characterize it in the very generalized sense of the decay of one tradition and the gradual movement toward new factors capable of superseding it. The ultimate shape these developments will assume is still by no means definitive in its outlines; but both their causes and their present trends are in certain respects quite clear, as are the specific questions posed by the latter.

It seems clear, for example, that the development of harmony as we have traditionally conceived it has probably reached a dead end. First of all, composers have for many years felt able to utilize all possible vertical combinations of tones, and have so abundantly availed themselves of that possibility that any new discoveries in this regard are virtually unthinkable. Even this fact, however, tells only a part of the story, since the possibilities are not so rich as this purely statistical assumption would indicate. As more and more tones are added to any chord, each added tone contributes less to the character of the chord, or, in other words, to the factor that differentiates it from other combinations of tones. The decisive development of harmony, therefore, depends overwhelmingly on combinations of a relatively small number of tones; beyond that number, so to speak, the ear refuses to interest itself in strictly harmonic effect. It is not so much a question of possibilities as such, as of possibilities that are in any way decisive. The real point is that composers seem by and large no longer interested in chords as such, and that this is a tacit recognition that there is nothing left to be discovered, in the sphere of harmony, that arouses any feeling of excitement on their part.

Something similar had of course taken place already in regard to functional harmony. Based very clearly on a triadic premise, the principle of root progression had given way before the proliferation of "altered chords" that was so characteristic a feature of harmonic evolution in the nineteenth century. The process is a perfectly familiar one which need not be summarized here. Suffice it to say that what is often called "atonality" was a very gradual development—so gradual in fact, that, aside from the literal meaning of the term itself, it is impossible to define it with any precision whatever. It is in other words impossible to show exactly where tonality ends and "atonality" begins unless one establish wholly arbitrary lines of demarcation in advance.

This is not the main objection to the term, however. "Atonality" implies music in which not only is the element of what is defined as "tonality" no longer a principle of construction, but in which the composer deliberately avoids all procedures capable of evoking "tonal" associations. Actually this is virtually impossible, owing to the mere fact that we use tones, and hear them in relation to each other. In other words, whenever a series of tones is heard, the musical ear assimilates it by perceiving a pattern composed not only of tones but of intervals; and neither the process nor the sensation is different in any essential principle from the process by which one assimilates music that is unimpeachably "tonal." I am reliably informed that Anton Webern himself insisted on this point, and even on specifically tonal references in his own music.

Whatever real sense the word "atonality" may have derives from the fact that the further a chord departs from a strictly triadic structure, the less unequivocal it becomes in terms of a specific key; and that, in the proportion that such harmonies become predominant in musical usage, it becomes more difficult to establish genuine tonal contrast, and the effort to do so becomes more forced. As the cadence, in the early years of this century, came to acquire for composers more and more the aspect of a cliché, and as the composers found themselves more and more obliged to discover other means of achieving musical articulation, they found themselves obliged to discover new principles of contrast as well. They discovered that in the absence of strictly triadic harmony it was virtually impossible to establish a feeling of key sufficiently unequivocally to make possible a genuine and definitive change of key, and that hence tonality was for them no longer sufficient as a principle of structure. It was this discovery perhaps above all that led to both the adoption of the serial principle by Schoenberg and the attempt to find ways toward the revitalization of tonal principles that was embodied in the "neoclassicism" of Stravinsky.

The above does not mean, of course, that harmony has ceased to exist in any music, or that it has become an element that can be ignored. Our harmonic sense is essentially the awarenss of one of the dimensions of music; having acquired that awareness, we cannot do away with it, and it would be ridiculous folly to try to do so. If art is to develop, awareness of every aspect of the art must increase rather than diminish. But harmonic effect as such has clearly ceased to be a major interest of composers, just as tonality has ceased to be an issue or a point of reference against which issues can be adequately discussed. To be sure, the question still arises constantly in the public discussion of music; but such discussion can have no meaning except on the level of very precise technical definition. We are dealing with facts, not with slogans, and the facts have to be referred to basic esthetic and acoustical considerations, rather than to specific historical embodiments of these. If by "tonality" we mean, in the most general terms, the sense of pitch relationship and of the patterns and structures that can be created out of such relationships, the word "atonality" can have no meaning, as long as we use tones. If we mean, on the other hand, a precise set of technical principles and hence of procedures, it is easy to see in retrospect that the very vitality with which it developed led ultimately beyond the principle itself.

If the cadence, as conventionally defined, came finally to seem to many composers, in the context of their own music, little more than a cliché, it was because they came to feel a definite disparity between the harmonic vocabulary native to them and the harmonies necessary to establish the cadence. While the composers of the late nineteenth century—one senses the problem already in the music of Wagner—succeeded in overcoming this disparity, often through sheer technical ingenuity and sometimes with visible effort, their successors often found this impossible to achieve without stylistic violence. It was necessary either to turn backward or to seek new principles.

As we all know, a similar development took place in the rhythmic sphere. It took place more quietly and with far less opposition, if indeed there was any appreciable opposition whatever. There is no need to dwell on the rhythmic question here. Though the changes that have taken place have been equally far-reaching, they have been in a sense less spectacular and less esoteric, if only for the reason that they owe so much to the influence of popular music and of Gregorian chant. They have found incomparably more ready acceptance, both from musicians and from the general public, than the developments of which I have spoken in the realm of harmony. Furthermore, the rhythmic aspects of music are bound closely and inevitably to the other elements of the musical vocabulary; in this sense one can say that the development of music away from the tonal and cadential principle has also created a whole new set of rhythmic premises and requirements.

In any event, the focal point of the more advanced musical thought of today is polyphonic, and more concerned with problems of texture and organization than with harmony in the hitherto accepted meaning of the term. Once more, this does not mean that composers have ceased to be acutely aware of vertical relationships between tones, of progressions from one vertical conglomerate to another, or even of the patterns formed by such progressions. But it is certainly true, I think, that they tend more and more to think of these matters in terms of texture rather than harmony as hitherto defined. The current trend is to refer to such vertical conglomerates as "densities" rather than as "chords" or "harmonies"; but it must be stressed that there is no satisfactory substitute for awareness of their entire musical context, and that the replacement of one term by another is useful in so far as it increases that awareness, and does not connote the evasion of one issue in favor of another.

It is, of course, fashionable to regard Webern as the patron saint of the dominant contemporary trend, and to invoke his name as a rallying point for all that is most aggressively anti-traditional in contemporary music. As is so apt to be the case, there is a discrepancy at many points between Webern the symbol and Webern the actual figure. The latter, however individual his musical style, was of course as deeply rooted in the Viennese tradition as Schoenberg himself, and probably more narrowly; and without in any sense meaning to detract from his musical stature, one can say that he remained a loyal disciple to the extent of being more Schoenbergian than Schoenberg himself. In the last analysis he was at least as much the Romantic Expressionist as Alban Berg, if not more so. Above all, and most important, he was a musician of the ripest culture, at once the most daring and the most realistic of artists. The teacher who at times finds himself obliged to stress the fact—so easily lost from view in the heat of speculative enthusiasm—that musical values are, first and last, derived from tones and rhythms and the effects they produce, and not from their theoretical consistency or analytical plausibility, can find no better or more demonstrable evidence in his own behalf than that furnished by almost any score of Webern.

At the same time, however, one may find oneself impelled to question the sufficiency of the post-Webernian trend as a firm and comprehensive basis for new departures in music. This brings us to the large question of serialism, which I have deliberately postponed till after discussing some of the factors that have been given rise to it. One cannot, of course, stress too much that serialism is neither the arbitrary nor the rigid set of prescriptions that it is often supposed to be, not only by its foes but unfortunately also by some of its friends. It is rather the result of many converging trends of musical development, of which I have mentioned a couple of the most important and the most general ones. Above all, perhaps, it is the result of the decreasing validity of the harmonic principle as an organizing force, and the necessity of adopting consistent relationships between tones, which can serve as a constructive basis for the organization of musical ideas, along both the horizontal and the vertical dimensions.

Quite as important is to stress that serialism is in full process of development, and that the shapes it has taken are already manifold. It is no longer the exclusive possession of any one "school" or group of composers, nor is it bound to any one mode of expression, Viennese or otherwise. Need one cite evidence, at this date? In other words, it is a technical principle that a wide number and variety of composers have found useful for their own purposes, both because of the organizing principles they have derived from it and because of the musical resources it has opened up for them. Like any other technical principle, it yields nothing in itself; it is always for the imagination of the composer to discover what it can give him, and to mold it to his own uses. Like any other technical principle, it has to be thoroughly mastered, in terms of the composer's creative vision; a half-baked relationship to it in this respect can produce only less than half-baked results. For this reason the young composer who has not grown up with it from the beginning—there are already a number who have done so, and to whom it is, so to speak, native—would be well advised to avoid it until he has become sure of his own musical identity, and can grow into it in full conviction and genuine musical maturity. It does not provide answers to all musical questions or in the last analysis to any; it is only a vehicle and a means, which, let us reiterate, many composers find useful. Once more like other technical principles, it has acquired its own brand—several brands, in fact—of academicism, and many varieties of cliché, which are none the less recognizable as clichés for being derived from a technical principle that has been in active existence for little more than forty years. Its value lies wholly in the music of the composers who have seen fit to adopt it, and the value of that music resides in the imaginative, emotive, and constructive force inherent in it, not in the ingenuities with which the system is applied, except in so far as these are the inherent result of a musical conception.

The serial organization of tones must be, and for the most part
is, today regarded as a settled fact—the composer is free to take
it or leave it, or to adopt it with varying degrees of rigor, as he
may choose. The results it can yield are open to all to see and
judge as they see fit. More problematical are some attempts that
have been made to extend serial organization to other aspects of
music—notably to that of rhythmic values and that of dynamics.
Any discussion of these matters must emphasize once more that
it is only results that matter; that the human imagination works
along channels that are frequently unexpected, and that a critical
scrutiny of technical premises does not release one in the slightest degree from the responsibility of holding one's mind, ear, and
heart open to whatever may reveal genuinely new vistas of musical expression and experience.

   With this caution in mind one can easily observe that tones are,
for the musical ear, fixed and readily identifiable points in musical space, and that the progress from one tone to another has
a clear point of departure and arrival. This is partly the result
of the fact that within the octave there are only twelve tones,
with which the musical ear has familiarized itself over the course
of many centuries; and the additional fact that our musical culture has taught us to regard as equivalent, tones that occupy the
same position within the various octaves. *A*, for instance, is recognizable as *A* whether it be played on the open *A*-string of the
double bass, of the 'cello, or of the violin—or, for that matter,
in the high register of the flute or the piccolo. Time values, on
the other hand, are by no means fixed; their range is to all intents and purposes infinite. This does not at all exclude the possibility of adopting an arbitrary series of time values for the
purposes of any single composition, but it does raise very valid
questions regarding the serialization of time values as a general
principle. The serialization of dynamics, however, raises questions of a much more fundamental nature. Dynamic values are
by their very essence relative, both in an objective and a subjective sense. They have quite different meanings for different
media and under different conditions. How can we regard as
equivalent, except on the most practical level of balance, a given
nuance on, say, the oboe and the violin, or for that matter, the

same nuance in different registers of the same instrument; or on the same note on the same instrument, sounded in a small room, a large concert hall, and the open air? What does the indication p actually mean, and how can we as listeners distinguish in clear terms a transition from mf to f, or even from mp to ff?

The basic question of all is of course—as is often the case—"Why?" The principle of so-called total organization raises many questions and answers none, even in theory. First of all, what is being organized, and according to what criterion? Is it not rather a matter of organizing, not music itself, but various facets of music, each independently and on its own terms or at best according to a set of arbitrarily conceived and ultimately quite irrelevant rules of association? Was the music of Beethoven, or who you will, not totally organized in a sense that is much more real, since it is an organization of musical ideas and not of artificially abstracted elements?

The subject of "total organization" leads naturally to the consideration of electronic media, since the latter make possible the exact control of all musical elements, and make possible in a sense also a partial answer to some of the questions I have raised. Since the potentialities of electronic media in the realm of sound are, at least to all intents and purposes, infinite, it is possible to measure all musical elements in terms of exact quantity, and in fact necessary to do so, since such measurement is the very nature of the instruments and the method by which they are used. A dynamic nuance thus not only can, but must, become a fixed quantity, as can and must, also, any one in the whole range of pitch or color gradations. Every moment of music not only can but must be the result of the minutest calculation, and the composer for the first time has the whole world of sound at his disposal.

That electronic media will play a vital and possibly even decisive role in the future of music is not to be doubted. I must confess however to skepticism as to what that precise role will be. Two questions seem to me to be crucial. First of all, it is not sufficient to have the whole world at one's disposal—the very infinitude of possibilities cancels out possibilities, as it were, until limitations are discovered. No doubt the limitations are there, and if not there they are certainly in human beings. But the musical media we know thus far derive their whole character and their usefulness as musical media precisely from their limitations—stringed instruments derive their character and utility from not only the fact that they are stringed instruments, that the tone is produced by stroking strings, but from the fact that they are not wind or percussion instruments; and we have learned to use them with great subtlety of effect and power of expression because of that. The dilemma of electronic musical media is a little like that of the psychologist who is reputed once to have said to one of his friends, "Well I have got my boy to the point where I can condition him for anything I want. What shall I condition him for?"

The other question has to do with the essential nature of music itself. Is music simply a matter of tones and rhythmic patterns, or in the final analysis the organization of time in terms of human gesture and movement? The final question regarding all music that is mechanically reproduced seems to be bound up with the fact that our active sense of time is dependent in large degree on our sense of movement, and that mechanical repetition mitigates and finally destroys this sense of movement in any given instance; it destroys also our sense of expression through movement, which plays so large and obvious a part in our musical experience. This is what lies behind the discussions of the element of "chance," which has so bothered the proponents of "total organization." But the element that "total organization" leaves out of account is not chance at all. It is the organic nature of movement as such, of the fresh and autonomous energy with which the performer invests each musical phrase, every time he sings or plays it, and which gradually disappears for our awareness if we listen so often to a mechanical reproduction of it that we become completely familiar with it, to the point of knowing always exactly what is coming next. It is more than the element of mere "surprise"; it is rather that if the expression of movement is to become effective, we require not only the evidence of movement from one point to the next, but a sense of the motivating energy behind it.

To raise these questions is not in any sense to reject the principle of electronic music as such. In the first place, composers are beginning to feel the need for new instruments. The existing ones, for all their technical perfection, are beginning at times to seem vaguely obsolete as far as some of the composers' musical ideas are concerned. The possibilities electronic music suggests are altogether likely to make this situation more acute.

In my own opinion, electronic media more than justify their existence if only by the new insight one can gain from them into the nature of sound, musical and otherwise, and above all by a vast quantity of fresh experience they can provide, on the purely acoustical level. They are still in a clearly very primitive stage and it is impossible to say what they may contribute in the future. But they raise the above questions and many others, and the questions will certainly become more acute as the media develop.

One hears a good deal, these days, of the developing "dehumanization" of music and the other arts; and specifically in regard to the tendencies we discussed in detail at the Princeton Seminar last year, and which I have been discussing in these pages. This is all very well, and not without plausibility; but we are speaking of a movement that is widespread among the younger composers of Europe, that has begun to take root in the United States, and that above all is in constant development and evolution. Many ideas are being tested, and many are quickly discarded. If we regard certain manifestations with raised eyebrows, that is our privilege as members of an older generation, as it is always our privilege to point out flaws in logic. But if it is also our prerogative to insist on the primacy of the creative imagination, and to minimize the decisive importance of theoretical speculation, we are at the same time obliged to abide by our own premises, and look toward artistic results rather than toward the ideas by which these are rationalized. By the same token it is well to remember that art, considered on the most objective level, reflects the attitudes of the individuals that produce it. The danger of dehumanization is a real and patent one, and the individual can, and certainly should, resist any dehumanizing tendency with all his strength. But this cannot, and must not, blind us to the claims of whatever is genuinely new and vital in the arts, or, once more, cause us to forget that it is the product, not the process, that is of real importance; and that the creative imagination, at its most vital, has revealed itself through many and often surprising channels. There is no reason to believe that it will not continue to do so, as long as creative vitality—which for musicians means above all the intense love of music—continues to persist.

CHARLES

HAMM, composer and musicologist, has written seven

operas and a book on opera as a musical form. He was born in
Charlottesville, Virginia, in 1925. After graduating from the
University of Virginia he went to Princeton University for his
graduate studies, obtaining the degree of Master of Fine Arts
in 1950 and the Ph.D in 1960. Meanwhile he taught at the Cincinnati College of Music from 1950 to 1957, and while in Cincinnati he became interested in the study of early American music
in that area, on which he has written several valuable papers.
From 1959 to 1963 he was on the music faculty of Newcomb
College, Tulane University, in New Orleans, and in 1963 he
transferred to the University of Illinois.

His teachers in composition were Randall Thompson, Bohuslav
Martinu, and Edward Cone. Among his earlier compositions are
Sinfonia 1954 (commissioned by the Cincinnati Symphony), five
song cycles, two piano sonatas, and various chamber, piano, and
choral works. More recent works include *Mobile for Piano and
Tape* (1963), *Portrait of John Cage* for piano and three tape
recorders (1963), and *Canto* (1963) for singer, speaker, five instruments, and magnetic tape. Among his operas are *The Mon-
key's Paw*, *The Cask of Amontillado*, *The Secret Life of Walter
Mitty*, *The Salesgirl*, and *The Box*. His interest in American music has also led him to compose *American Harmony* for large
wind ensemble and *Three Folk Hymns* for a cappella choir.

The following trenchant essay on "Opera and the American Composer" was written especially for this book at the request of the Editor.

Opera and the American Composer / (1961)

There are those who pretend that the state of opera in this country is healthy, but they are mostly persons who would like to see the *status quo* maintained because of some financial, professional, or social involvement with opera. It should be clear enough to anyone else that Americans have firmly and repeatedly rejected opera as it has been offered them.

No statistics of phonograph recordings sold or huge radio audiences can obscure this. Opera on records and over the radio is not what composers have understood this complex art form to be, nor what people in other countries and at other times have known and enjoyed as opera. The most telling statistic is that this country of 170,000,000 persons and great wealth has exactly two professional opera companies, both in New York. We have professional opera of sorts in Cincinnati, New Orleans, San Francisco, Chicago, and elsewhere, but in none of these places is there anything approaching a full season of opera—nor an opera company. Singers are brought in from the Metropolitan or from abroad; orchestras are pieced together from those musicians who are in the city anyway, playing in the local symphony or teaching high school or selling insurance or living in retirement; a few local singers may be used in minor roles, being paid enough for this service to enable them to take a few more voice lessons; the chorus and dancers are drawn from local, frequently amateur, talent.

The contrast with the operatic life of certain European countries is startling. West Germany, for example, has over fifty professional opera companies, each requiring a group of principal singers, an entire opera orchestra, a chorus and a ballet troupe, and a complete technical and directional staff. At random, German cities with opera companies are Dortmund (about the size of Denver), Hagen (comparable, in size, to Little Rock), Freiburg (as large as Dearborn, Michigan), Kaiserlautern (with about as many people as Rock Island, Illinois), Karlsruhe (not much larger than Sacramento), and Chemnitz (with no more people than Richmond).

Imagine a comparable situation in the United States. Imagine full-time professional opera companies in Denver, Little Rock, Dearborn, Rock Island, Sacramento, Richmond, and the hundreds of other cities of comparable size, each company needing singers, and technical staffs. Imagine what such a healthy operatic state would mean to the deans of our conservatories and music departments, who now have the annual melancholy experience of seeing scores of graduates with the talent and training to become professional musicians forced to teach school or work in department stores or sell insurance or do one of a hundred other things having nothing to do with music. Imagine music as a legitimate profession in our country, with singers and instrumentalists who reach a certain level of proficiency able to find professional employment as a normal thing, not as an unlikely exception.

European opera companies are subsidized by the government, American companies are not. But this does not, as some suppose, explain the current state of opera in this country. Government funds are used for opera in Europe because citizens of various countries approve of this arrangement; government money is not used for opera here because the large majority of our citizens would protest. Opera is a popular art form in many European countries; it is not a popular art form here, and pouring government money into the type of production the Metropolitan Opera Association and other groups offer is not likely to make it any more popular.

Many explanations have been offered for the continued rejection of opera by the American public. It has even been suggested that our most prominent company, the Metropolitan, has much to do with it: that the long-range, high-powered publicity campaign conducted by this organization has succeeded in convincing most Americans that what goes on at the Metropolitan is the only thing that can and should happen on the operatic stage.

The Metropolitan is by no means the first opera company of its sort the world has known. There have been others, at other times and in other countries, orientated toward what could be called "aristocratic opera": opera performed for the amusement of a small select group, in a language or languages other than the vernacular, dependent on visual spectacle and the appeal of spectacular singing personalities, produced in such a way as to take advantage of no more than several of the many dimensions of opera. Companies of this sort did Italian opera in London in Handel's day; there were others in some south German and Austrian cities in the early eighteenth century, in Russia in the nineteenth century, in Paris in the pre-Lullian period; there are some today in South America.

Certain of the countries which now enjoy a healthy operatic life have had such companies; some of them still do. There is a place in our culture for the Metropolitan, certainly. As has often been pointed out, it functions as a sort of museum, keeping alive operatic works and traditions with no other chance of survival. And there is an audience for it, and the handful of similar groups scattered around the country, an oddly heterogeneous gathering of the wealthy and near wealthy who have been told that attending the opera is a proper thing to do, business and professional men who are untouched by what happens on the stage but who have a strong sense of civic pride, members of minority groups anxious to participate in prestige activities, immigrants seeking some contact with the homeland and their native tongue, singers and ex-singers and would-be singers and teachers of singers, students, and musicians with no illusions about what goes

on but who come because it is the only opera in town, and sometimes entire classrooms of students. The Metropolitan does not
prevent us from having more and better operatic activity, but it
is no substitute for such activity either.

Critics of the American operatic scene have spared no one in
their search for causes of the current situation. The managers
of our opera-producing groups have been blamed for their policy
of offering opera in languages other than English. Our stage
directors have been accused of producing opera with little regard
for modern stage techniques and a sometimes complete disregard
of the fact that for many composers opera was a dramatic form.
Our singers and voice teachers and opera coaches are criticized
for the fact that often when opera is offered in English not many
people realize it. Our architects have been blamed for erecting
structures in which it is difficult for an audience to enjoy anything, let alone opera. Our critics have been criticized for their
failure to point out the inadequacies and absurdities of some of
our operatic productions. Even the public has been accused: we
have been told that the forms and conventions of opera are, and
will remain, foreign to the nature of most Americans.

Many of these critics agree as to how the situation can be improved. *Carmen, Madame Butterfly, Don Giovanni,* and the like
should be superbly translated into English by brilliant scholar-
poet-musicians. They should be staged by men of genius (preferably with a background of successful Broadway productions)
who understand the dramatic nature of opera and the workings
of the American mind, employing the most modern techniques
of set design, lighting, costuming, and makeup (again with preference to those tricks which have proved to be successful on the
commercial stage). The cast should be composed of singer-actors
with impeccable English diction and the ability to give convincing character portrayals. Productions should be rehearsed as
long and carefully as Broadway shows, then given on television
or in halls much smaller and more suitable to opera than those
currently used. If all this could be done, we are told, Americans
could see and hear opera as it should be, and they would naturally
respond to it with the same enthusiasm as audiences in other
countries. Additional opera companies would have to be formed

to meet the growing demand; these would perform for ever-increasing numbers of Americans now able to understand and love opera for the first time.

Such productions would be a delight and might attract more people to the opera house, but they would never build a popular following for opera such as is found in Italy and Germany and even Russia. The history of opera tells us, clearly and repeatedly, that the popularity of opera in these countries can be traced back to successful attempts by composers to create operas completely comprehensible to audiences in these countries, comprehensible not merely because they are written in the vernacular but because they have something to do with the culture of the country.

We have our aristocratic opera with its limited audience, but we do not have and have never had opera which reaches beyond the trained musician and student and snob to the far larger group of reasonably intelligent and potentially receptive people who would respond to opera of another sort. It is unlikely that *Carmen, Madame Butterfly* and *Don Giovanni,* no matter how well done, can ever be of much interest to Americans with no prior acquaintance with opera. They are from another time and another culture. But if American audiences were to become familiar with the forms and conventions of opera through performances of native operas which they could understand and enjoy as naturally as they understand and enjoy productions of native dramas, they could gradually come to understand the nature of opera enough to *then* be ready for such works as *Carmen, Madame Butterfly,* and *Don Giovanni.*

But American audiences have not had the opportunity of witnessing native operas which they can understand and enjoy. Operas have been written by our composers, by the dozens and now by the hundreds, but almost none of these have been operas which have made our audiences want to hear them again, or want to hear other operas, or want to have a hand in raising money for more and better opera companies and opera houses, or want to write letters to Washington urging subsidy of opera.

We do not have a healthy operatic life in this country because our American composers have not given us the works necessary for the creation of such a life. The final blame for the rejection of opera by our audiences must be put not on managers, directors, singers, teachers, critics, and audiences, *but on our composers for their failure to give us enough good operas.*

Having said this, I must immeditely explain that I by no means agree with the opinions offered by Henry Pleasants in his notorious *The Agony of Modern Music.* In one chapter he disposes of all recent opera ("Up to the time of *Der Rosenkavalier,* opera was a living art and . . . since then it has not been") by offering the thesis that the foundation of opera is melody, whether this melody be given out by voices (as in Italian opera of the eighteenth and nineteenth centuries) or by the orchestra (as in Wagner and late Verdi) ; "modern opera" fails, says Mr. Pleasants, because it has no melody. "The singer is restricted to declamation in order that the text may be understood," he reports ; "parlando recitative or dry declamation has replaced the aria and the concerted piece. Even the orchestra . . . has become an humble provider of commas, periods, exclamation points, descriptive color, inflated dynamic contrasts, and mood painting. . . ."

There may be a few recent operas in which the voices are restricted to declamation and the orchestra to interjection, but most "modern operas," certainly the best ones, sing. It may be true that the operas of Britten, Stravinsky, Menotti, Weill, and Schoenberg do not sing as well as those of Rossini, Mozart, and Verdi, but the difference is not in the intent of the composer but in the success with which operatic forms are handled.

There are differences between "modern opera" and works of the more distant past, but Mr. Pleasants does not so much as hint at these in his book. A reading of this chapter, and of the entire book, leaves one with the melancholy suspicion that one very good reason Mr. Pleasants does not like "modern music" is that he knows so little about it.

But it is surprising, on the surface, that our composers have given us so few good operas. They turn out hundreds of string quartets, symphonies, and piano sonatas, some of these as good as any music being written today. They are highly educated, well drilled in the techniques of composition, better acquainted with the great music of the past than composers have ever been before, reasonably well cared for financially (though they do not

like to admit it), and they have no particular difficulty in getting
performances of their music once they accept the fact that there
are performing groups and individuals outside the city limits
of New York, Boston, and Philadelphia. If our composers are
not producing good operas it is not because they are deficient in
talent, training, or technique.

Nor is it because they are unable to hear their own operas and
other new operas. Our college opera workshops and community
opera groups perform hundreds of contemporary works each
year, most of them by American composers. Local telecasts of
new American operas are becoming commonplace, and each season one or more of the national networks offers a new opera or
two, as carefully prepared and thoroughly professional as performances can be these days. New operas are given in concert
form, sometimes even partially staged, on the concert series of
some of our major orchestras. Summer festivals offer contemporary operas. Even our professional opera companies do a new
work from time to time, and will do more in coming years with
the encouragement of the Ford Foundation. Operas have also
been known to turn up in off-Broadway theaters.

Opportunities for performance of new American operas exist
right up the line, from the humblest amateur groups to our top
professional companies. Many opera-producing groups, far from
being antagonistic to the idea of doing new American works,
would welcome nothing so much as a truly first-rate opera by an
American composer.

Most of the operas written in this country today are performed; most of these performances are at least as good as the
quality of the work deserves. And most of these operas prove to
be, upon performance, poor works. One expects inferior composers to write inferior music and mediocre composers to turn
out mostly mediocre music. But it is distressing to find scattered
among the bad operas which turn up each year works by composers of genuine talent.

But is it surprising, after all, that our composers have such
bad luck with opera? As thorough as their training is in most
areas, a significant deficiency in their preparation for composing
opera shows up in a comparison with the training of those men

who have succeeded, in the past, in composing the best operas. No matter how different the personalties and backgrounds of Gluck, Mozart, Verdi, Weill, Handel, and Wagner may have been, a common pattern can be traced in their preparation. After mastering the rudiments of music theory and practice, each set out to acquire as intimate a knowledge of opera as possible. They studied, in score and on the stage, the currently successful works; they sought out as teachers men who had demonstrated an ability to write workable operas themselves; they learned about the practical side of opera by singing, conducting, coaching, or playing in an opera orchestra; they cultivated some of the better singers of their day in order to learn what they could about the curious and complex art of singing; they thought and talked and wrote about opera, from the sociological, philosophical, practical, or national point of view. These men approached the composition of opera as a highly specialized craft which would take years to learn and many more to master. Their hope was that if they were diligent enough in learning this craft and in serving a period of apprenticeship, they might finally come up with a successful opera on the fourth or seventh or eleventh try.

Contrast this with the training of our young opera composer of today. He will study at a conservatory or in the music department of some college or university, as all our young musicians must these days, receiving rigorous schooling in harmony, form, counterpoint, orchestration, and analysis. He may take a course in the history of opera. His teachers will not be successful opera composers, since we have almost none of these around today, certainly not in our schools. He will write piano pieces, songs, and a trio or quartet; if he perseveres to the graduate level he will eventually work out a piano concerto or even a huge cantata-like piece with orchestra, chorus, and soloists. His first opera will be written after he has left school and has a job directing a high school band or selling insurance, since the writing of operas among composition students is frowned upon. He will persuade his wife or a fraternity brother who majored in English to do a libretto, which he will use as the basis for a score abounding in harmonic subtleties, rhythmic complexities, contrapuntal cunning, and cleverly concealed permutations. He will persuade his old school or a small, local opera group to do the work. He will be dumbfounded at its failure—after all, he knows much more about harmony, form, counterpoint than Rossini, Puccini, Gounod, and Bizet ever knew—and will of course blame the singers, the producer, the audience, and any critics who might have been persuaded to come.

It is not just our young composers who have difficulty with opera. Recently a number of our more mature writers, men who have turned out successful orchestral and chamber music and some of whom know enough about the mechanics of music to have written books, are turning to opera. These men have been equipping themselves with fellowships and grants, with librettos by poets who have struggled up some of the steps of the ladder of literary fame and are unhampered by knowledge of the limitations of the libretto as a form, and they have been writing operas full of music just as good as that found in their earlier works. Puzzled and hurt by the failure of these operas, they have lashed out at producers and the public for their lack of interest in contemporary American opera.

American composers have failed to turn out good operas because they have not understood that the composition of opera is a specialized skill having little to do with composition in other forms.

American composers have written poor operas because they have not understood that opera is a complex and intricate art form with conventions and techniques which often have little or nothing to do with the conventions and techniques of the sonata and the quartet and the symphony and the concerto. They have not understood that the ability to compose successfully in other forms does not insure success in the composition of opera. They have not understood that an opera may be full of good music and still be a bad opera.

American composers have written poor operas because, despite their skill in many of the techniques of composition, they have been unprofessional in this particular area. They can write spectacular virtuoso passages for individual instruments and handle large orchestras with ease—but they cannot score for an opera orchestra so that a human voice and the words this voice is singing can be heard against it. They can devise some of the most intricate rhythmic patterns Western music has known—but they cannot find a rhythmic setting for a line of text which does not distort and exaggerate the fundamental rhythm of this line.

They are literate enough to discuss and write about complexities of row manipulation and the history of the clarinet and the place of the creative artist in modern society—but they will spend years setting to music a text so innocent of the techniques and conventions of the libretto that no composer could make it into a workable opera.

In their instrumental works they handle baroque, romantic, classical, and even mediaeval forms fluently—but in their operas they ignore the fundamental concept of the recitative-aria as a dramatic, not a musical, form. They do not seem to understand the different dramatic functions of recitative, arioso, song, and aria, nor that each of these demands a different type of text. They disregard the effect of range and type of voice on projection of the text. They know little of the technique of setting English, as opposed to setting French or German or Italian. They are unaware of the basic operatic technique of having dramatic climaxes and musical climaxes occur at different times.

Their mishandling of operatic forms and their misunderstanding of operatic conventions stems not from lack of talent or technique, but from simple ignorance—ignorance of opera, ignorance of its nature and fundamental techniques. This same ignorance colors their reactions to other new operas and their selection of models.

Composers and critics of all persuasions have joined forces in hailing Berg's *Wozzeck* as an authentic masterpiece; it has influenced more opera composers than has any other work of the last thirty years. As music, it is a work of genius, and some of it is effective on the stage, but almost no one has bothered to notice that long stretches of it do not work as opera. The second scene of the second act, for example, a longish scene with the Captain and the Doctor and later Wozzeck, reads well and analyzes better, but even when done by singers with excellent diction in whatever language is being used it cannot possibly come across dramatically. The three stand and talk, their conversations cleverly firming up the personalities of these central characters—but in performance Berg's extreme ranges, jagged melodic lines, rhythmic distortions, and monstrous orchestra make it impossible for more than a small fraction of this clever and essential section of the text to come across. Reading a summary of the plot beforehand is no substitute for following this involved conversation line by line, and the other alternative, keeping one's eyes glued to the libretto, is as contrary to the whole idea of opera as anything could be.

The great operatic masterpieces of the past can be enjoyed to the maximum in the opera house, but much of *Wozzeck* can be enjoyed to the maximum by listening to a recording while following a score (preferably marked with colored pencils), savouring details of the libretto and of the handling of musical material which get lost in the opera house.

Lulu is an even more fascinating work, musically, but most of it has nothing much to do with opera. Some of the mass scenes in Schoenberg's *Moses and Aaron* are fine examples of one of the things opera can do better than any other art form, but most of the work cannot be followed in performance in the way that opera has been followed since the very early seventeenth century. The late Strauss operas are full of private communication between composer and librettist which can be shared by anyone who takes the trouble to study the score and the libretto closely but which is lost on anyone who goes to a performance unprepared. Stravinsky is too good a composer to ever write poor music and he has some of the proper instincts for opera, but his *The Rake's Progress* is burdened with a libretto which looks like a libretto but which does few of the things a libretto can and must do.

These are works which have been tested, which have failed as operas (though not necessarily as music), but which are taken as models by aspiring opera composers, young and old.

Most composers and critics and theorists today evaluate an opera on the basis of harmonic usage, formal structure, and contrapuntal treatment. The very things which make opera a unique art form are ignored in criticism, in analysis, and even in the composition of new operas. Opera is analyzed and criticized and composed today as though it were symphony or concerto or sonata, as though it were no different from any other form of music. This robs it of its reason for existence.

It is a curious misfortune that most of our more "radical" composers have been insensitive to the traditions and techniques of opera—a misfortune because most of our better composers fit in this category. Opera is not incompatible with innovations in harmony and form and instrumentation; to the contrary, it has traditionally been a hotbed of radicalism, from the days of Monteverdi right through those of Wagner and Strauss. Opera is not incompatible with recent trends in serial organization, rhythmic modulation, chance, harmony and form, and the electronic production of sound; to the contrary, such devices and techniques could be assimilated into opera and would be more readily accepted if used for dramatic effect, just as harmonic and formal and instrumental innovations have always been more readily accepted in the opera house than in the concert hall. But our best composers, the men with the talent necessary to create successful operas, have either stayed away from the form or refused to master its peculiar techniques. Our best American music has been written by such men as Sessions, Copland, Elliott Carter, and Ives; our best operas by Menotti and Weill and perhaps even Douglas Moore.

We have in this country today all of the necessary ingredients for a thriving operatic life. We have excellent singers, instrumentalists, directors, technicians, and the largest potential audience of well-educated people with time and money to spare that the world has ever known. And we have composers with enough talent to write first-rate operas. All that is needed is for some of the latter, some of the best of them, to become interested enough in opera to spend some years studying its traditions and techniques, studying the most successful operas of the past, involving themselves in opera in a practical way in order to begin to learn what does and what does not work on the stage, studying the nature and structure of the libretto, studying singers and singing, studying ancient and modern stage techniques. We need composers of genius who will have enough respect for opera not to presume to write in the form until they understand it and have mastered some of its techniques. We need composers who are not in a hurry, who do no feel a compulsion to try to get everything they write performed and published immediately, who are willing to write half a dozen or more unsuccessful operas in the process of acquiring a technique.

There is nothing wrong with the operatic life of this country that a succession of first-rate, thoroughly professional American operas would not cure. But we are not likely to get such works so long as our composers continue to refuse to master the peculiar skills necessary for writing such operas.

EARLE
BROWN was born in Lunenburg, Massachusetts, on December 26, 1926. At Northeastern University in Boston he majored in engineering; but music soon became his main interest. From 1947 to 1950 he studied counterpoint and composition with Roslyn Brogue Henning; from 1946 to 1950 he also undertook advanced work in the Schillinger techniques of composition and orchestration with Kenneth McKillop. As an authorized teacher of the Schillinger System of Musical Composition he taught at Denver, Colorado, from 1950 to 1952. In the latter year he went to New York, where he was associated with John Cage, David Tudor, and others in the "Project for Music with Magnetic Tape." From 1955 to 1960 he was employed as editor and recording engineer at Capitol Records; after that he was appointed Artists and Repertoire Director of the "Contemporary Sound Series" for TIME Records. Making his home in New York City, Brown has traveled extensively as conductor, as lecturer, and as a recording engineer for special projects.

Among Earle Brown's principal compositions are *Folio* (1952–53), *Four Systems* (1954), *Pentathis* for nine solo instruments (1957–58, commissioned by Pierre Boulez for "Domaine Musicale," Paris), *Hodograph* for flute, piano or celesta, and percussion (1959), *Available Forms I* for eighteen instruments (1961), commissioned by the city of Darmstadt, Germany), *Available Forms II* for large orchestra with two conductors (1962, commissioned by the Rome Radio Orchestra; performed by the New

York Philharmonic in February, 1964), *Times Five* (1963, commissioned by the French Radio-Television Service) for five instruments and four channels of tape, and Calder Piece (1964–65) for four percussionists and Calder Mobile (functioning as conductor). Brown's compositions have been performed in Brussels, Stockholm, Darmstadt, Cologne, Bonn, London, Milan, Venice, Vienna, Paris, The Hague, Athens, Zagreb, Montreal, and Tokyo. In 1962 he conducted the first performance of his *Novara* for eight instruments at the Berkshire Music Festival in Tanglewood, Massachusetts. He has also conducted his own works in Italy, in Germany, and in France.

Some Notes on Composing / (1963)

Spontaneous decisions in the performance of a work and the possibility of the composed elements being "mobile" have been of primary interest to me for some time.[1] The mobility of the elements in my compositions—for example, in *Twenty-Five Pages* (1953)—was inspired by the mobiles of Alexander Calder, in which, similar to this work of mine, there are basic units subject to innumerable different relationships or forms. My insistence that the work be conducted and formed spontaneously in performance was to a large extent inspired by the working process

1 The Editor assumes full responsibility for the arrangement and continuity of these "Notes," assembled from material written at different times and for various occasions. [Ed.]

and the works of Jackson Pollock, in which the immediacy and directness of "contact" with the material is of such importance and produces an intensity in the working and in the result. The performance conditions of this work are similar to the situation of a painter working spontaneously with a given palette. Such comparisons are extremely dangerous, and I must emphasize that I do not refer to the quality of the results, but to the nature of the working process and the formal possibilities.

I have felt that the conditions of spontaneity and mobility of elements with which I have been working create a more urgent and intense "communication" throughout the entire process, from composing to the final realization of a work. I prefer that the "final form" which each performance necessarily produces, be a collaborative adventure and that the work and its conditions of human involvement remain a "living" potential of engagement.

These concepts and principles are illustrated in *Available Forms II,* for divided orchestra with two conductors, which was first performed by the Rome Radio Orchestra at the Venice Biennale in April, 1962. Apart from the composing of the basic materials of this work (which I call the "events"), the aspect of the work that interests me most is the attempt to provoke a performance situation in which there is an intensification of the working process in the performance itself. I do not believe in a final best form for these materials and they were composed "in the abstract," so to speak, that is to say, as basic structural possibilities having more than one conceivable function within their implied context. There is obviously a "best form" for a work that is based upon thematic development or a programmatic continuity. I prefer, however, to base the work and its formal future on the immediate and spontaneous responses which occur to the conductors in relation to the composed basic material—the "events"—and to the unique qualities of the conductors and the conditions of each performance. With the exception of the basic materials, these are all variables, and my intention is that they become creative correlatives between the composer, the materials, the conductors, the musicians, and the audiences—as one constantly changing and continuing "process" in the nature of the work.

No two performances will arrive at the same formal result, but the work will retain its identity from performance to performance through the unchanging basic character of the events.

. . . . . .

The question of aesthetics or what I think about the musical situation at the present moment could be a subject for very extensive discussion. Let me begin by saying a few words about the influence of Joseph Schillinger [2] in my work. Although I have not used serial techniques since 1952, some of my works have employed other principles of organization, control, and structural determination; on the other hand, some of my works have used virtually no principle of order and coherence other than the fact that time goes on and different events take place—and this can be said to create its own order. Among the principles of Schillinger that continue to be of interest to me are: structural density, strata, the use of graphs in preliminary scoring, coordination of time structures, acoustic distribution of elements, and multicoordinate systems of defining and organizing the sound continuum. I did not always choose to "organize" to the extreme degree suggested by Schillinger as being essential to musical coherence, because I do not agree with the overly mechanistic and mathematical basis of his aesthetic orientation. I am, however, very much indebted to my studies of the Schillinger method (from 1946 to 1950) for making me question the definitions of music, art, and academic practice and for allowing me to reevaluate and begin building from the fundamental principles of SOUND—its physical characteristics and vocabulary of measurements—as the material from which music is made.

Schillinger did one other thing for which I am grateful. His extreme emphasis on the physical properties of sound and on the integral possibilities of numerical generation, modification, and

2 Joseph Schillinger (b. Kharkov, Russia, 1895; d. New York City, 1943), mathematician, composer, theorist, and teacher, came to the United States in 1929. He developed a highly successful method of teaching composition and orchestration. After his death two of his pupils, Lyle Dowling and Arnold Shaw, published *The Schillinger System of Musical Composition* (2 vols.; New York, 1946). His general theory of aesthetics was also published posthumously in 1947 as *The Mathematical Basis of the Arts* (New York). [Ed.]

expansion, and his implication that a rational, mathematical formula-system could ensure the production of musical works of art, produced an opposite reaction that led to my involvement in rather extreme experiments in purely intuitive and spontaneous actions. These began with my own actions (1950–51), followed by attempts (in 1952) graphically to motivate similar actions from performers of my music. The reaction also spread into the area of compositional systems involving tables and sets of random numbers, and other techniques applicable to an aesthetic based on a desire objectively to explore and observe possible sound relationships rather than to make emotional or intellectual patterns.

The aesthetic validity of this last-mentioned inclination seems to be highly controversial, in spite of a long history in arts other than music—mainly in the visual arts and in literature. At the moment I am not inclined to get involved in a defense of this position; first, because I don't believe it needs to be defended— the work itself either defends or convicts itself on the basis of its being an exciting (not an excited) sound experience (philosophical justification is not sufficient) ; secondly, because it doesn't interest me to work that way any more. I am more interested, at this moment, to work from a basis of extreme personal involvement—which tends to approach objectivity again and is not the same as subjectivity—rather than from a position of disinvolvement.

There are some sketches of piano pieces and pieces for string quartet dating from 1950 and 1951 which are the beginnings of my interest in notation and in new approaches to performance concepts. These are the first pieces that were inversely inspired by the mechanistic approach of Schillinger. They are attempts to produce pieces in which decisions as to the validity and rational function of details, such as pitch and vertical aggregates—in general, the "editorial" aspects of composition—were minimized as much as possible, while qualities of spontaneity and immediacy were considered to be the most direct and essential aspects of the work. The intent was to realize graphically the essence of the piece: the initial, intuitive conception, before it has been molded to conform to technical and aesthetic concepts of structure, form, continuity, art, beauty, and other acquired habits and prejudices of taste and training.

These pieces are in the standard notation and are to be performed as usual, but were written in an extremely rapid, direct, and intuitive manner. The entire piece would be sketched within a few minutes (relative frequency, intensities, durations, and contours), and then notated and "punctuated" as music. There was an attempt to bring the time needed to compose the piece closer to the time needed to perform the piece. This "technique" of composition was very much influenced by the work of Jackson Pollock, and his manner of working, which I first remember seeing around 1949 or 1950. I was very much moved by the life, energy, and immediacy of his work, and thought that these qualities should also be in music.

The influence of the visual arts on so-called "experimental" music in America is an extremely significant thing. In 1950 it was very difficult to see or hear or read about new music in the United States (at least, it was so in Boston and in Denver, Colorado), but there were very exciting things happening and being publicized, in painting and sculpture. There can now be questionings and profound arguments as to whether or not there was a general misapplication and naïve transposition of approach between spatial and temporal arts; but I believe that the transposition was concerned with the general aspects of communication in art rather than with the material nature of the different arts.

. . . . . .

Let me now briefly describe the scoring and performance characteristics of the pieces that are grouped together under the collective title *Folio*. This work contains approximately twelve pieces, each on a separate page; mostly of different sizes. There are six different notations; each notation is to be approached as a unique graphic event and performed in a manner which the performers feel to be one of the infinite number of valid possible realizations in sound of the graphical implications. The pieces in *Folio* were composed between September, 1952, and the spring of 1953. The "progress" of the notation is roughly a change from the use of traditional notation symbols in very "un-fixed" spatial configurations (unable to be understood metrically) to invented (untraditional) symbols in spatial fields that are undefined as to frequency and time (but implying both dimensions by relative size, length, and position in the field). The latter procedure, applied in the piece called *December, 1952,* seems to me to be the most graphically pure expression of an implied "essence." Hence this piece is the most interesting one to me and has had the most effect on my subsequent working techniques and concepts.

There was both success and failure in these *Folio* pieces, but they were of importance to me because they were concerned with what I feel to be the primary problems of music today. One of these is the problem of graphics, which is not a superficial matter but a concern with how to indicate the technical complexity that is conceivable now, in terms that communicate unverbal and unhistorical intentions to a performer or a group of performers. Sounds and relationships that are aesthetically acceptable and artistically necessary today (largely as a result of the accelerated process of innovation and change brought about by our awareness of electronic possibilities) were never in the vocabulary of music when the traditional notation was devised. The function of the latter was based on sonorous and rhythmic patterns that have been superseded by more inclusive concepts of technical and aesthetic "function." The notation could survive the change from harmonic to atonal concepts, but it cannot survive the change from atonality and serial concepts to the concept of *sound* as the "subject" of present and future music. This is because a notation based on the indication and measurement of discrete steps on the time and frequency coordinates is incompatible with the concept of a sound continuum.

Another problem that seems to be dealt with in *Folio* is that of discovering the limits within which a performer can work with immediacy as a principle of performance. While I am no longer as urgently involved with these problems as I was in 1952, they still concern me very much. With *Folio* I seem to have gone to the extreme points, and since then I have worked with what I have observed from these experiments, but in ways that were more inclined to produce sound events compatible with the concepts—and a little less frightening to performers!

I became interested in performance based on intuitive "time-sense perception" (in relation to events within a given time span) after seeing a company of six dancers perform a non-metric type of choreography, without music or any exterior methods of timing and coordination. The dance was intended to be fifteen minutes in duration. With only this interior time sense and a familiarity with the movements in relationship to each other, the dancers finished together at 14 minutes and 51 seconds. To me it seemed that a sense of time and of relationships produced the flexible yet accurate and intense quality that I consider essential in musical composition today.

bibliography

General

BARZUN, JACQUES. *Music in American Life.* (New ed.) Bloomington: Indiana University Press, 1962.

CHASE, GILBERT. *America's Music: From the Pilgrims to the Present.* 2nd ed., rev. New York: McGraw-Hill Book Co., 1966.

COPLAND, AARON. *Our New Music: Leading Composers in Europe and America.* New York: McGraw-Hill Book Co., 1941.

COWELL, HENRY (ed.). *American Composers on American Music.* A Symposium with a new introduction by the author. New York: Frederick Ungar Publishing Co., 1962.

EDMUNDS, JOHN, and GORDON BOELZNER. *Some Twentieth Century American Composers: A Selective Bibliography.* With introductory essay by PETER YATES. 2 vols. New York: The New York Public Library, 1959–60. Includes portraits.

GOSS, MADELEINE. *Modern Music-makers: Contemporary American Composers.* New York: E. P. Dutton & Co., 1952.

HOWARD, JOHN TASKER. *Our American Music: A Comprehensive History from 1620 to the present.* 4th ed., rev. New York: Thomas Y. Crowell Co., 1965.

HUGHES, RUPERT. *Contemporary American Composers.* Boston: L. C. Page & Co., 1900.

LANG, PAUL HENRY (ed.)., *One Hundred Years of Music in America.* New York: G. Schirmer, Inc., 1961.

LOWENS, IRVING. *Music and Musicians in Early America.* New York: W. W. Norton & Co., 1964.

MARROCCO, W. THOMAS, and HAROLD GLEASON. *Music in America. An Anthology from the Landing of the Pilgrims to the Close of the Civil War, 1620-1865.* New York: W. W. Norton & Co., 1964.

MASON, DANIEL GREGORY. *Tune In, America! A Study of Our Coming Musical Independence.* New York: Alfred A. Knopf, 1931.

MELLERS, WILFRID. *Music in a New Found Land. Themes and Developments in the History of American Music.* New York: Alfred A. Knopf, 1965.

REIS, CLAIRE. *Composers in America; Biographical Sketches of Contemporary Composers with a Record of Their Works.* New York: The Macmillan Co., 1947.

RITTER, FREDERIC LOUIS. *Music in America.* New York: Charles Scribner's Sons, 1883.

ROSENFELD, PAUL. *An Hour with American Music.* Philadelphia: J. B. Lippincott Co., 1929.

SESSIONS, ROGER. *Reflections on the Music Life in the United States.* New York: Merlin Press, 1956.

SPAETH, SIGMUND. *A History of Popular Music in the United States.* New York: Random House, 1948.

STEARNS, MARSHALL W. *The Story of Jazz.* New York: Oxford University Press, 1955.

ULANOV, BARRY. *A History of Jazz in America.* New York: The Viking Press, 1952.

WILLIAMS, MARTIN T. (ed.). *The Art of Jazz; Essays on the Nature and Development of Jazz.* New York: Grove Press, 1960.

Individual Composers

ARMITAGE, MERLE. *George Gershwin, Man and Legend.* New York: Duell, Sloan, & Pearce, 1958.

BARBOUR, J. MURRAY. *The Church Music of William Billings.* East Lansing: Michigan State University Press, 1960.

BERGER, ARTHUR. *Aaron Copland.* New York: Oxford University Press, 1953.

COWELL, HENRY, and SIDNEY COWELL. *Charles Ives and His Music.* New York: Oxford University Press, 1954.

DUNN, ROBERT. *John Cage.* New York: Henmar Press, Inc., 1962. Catalogue of Compositions, Facsimiles, Interviews, Critical Excerpts, Bibliography.

ELLSWORTH, RAY. "The Weird, Wonderful World of Harry Partch," *American Record Guide,* XXV, No. 2 (October, 1958).

ESKEW, HARRY. "William Walker: Popular Southern Hymnist," *The Hymn,* XV, No. 1 (January, 1964).

EWEN, DAVID. *A Journey to Greatness: The Life and Music of George Gershwin.* New York: Henry Holt & Co., 1956.

GILMAN, LAWRENCE. *Edward MacDowell, A Study.* New York: John Lane Co., 1908.

GOLDBERG, ISAAC. *George Gershwin, A Study in American Music.* New ed., supplemented by Edith Garson, with a Foreword and Discography by Alan Dashiell. New York: Frederick Ungar Publishing Co., 1958.

GOLDMAN, RICHARD FRANKO. "The Music of Elliott Carter," *The Musical Quarterly,* XLIII, No. 2 (1957).

GOTTSCHALK, LOUIS MOREAU. *Notes of a Pianist.* Ed., Jeanne Behrend, with a Prelude, a Postlude, and Explanatory Notes. New York: Alfred A. Knopf, 1964.

HASTINGS, GEORGE E. *The Life and Works of Francis Hopkinson.* Chicago: University of Chicago Press, 1926.

HOOVER, KATHLEEN, and JOHN CAGE. *Virgil Thomson: His Life and Music.* New York: Thomas Yoseloff, 1959.

HOWARD, JOHN TASKER. *Stephen Foster, America's Troubadour.* New ed. New York: Thomas Y. Crowell Co., 1953.

JABLONSKI, EDWARD, and LAWRENCE D. STEWART. *George Gershwin.* Introduction by Carl Van Vechten. Garden City, N. Y.: Doubleday, 1958.

LOGGINS, VERNON. *Where the World Ends: The Life of Louis Moreau Gottschalk.* Baton Rouge: Louisiana State University Press, 1958.

LOMAX, ALAN. *Mister Jelly Roll.* New York: Duell, Sloan, & Pearce, 1950.

MASON, DANIEL GREGORY. *Music in My Time, and Other Reminiscences.* New York: Macmillan Co., 1938.

SCHUBART, MARK. "Roger Sessions; Portrait of an American Composer," *The Musical Quarterly*, XXXII, No. 2 (1946).

SESSIONS, ROGER. *The Musical Experience of Composer, Performer, Listener*. Princeton: Princeton University Press, 1950.

SLONIMSKY, NICOLAS. "Roy Harris," *The Musical Quarterly*, XXXIII, No. 1 (1947).

SMITH, JULIA. *Aaron Copland: His Work and Contribution to American Music*. New York: E. P. Dutton & Co., 1955.

UPTON, WILLIAM TREAT. *Anthony Philip Heinrich*. New York: Columbia University Press, 1939.
    William Henry Fry, American Journalist and Composer-Critic. New York: Thomas Y. Crowell Co., 1954.

WEISGALL, HUGO. "The Music of Henry Cowell," *The Musical Quarterly*, XLV, No. 4 (1959).

WILKINSON, MARC. "An Introduction to the Music of Edgard Varèse," *The Score and I.M.A. Magazine*, No. 19 (March, 1957).

Sources

BABBITT, MILTON. "Who Cares If You Listen?", *High Fidelity Magazine*, VIII, No. 2 (February, 1958.)

BERGER, ARTHUR. "Stravinsky and the Younger American Composers," *The Score and I.M.A. Magazine*, No. 12 (June, 1955).

BILLINGS, WILLIAM. *The Continental Harmony*. Boston: I. Thomas and E. T. Andrews, 1794. New facsimile ed. by Hans Nathan; Cambridge: The Belknap Press, Harvard University Press, 1961.
    The New-England Psalm-Singer, or American Chorister. Boston: Printed by Edes and Gill, n.d. [1770].

CAGE, JOHN. *Silence* (Lectures and Writings). Middletown: Wesleyan University Press, 1961.

COPLAND, AARON. *Our New Music: Leading Composers in Europe and America*. New York: McGraw-Hill Book Co., 1941.

COWELL, HENRY. *New Musical Resources*. New York: Alfred A. Knopf, 1930.

FARWELL, ARTHUR. "An Affirmation of American Music," *The Musical World*, III, No. 1 (January, 1903).

FRY, WILLIAM HENRY. *Leonora: A Lyrical Drama in Three Acts*. The words by J. R. Fry. The music by William H. Fry. First

performed at the Chestnut Street Theatre, Philadelphia, June
4th, 1845. . . . Piano forte arrangement. New York . . . and
Philadelphia . . .: E. Ferret & Co., 1846.

GERSHWIN, GEORGE. "The Composer in the Machine Age," in Oliver
M. Sayler (ed.), *Revolt in the Arts.* New York: Brentano's,
1930.
GILBERT, HENRY F. B. "The American Composer," *The Musical
Quarterly,* I, No. 2 (1915).
GOTTSCHALK, LOUIS MOREAU. *Notes of a Pianist.* Ed. Clara Gott-
schalk, his sister. Philadelphia: J. B. Lippincott Co., 1881.

HARRIS, ROY. "Problems of American Composers," in Henry Cowell
(ed.), *American Composers on American Music.* Stanford: Stan-
ford University Press, 1933.
HEWITT, JOHN H. *Shadows on the Wall, or Glimpses of the Past.* . . .
Also the Historical Poem of De Soto, or the Conquest of Florida,
and Minor Poems. Baltimore: Turnbull Brothers, 1877.
HOPKINSON, FRANCIS. *Seven Songs for the Harpsichord or Forte-
Piano.* Philadelphia: n.p., 1788. Facsimile edition by Harry
Dichter; Philadelphia: Musical Americana, 1954.

IVES, CHARLES. *Essays Before a Sonata* (Second Pianoforte Sonata).
New York: privately printed, n.d. [1920]. 2nd. ed.; New York:
Arrow Music Press, 1947. New ed. by Howard Boatwright; New
York: W. W. Norton & Co., 1961.

MACDOWELL, EDWARD. *Critical and Historical Essays.* Ed. W. J.
Batzell. Boston: Arthur P. Schmidt Co., 1912.
MASON, DANIEL GREGORY. *The Dilemma of American Music.* New
York: Macmillan Co., 1928.
MORNEWECK, EVELYN FOSTER. *Chronicles of Stephen Foster's Family.*
2 vols. Pittsburgh: University of Pittsburgh Press, 1944. Pub-
lished for the Foster Hall Collection.

PARTCH, HARRY. *Genesis of a Music.* Madison: University of Wisconsin Press, 1949.

SCHULLER, GUNTHER. "The Future of Form in Jazz," *The Saturday
Review* (January 12, 1956).
SESSIONS, ROGER. "Problems and Issues Facing the Composer Today,"
The Musical Quarterly, XLVI, No. 2 (1960).

THOMSON, VIRGIL. *The State of Music.* 2nd ed., rev. New York: Random House (Vintage Books), 1961. Originally published in 1939.

WALKER, WILLIAM. *The Christian Harmony; Containing a Choice Collection of Hymn and Psalm Tunes, Odes and Anthems.* Philadelphia: E. W. Miller and Walker, n.d. Preface dated October, 1866.

index

DATE DUE

GAYLORD			PRINTED IN U.S.A.